Contemporary Issues in Consumer Bankruptcy

Wolfram Backert / Susan Block-Lieb /
Johanna Niemi (eds.)

Contemporary Issues in Consumer Bankruptcy

PETER LANG
EDITION

Bibliographic Information published by the Deutsche Nationalbibliothek
The Deutsche Nationalbibliothek lists this publication in the Deutsche Nationalbibliografie; detailed bibliographic data is available in the internet at http://dnb.d-nb.de.

Library of Congress Cataloging-in-Publication Data

Contemporary issues in consumer bankruptcy / Wolfram Backert, Susan Block-Lieb, Johanna Niemi (eds.).
pages cm.
ISBN 978-3-631-63917-7
1. Bankruptcy. 2. Consumer credit--Law and legislation. I. Backert, Wolfram, editor of compilation. II. Block-Lieb, Susan, 1958- editor of compilation. III. Niemi-Kiesiläinen, Johanna, editor of compilation.
K1370.C655 2013
346.07'8--dc23
2013030630

ISBN 978-3-631-63917-7 (Print)
E-ISBN 978-3-653-03656-5 (E-Book)
DOI 10.3726/978-3-653-03656-5

PKL Academic Research is an Imprint of Peter Lang GmbH.

Peter Lang – Frankfurt am Main · Bern · Bruxelles · New York · Oxford · Warszawa · Wien

www.peterlang.de

Contents

Contents

Introduction

Wolfram Backert *Susan Block-Lieb* *Johanna Niemi*

The financial crisis hit households and individuals hard, yet the political discourse has focused nearly exclusively on the banking system and the debt crises of certain European nations. When policymakers focus on consumer debtors, the debate is mostly limited to a discussion of individual responsibility. But as the current situation in many European countries shows, over-indebtedness is closely related to macroeconomic changes at global and national levels.

During the last twenty years, many countries have taken up legal measures to alleviate the situation faced by over-indebted individuals and households. Especially in Europe, debt adjustment laws that resemble Anglo-Saxon consumer insolvency procedures leading to partial or total discharge of excessive debt have been adopted. In this book, legal developments and experiences in the Netherlands, Sweden, Austria, and Germany are reported. In the Netherlands, debt adjustment is connected with the idea of prevention and consumer protection. Traditionally, debts have been renegotiated successfully. Nadja Jungmann and Nick Huls analyze the problems related to this renegotiation approach in a new environment of credit and court imposed discharge. The Swedish attitude toward the discharge of debt instead has been quite restrictive. Annina H. Persson takes up the recent reform of this debt adjustment law, in which the institutional setting has been changed to open access to the procedure. In Austria, emphasis has been on individual debtors' repayment schemes, a bankruptcy process that has been in force for a decade now. Georg E. Kodek provides empirical evidence to suggest that the procedure has been a success.

Besides debt adjustment procedures, consumer protection measures have a role in the prevention and alleviation of consumer over-indebtedness. In Europe, the new consumer credit directive (2008) does not address over-indebtedness, nor do any other European Union instruments. Johanna Niemi sees over-indebtedness as a problem that should be addressed with the integration of the markets. She takes up the Council of Europe Recommendation as an example of how a common policy might be pursued. Michelle Kelly-Louw discusses problems encountered with raising interest levels in South Africa. Interest rate increases pose serious problems to individual debtors and households, especially at times of economic insecurity. Souichirou Kozuka analyzes how consumer protection law, both judge-made law and legislation, has developed and interacted in Japan to approach consumer over-indebtedness.

Stephanie Ben-Ishai and Saul Swartz take up the role of the public sector creditors in the processes of indebtedness. In welfare societies, the government and public sector are important sources of economic support, both to households and businesses. Government subsidies are in some cases paid on conditions that remain unfulfilled and the subsidy will be collected back. The public also plays a role as a creditor in its function of tax collector. The role of public creditors has largely been unacknowledged in research on over-indebtedness so far.

We also need more empirical and qualitative research on over-indebtedness as a social problem. Several studies report on different factors leading to over-indebtedness. In this book, research by Michael Knoblauch and by Eva Münster et al. from Germany as well as by Cláudia Abreu Lopes, Catarina Frade and Fernanada Jesus from Portugal report that loss of employment, small business failure, health problems, changes in family relations, and inadequate handling of financial affairs are common factors in the cases of over-indebtedness. These factors are often seen as factors leading to over-indebtedness and insolvency but recent studies, such as that by Eva Münster et al., indicate that over-indebtedness is also a cause of or at least a factor contributing to, for example, health problems. When this causal link is acknowledged, the enormous cost of over-indebtedness to societies becomes more visible.

The contributions in this book are based on presentations at the conference Over-indebtedness: Everyday Risk in Modern Societies? Theoretical Aspects and Empirical Findings in International Perspective, organized by the Department of Sociology at Chemnitz University of Technology, between March 26 and 28, 2009. The conference gathered together an international network of scholars conducting socio-legal and comparative research in issues of consumer over-indebtedness and insolvency.

We thank Fritz Thyssen Stiftung for financing this conference. We also thank Alice Neffe, of the Helsinki University, and the many students at Chemnitz Technical University who assisted the editors with the technical part of editing this book.

Two chapters are based on earlier published work. We thank the US-China Law Review and the Queen's Law Journal for the permissions to reprint the articles.

Berlin, Helsinki and New York

Wolfram Backert, Susan Block-Lieb and Johanna Niemi

Never too Small to Fail: Insolvency of Consumers as an International Concern

Johanna Niemi

Introduction

Individual debtors in the rescue discourse[1]

We live in the midst of the worst economic crisis since the 1930s. The crisis that started in 2007 and was first characterized as the bursting of the housing bubble in the United States has now spread all over the world. In late 2008, after the collapse of the investment bank Lehman Bros., the crisis discourse was framed as a debate over the default or the rescue of banks and the banking system. The possibility of certain large banks' failure was seen as a threat to the whole financial system – hence the notion that some banks were too large to fail.[2] Fears of the collapse of the financial sector have been prevailing since. A third turn in the framing of the crisis discourse took place in 2010 in Europe when first Greece and then Ireland were unable to meet its credit obligations. Portugal and Spain now have also received bailout funds. The problems of national economies, particularly those in the Euro zone, have started to denominate the discussion and the framing of the crisis.

Individual debtors have been strangely absent from the public discourse, although they were first pointed out as the precursor of the crisis with the housing bubble. That the financial crisis hit individual debtors is a generally known fact, but it may take a long time before the full effect of the economic crisis on ordinary households is revealed. Articles in this book, as well as previous research, demonstrate the mounting distress and suffering of over-indebted consumers.[3] In this book, Eva Münster et al. show how health problems are strongly correlated to individuals' debt problems, both as a cause and a consequence. Claudia

---

1 I thank Wolfram Backert and his colleagues at Chemnitz University of Technology for organizing the conference, at which this paper was first presented, and also the participants of that conference for comments and exchange of ideas. I also thank Susan Block-Lieb for valuable editing of this chapter.

2 Stiglitz 2010.

3 See, for example, Sullivan et al. 1989 and 2000; Niemi-Kiesiläinen et al. (eds) 2003 and 2009; Towards a common operational European definition 2008. In this chapter, the term consumer debtor refers in the context of insolvency law to any debtor who is seeking relief in his or her private capacity. The debts are not necessarily incurred by consumption. There may be housing debts, tax debt and debts from an already closed business etc. In the context of insolvency law, the term consumer is used in this broad meaning.

Lopes, Catarina Frade and Fernanda Jesus describe the problems that over-indebted Portuguese debtors have suffered in a time of growing unemployment before the debt situation of Portugal became front page news in the spring 2011. Michael Knoblauch and Götz Lechener analyze in their respective articles the situation that German debtors face, both when they come and seek help from debt advisors and when they file for consumer insolvency in the courts.

The possibility that troubled banks' insolvencies would drag down entire economies led to demand for bank bailouts. Ordinary debtors' insolvencies have not evoked equally strong demands for rescue as have banks' troubles. Ordinary debtors have never been too small to fail.

As Joseph Stiglitz has argued, the current crisis may be a symptom of deeper changes in the economic and political system.[4] Deregulation of the financial system has led to an increasing instability of the global economic order since the Second World War. As a consequence, different parts of the world have experienced successive economic crises: Latin America in the beginning of the 1980s; many parts of Europe in the late 1980s and early 1990s; East Asia 1997-98 and Europe and the United States in the early 2000s (Internet bubble); and now this nearly global crisis, which began in 2007 or 2008. All these preceding crises can be attributed, at least in part, to the deregulation of the credit markets and overheating of investments in specific assets in certain parts of the world. Therefore, it was natural to interpret the current crisis as a symptom of inflated housing prices and an unregulated market in sub-prime mortgages and residential mortgage backed securities.

For ordinary people, deregulation of the financial services industries has meant the democratization of consumer credit by making credit available to a wider breadth of people than before. But increased access to credit has also made a wider swath of people vulnerable to default when the economy hit a downturn. Indeed, each of the mentioned economic crises has brought with it an increase in the number and distribution of households with serious debt problems. As the articles in this book show, many States that have been hit by an economic crisis have taken steps to solve the problem of over-indebtedness. There seems to be a fundamental difference in the approaches that governments apply when seeking to resolve the financial difficulties faced by banks, nation-states and ordinary people.

Political discourse on the crisis of the banking system focused on rescue. Banks' threatened illiquidity invoked strong demands for rescue operations by national governments. In many countries, governments infused capital into the

---

4 Such analysis is presented also by Ferguson 2008 and Rajan 2010.

banking system in order to sustain the overall functioning of the financial sector. In the United States, TARP (Troubled Asset Relief Program) funding was made available to nearly all banks, no questions asked. Even before Congress authorized TARP funding, the US Federal Reserve System bolstered the liquidity in this sector by lending on the most favourably terms through its discount window. The Bank of England similarly provided liquidity support for failing financial entities, such as Northern Rock. In Europe, Member States of the European Union and the European Central Bank have combined their efforts to adopt a variety of liquidity measures. There have been differing solutions. The European Union has issued bonds to consolidate Member States' loans; the governments of some Member States unilaterally have strengthened the share capital of some banks; in others, the government bought bad loans. Rescue operations are always urgent; in the heat of the moment the conditions for loans and capital cannot be deliberated upon in great detail.

We have not seen equally urgent rescue packages for individual debtors. The problem of individuals' over-indebtedness is examined solely in the national context. National legislatures have, indeed, taken steps to help over-indebted consumer debtors and households, but usually only after the urgency of the crisis is over. This book, as well as prior comparative research on consumer insolvency, shows that the measures taken to enable consumers access to an insolvency regime, or to reform the terms on which such access is granted, vary a great deal, depending on the economic system, legal traditions and culture, and the depth of the crisis. Chapters in this book give several examples of national legislatures' responses to the problems of the over-indebted debtors. Chapters by Michelle Kelly-Louw and Souichirou Kozuka contain several examples of the ways in which consumer protection and consumer credit laws have been amended in South Africa and Japan to prevent or otherwise address debt problems and the potential for unintended consequences as these laws are implemented.[5]

Rescue through personal insolvency

In many cases, rescue has taken the form of consumer debt adjustment laws. Consumer debt adjustment law or, in the American legal usage consumer bankruptcy law, means, in this context, a judicially supervised procedure, in which the debtor can receive relief from part of her debts through confirmation of a payment plan that obliges the debtor to pay the remaining portion of her debt.

Before the 1990s, this legal institution was seen in other parts of the world as an Anglo-Saxon curiosity. The insolvency laws in other parts of the world

---

5 Kelly-Louw et al. 2008. See also discussion and examples in Niemi-Kiesiläinen et al. 2009.

focused on business bankruptcy; relieving natural persons from their debt obligations was not recognized at all. The economic crises that several European countries underwent during the 1990s and 2000s led, among other things, to the enactment of consumer debt adjustment laws. The US consumer bankruptcy system and especially its Chapter 13, which enables individuals to receive partial relief from their debt after completion of a court-confirmed debt repayment plan, influenced these legislators. The idea of a quick "fresh start" after bankruptcy, like that available in a US Chapter 7 liquidation, was never really embraced by European legislatures. Although they rejected the notion of a complete discharge from debt, European lawmakers widely adopted laws providing for consumer debt adjustment. Today, a majority of European countries have enacted a consumer debt adjustment act.[6]

Table 1: European countries that have enacted a consumer debt adjustment act.

- Denmark 1984
- Finland, Norway 1992
- Sweden 1994
- Austria 1993
- Germany 1994/1999
- Belgium 1998
- The Netherlands 1998
- Luxembourg 2000
- France 1990/2003/2010
- UK 1881/2002
- Estonia 2003/2010
- Portugal 2004
- Slovakia 2004/2006
- Czech 2006/2008
- Slovenia 2007
- Latvia 2007
- Poland 2008
- Greece 2010

Within Europe, consumer debt adjustment laws are characteristically national laws. There has been no coordination between the legislatures of the European countries, even if law-makers have naturally looked to the laws of their neighboring countries for inspiration. The US Bankruptcy Code has also provided a source of information for drafters of some of the consumer debt adjustment laws enacted in Europe.

As a consequence, these national laws differ from each other a great deal. Scholars in the field have classified these systems in different ways.[7] One possible classification differentiates based on the context of the legislation: either bankruptcy law; consumer protection law; or law relating to the specific social policies of the country in question.

6 Niemi-Kiesiläinen 1999; Niemi-Kiesiläinen and Henrikson 2006; Ziegel 2003; Kilborn 2007.

7 See Huls et al. 1994; Ramsay 1997 and 2007; Niemi-Kiesiläinen 1999 and 2003.

Like the US, several European countries have incorporated consumer insolvency in their insolvency or bankruptcy codes. This is the case in Germany, Austria, Estonia, Portugal, the UK[8] and Ireland.[9] Georg Kodek's chapter in this book describes the Austrian "Privatkonkurs" -- a simple bankruptcy proceeding leading to a mandatory payment plan of at least ten percent of the total debt and a discharge of the rest. Even if the plan is lengthy and arduous, Austrian debtors seem to have fulfilled the plans relatively well.

Francophone countries have chosen an approach that puts consumer over-indebtedness and relief into the context of consumer protection and prevention against over-indebtedness. Their legislations also include a number of other provisions on consumer credit aiming to prevent over-indebtedness. Even in the case of over-indebtedness, emphasis is on the renegotiation and rescheduling of debt. Nadja Jungmann and Nick Huls give in this book a rather critical account of the emphasis on counseling and negotiation between the debtor and her creditors in the Netherlands. This model, which was considered quite successful before a formal court-based debt adjustment process became available in 1998, seems rather bureaucratic today.

Finally, the Scandinavian laws, with a characteristically pragmatic approach, offer the debtor a full insolvency procedure but emphasize rehabilitation as an important social policy goal. They tend to offer debtors counseling on their debt as well as other problems. Annina H. Persson gives us a picture of the Swedish debt adjustment procedure, in which the state debt enforcement authority plays a central role.[10] Although the Swedes have diminished their reliance on counseling lately, the role played by the enforcement officers is also somewhat ambivalent. The number of filings has been relatively low in Sweden recently and the number of accepted applications very low. Whether this is due to the cumbersome system or to the sound economic condition of Sweden is hard to tell.

These new laws put the rescue of the individual in the center. But unlike bank and state rescue, governments are not directly injecting money to debtors. Indirect support to the debt adjustment process, though, is commonplace. States finance debt counselling by state, municipality or third sector agencies in several, but not all, European countries. Also the courts (or administrative bodies) that handle debt adjustment filings are financed by governments and, in most

---

8 While there are several insolvency options available to consumers in the UK, the access conditions are rather high in each of them. See Green 2009.

9 The Irish Bankruptcy Code includes a theoretical option for debt relief. The conditions, however, are so hard that it cannot be counted as a consumer debt relief option.

10 See Persson in this book. Another view of the Swedish system, emphasizing the moral tone of it, is given by Carlsson and Hoff 2000.

European countries, debtors are not required to pay a court fee to access the insolvency procedure.[11]

It goes without saying that the government should not step in and help individuals by paying their debts.[12] The risk of moral hazard would be too obvious. Actually, one of the main legitimating arguments for consumer debt adjustment is that social contributions are sometimes indirectly used to pay off private creditors and such situations should be avoided. For example, if creditors garnish a debtor's wages and the debtor is left with too little to support his or her family, the debtor's family may receive government subsidies, even if her income is otherwise high enough to support the family. One of the purposes of consumer debt adjustment laws is to decrease this type of indirect public support for the repayment of privately held debt.

There may be obvious risks in juxtaposing bank rescues with initiatives intended to help individual debtors. It is clear that bank failures have very serious macroeconomic consequences, both as relates to depositors and debtors. The instability of the banking system causes enormous problems to ordinary people as savers, debtors, shareholders, guarantors and mortgagors. In a strange way, the housing bubble demonstrates that ordinary people want to invest in secure assets that retain their value over the long term. The fact that many individual's investment in their own homes was insecure is a sign that ordinary, prudent people can be touched by the insecurity of the financial markets.

The stability of the credit market has value to financial institutions, capital markets investors and debtors alike. Ordinary debtors run the risk of losing, not only their money, but also their homes, jobs, communities and social relationships. As the ultimate losers in a financial crisis of systemic proportions, ordinary debtors have a strong interest in the security of credit markets. At the same time, they have the least possibility to influence market innovations, such as securitization and securities trading, that were central to the culmination of the current crisis. If Joseph Stiglitz is right when he argues that the current financial crisis is a symptom of long-term global imbalances in the supply and demand of credit, ordinary debtors may expect instability in their credit relations for many years to come.

---

11 About the social policy thinking behind these kinds of legislative choices, see Niemi-Kiesiläinen 2003.

12 Except in very exceptional situations, such as guarantees for student loans, in which case the state body has recourse against the debtor.

Internationalization of over-indebtedness and insolvency

The internationalization of credit markets is obvious in the current turmoil of the Euro countries. Not only are troubled countries indebted on the international financial market, but also the rescue efforts unite all European Union Member States financially and create additional incentives for them to work together to resolve their (now) joint financial crisis.

It has not been recognized until recently that the debt of ordinary people has an international dimension. Most people use credit cards internationally, whether they were issued by local or foreign banks. Cross-border debt relationships may be entered into when making purchases online through the Internet. A large number of housing loans originate from foreign banks. As creditors act globally, also debtors move across borders. Debts may be incurred on a trip abroad. Debtors move to other countries seeking better job opportunities. More and more people work in one state and live or have family in another. Consequently, even individual debtors often have creditors that are domiciled in other countries. Thus the problem of ordinary debtors' over-indebtedness may be international in nature. Not only insolvent companies but also individuals with insolvency problems may be indebted to creditors in a number of countries, just as they may expect revenue from various countries.

As you may imagine, a situation in which an insolvent debtor has creditors in other countries involves a number of legal issues. These kinds of legal problems have been known for quite a while. The first international bankruptcy cases are known from the 14th Century; the most famous case from that time concerns a bank, called Ambrosius. Ever since discussions on the cross-border effects of insolvency have focused on the insolvencies of big multinational companies. Despite the huge consequences of such an insolvency, the development of international insolvency law has been somewhat delayed in the legal field. The reason might be that there are a number of legal and other policies in place to prevent such insolvencies. It was not until the 1990s and 2000s that two major international documents on international insolvency law were adopted, the European Insolvency Regulation[13] and the UNCITRAL Model Law on Cross-Border Insolvency.[14]

There are basically two approaches to diminish the harmful consequences of international insolvencies: the harmonization and the regulation of cross-border effects. Both the European Insolvency Regulation and the Model Law represent

13 Council Regulation (EC) No 1346/200 May 29th, 2000 on Insolvency Proceedings (Insolvency Regulation).

14 Model Law on Cross-Border Insolvency of the United Nations Commission on International Trade Law, adopted by the UN General Assembly as A/RES/52/158, Jan 31, 1998.

the latter. They regulate issues such as jurisdiction (in which country the courts may take up a case), applicable law (the law of which country should be applied to resolve disputes arising in an insolvency setting), coordination of parallel insolvency proceedings in two states, and the competence of the trustees in insolvency. The European Insolvency Regulation is directly applicable in all European Union Member States (save Denmark).[15] Besides the Regulation and a handful of international conventions,[16] such matters are regulated in national laws. The Model Law has been implemented as the basis of national law in nearly 20 countries by now, including a few European countries, in which the national law regulates insolvency issues in relation to countries outside the European Union.

Harmonization of insolvency law would be a more far reaching integration policy. There are historical examples of such development. One of them is the unification of Germany in the 19th Century. One of the first significant federal codifications was the German bankruptcy act, Konkursordnung in 1863, which remained in force until the 1990s. Likewise, at the birth of the United States, its Constitution provided in 1789 that bankruptcy law falls within the legislative powers of the federal rather than the state government. With the rise of a national market economy in the US in the 19th Century, a series of economic crises saw the birth of successive US bankruptcy laws, as well as their abolition after a few years as soon as the crisis was over. In 1898, a permanent federal bankruptcy act was legislated; it remained in force until nearly 1980.[17] In these integration processes, the creation of bankruptcy legislation formed an integral part of the formation of a unified market.

One would expect that the integration of the European markets also would have led to the harmonization of insolvency laws. This has not happened, which is not for the want of attempt. Attempts to harmonize bankruptcy laws within the European Community in the 1980s failed due to differences in provisions on the

---

15 The Insolvency Regulation had a peculiar legislative history. In the late 1990s, treaties on insolvency law were drafted, first in the Council of Europe, and then in the European Community. Willingness to cooperate was not high at the time. Because of the Mad Cow Disease, some member states felt that they were discriminated against and as retaliation did not want to be bound by the treaties; therefore, the insolvency convention never entered into force. Instead, the convention was re-drafted as a Regulation on Cross-Border Insolvency. The EU Regulation was adopted as soon as the qualified majority procedure in legal matters became possible after the Amsterdam Treaty entered into force in 1999. Fletcher 2002.

16 The Nordic countries (1933) and the Latin American countries have conventions on international aspects of insolvency law. There are also bilateral conventions between countries on the topic.

17 The history of the US bankruptcy law has been told many times. See for example Skeel 2001 and Mann 2002.

rights of in rem of creditors or third parties.[18] In the beginning of the 2010s the harmonization idea has re-emerged on the EU agenda, now in a form of a policy paper that examines the differences among insolvency laws of a number of European countries, which brings to light problems caused by these differences and discusses the need for consistent regulations.[19]

In all these developments, the focus has been on multinational companies. Formally, neither the EU Regulation nor the Model Law excludes natural persons from their scope of application. However, they regulate insolvency proceedings in which the debtor is deprived of the control of her assets,[20] and this is not the case in many consumer debt adjustment proceedings. The Model Law covers proceedings that aim at the liquidation or reorganization of the debtor, not mentioning rehabilitation.[21] In addition, most of the issues they regulate are obviously irrelevant in the context of over-indebted ordinary people. The policy paper by the European Parliament explicitly restricts its discussion to business insolvency.

The scope of the EU Regulation is a tricky issue. The Regulation does not automatically cover consumer insolvency proceedings, such as debt adjustment or other procedures similar to "consumer bankruptcy." In the annex to the regulation, the member states identify the applicable national insolvency proceedings. The Finnish insolvency proceedings applicable to consumers, for example, and those of the other Nordic countries are not included in the Annex. In contrast, the German Restschuldenregulierung, that consumer debtors can access, is incorporated into the bankruptcy law and falls within the scope of the insolvency proceedings of the regulation. As a consequence, the consumer debt adjustment laws of some EU countries are covered by the EU Regulation and some others are not, in a somewhat arbitrary manner.[22]

The European Court of Justice has recently issued a judgment on consumer insolvency, in which it takes as a starting point the notion that over-indebtedness is a matter relevant to the free movement of persons and that may, as such, fall

---

18 After the failure, the EU shifted its agenda to the regulation of cross-border effects only.

19 Harmonization of Insolvency Law at EU Level, a note by the European Parliament, Directorate-General for Internal Policies, Policy Department on Citizens' Rights and Consitutional Affairs. The note is based on a report by INSOL Europe, an organization of insolvency practitioners and lawyers.

20 Moss et al., 3.06, at 43; Linna 2009.

21 Wood 2007, at 29-059. Generally, the literature on international insolvency law pays relatively little attention to natural persons as debtors. Quite recently, the World Bank has paid attention to the insolvency of natural persons and set up a working group to draft a report on this issue. A draft report has been published online, see World Bank 2012.

22 Niemi 2012.

within the jurisdiction of the European Union.[23] The Swedish law that included an unconditional requirement of domicile in Sweden was considered as "...capable of dissuading an insolvent worker, whose indebtedness is such that that he cannot be presumed to have the means to pay his or her debts within a foreseeable period, from exercising his right to freedom of movement."[24] However, a measure that constitutes an obstacle to the free movement of persons may be legitimate if it is justified by the public interest and if it is effective to achieve such purpose and it does not go beyond what is necessary. These conditions were not deemed to have been fulfilled in the *Radziejevsky* case.

The full implications of this case are still to be seen. It is likely that *Radziejevsky* will direct interest toward natural persons' insolvencies in the evaluation and reform process of the EU Regulation that is pending at the moment.

The issue of over-indebtedness has been likewise neglected in the development of consumer credit law at the European level. The Consumer Credit Directive of 1978 was replaced in 2008 by the Directive on credit agreements for consumers. Both Directives have served to harmonize the legislation in member states, the former at a minimum level and the latter by setting a common standard (maximum harmonization).[25] Neither Directive focuses on questions of over-indebtedness or aims at preventing over-indebtedness. In preparing for the 2008 Directive, over-indebtedness was discussed, especially the use of credit data to prevent over-indebtedness. Attempts were made to oblige creditors to use credit data for that purpose. In its final form, the Directive requires creditors to obtain from debtors details that affect their payment ability, if appropriate, and from credit data, if necessary (article 8).

While consumer insolvency proceedings have not been the focus of EU-wide legislation, the EU has shown interest in these matters by commissioning studies on the subject. It has until now commissioned and financed at least four important studies:

- N Huls, U Reifner and T Bourgoinie, Overintebtedness of Consumers in the EC Member States: Facts and search for solutions, 1994;

---

23 C-461/11 Ulf Kazimierz Radziejewski v Kronofogdemyndigheten i Stockholm, at 25-27.

24 C-461/11 Radziejevsky v. Sweden, at 28.

25 Directive 2008/48/EC on credit agreements for consumers, which replaced Consumer Credit Directive 87/102/EEC. For the legislative process, see Franken 2009.

- B Gianni, D Neil, RM Christina, V Vijay and Y Yaping, Study of the Problem of Consumer Indebtedness: Statistical Aspects. European Commission, 2001;
- U Reifner, N Huls, J Niemi-Kiesiläinen and H Springeneer, Study on the Legislation relating to Consumer Overintebtedness in all European Union Member States, 2003[26];
- Towards a common operational European definition of over-intebtedness. Observatoire de l'Epargne Europeenne, Centre for European Policy Studies and Personal Finance Research Centre. European Commission 2008.

Despite these studies, the EU has not adopted programmes relating to consumer over-indebtedness. The EU Consumer Policy strategy 2007 – 2013, for example, does not mention over-indebtedness.[27] According to Sander Osterloo, a spokesperson for the Commission, a study on lending practices and promotion of economic advice are envisaged, as is a working group to discuss the uses of credit information, but there are no projects directly relating to over-indebtedness.[28] The current crisis has made the EU more attentive to the problems of over-indebted households, however.

Consumer insolvency is a particular challenge to the prospect of formulating any international insolvency law. In the European Union, corporate insolvency belongs to the market regulation (DG Market), whereas the over-indebtedness of households has so far been conceptualized as a matter of social welfare and consumer protection (DG Sanco). This may be one of the reasons that over-indebtedness has not been a focus of the EU policies.

Even if the European Union has not been active in the field of over-indebtedness, it has enacted instruments that are of utmost relevance for individual debtors who are indebted to creditors in other Member States. The efficiency of debt enforcement has been the main interest of the EU in this field. The EU has for some time been concerned about cross-border enforcement of judgments. Initial efforts to devise a mechanism for cross-border enforcement of judgments within Europe began in 1968; subsequent amendments of the European Union Treaty have given the EU an even larger mandate in this field.[29]

---

26 Published as Reifner et al. 2010.

27 EU Consumer Policy Strategy 2007-2013, COM(2007) 99 final.

28 Oral statement at Responsible Credit Conference, London 13-14.11.2008.

29 This was achieved through the Brussels Convention on Jurisdiction and the Enforcement of Judgments in Civil and Commercial Matters 1968 and within the EEA countries through the Lugano Convention on jurisdiction and the enforcement of judgments in civil and commercial matters 1988, and subsequently through Council Regulation (EC) No 44/2001 of 22 December 2000 on jurisdiction and the recognition and enforcement of

European initiative

Council of Europe Recommendation

Against this background, the Council of Europe initiative was an important step in bringing the issues of consumer over-indebtedness on to the international agenda a few years ago. With its 47 member states, the Council of Europe reaches a far wider range of countries with varying cultural backgrounds than the European Union. As the Council of Europe has no goal to promote economic integration, it approaches over-indebtedness as an issue relating to the protection of human and basic rights. During the past two decades, the Council of Europe has also taken an active role in the development of the judicial systems of its member states.[30] In this area, the Council of Europe mainly works with soft law instruments, primarily recommendations. The recommendations have varying impact. Their main impact is political – as politicians become aware of instruments issued by the Council of Europe, they may initiate and promote political processes in their home countries. In many cases, recommendations have led to international treaties on the subject matter, either within the auspices of the Council of Europe or other international organizations, such as the European Union.

In June 2007, the Committee of Ministers of the Council of Europe adopted Recommendation (2007)8E on legal solutions to debt problems.[31] The Commit-

---

judgments in civil and commercial matters and through European Enforcement Order Regulation No 805/2004 (EEO). The latest development in the efficiency of enforcement in the EU is to harmonize summary proceedings to recover debts. Regulation (EC) No 861/2007 of July 2007 establishing a European Small Claims Procedure and Regulation (EC) No 1896/2006 of the European parliament and of the Council of 12 December 2006 creating a European order for payment procedure. Act on the European Small Claims Procedure 753/2008 and Act on the European Payment Order Procedure 754/2008. See Nylund 2008.

30 The Council of Europe has taken a broad view of judicial efficiency and set up a specific structure for monitoring the efficiency of the judicial systems of its member states. See Council of Europe Committee of Ministers Resolution Res(2002)12 establishing the European Commission for the efficiency of justice (CEPEJ), preamble.

31 In 2005 the Ministers of Justice of the member states convened in Helsinki, and the host country, which was responsible for the agenda, wanted to highlight two items: dispute settlement methods as alternatives to criminal proceedings on one hand, and debt problems on the other. Finland prepared for the meeting by addressing the Member States with a questionnaire to map out the related legislation in the member states. At the meeting in April 2005, the Ministers of Justice adopted a Resolution Seeking Legal Solutions to Debt Problems, which assigns the Secretariat the task of identifying legal instruments and proposing measures to prevent and solve problems relating to over-intebtedness. Not long afterwards, the Law Faculty of Umeå University, my employer at the time, was commissioned to carry out such a study. On the basis of the questionnaire, my colleague

tee of Ministers Recommendation is a significant document in a number of ways. First of all, it is the first resolution adopted by a key international organization to address consumer over-indebtedness as a serious problem that also has international dimensions.[32] Second, it contains several important recommendations for action, including the reform of national legislation on over-indebtedness. Third, it perceives over-indebtedness as a complex problem that requires measures over a wide spectrum of societal and legal policies. The Recommendation approaches the complexity of over-indebtedness from three aspects: prevention, alleviation of consequences, and rehabilitation.[33]

Prevention of debt problems

The Recommendation proposes a wide range of measures to prevent debt problems. One measure is for Member States to monitor lending and the development of debt problems. The Recommendation urges Member States to provide financial education and training to incorporate these in the curricula of schools, and to establish counseling and debt advice for debtors. These topics have drawn a lot of international attention lately, although consensus does not exist on their effectiveness.[34] Some countries, including Canada and the US, have incorporated a counseling requirement to their bankruptcy laws. For example, in 2005 the US mandated credit counseling before individuals are eligible to access bankruptcy procedure.

Moreover, the Recommendation provides that Member States should promote and ensure responsible practices in the various stages of the credit relationship, starting from the marketing of credit, as well as in the collection and use of information on credit and credit worthiness. As was mentioned earlier, the use of credit data was a heatedly debated issue in the preparation of the EU Consumer Credit Directive. The Council of Europe Recommendation is quite moderate in its approach, even hedging as someone might suggest, but moderation may be preferable considering the differences in legal provisions in the Member States.

Ann-Sofie Henrikson and I collaborated to produce a report and a set of recommendations. See Niemi-Kiesiläinen and Henrikson 2006.

32 The International Association of Restructuring, Insolvency and Bankruptcy Professionals made a similar recommendation. See INSOL International 2001.

33 In doing so, it largely follows the categorization of the above study. See Niemi-Kiesiläinen and Henrikson 2006. This categorization owes a great deal to the study for the EU by Reifner et al. in 2003 and 2010. Niemi-Kiesiläinen and Henrikson pay less attention to the legislation on credit contracts, which they consider important in the prevention of over-indebtedness but more indirect than the topics discussed in the report.

34 Braucher 2003; Gross 2003.

The term “responsible practices” used in the Recommendation also refers to the concepts of “responsible lending” and “responsible credit,”[35] all widely present on the international agenda and intended to draw general attention to the responsibility of creditors in granting credit in such a manner as not to lead an individual debtor into difficulties.

As a special issue, the Recommendation also mentions the position of guarantors. This is an interesting novelty. The position of individual guarantors came up into the spotlight in a number of countries, including Finland, during the recession of the late 1980s and early 1990s. Here, too, the Recommendation is cautious: it draws attention to a guarantor’s right to information and to the need for preventing irresponsible use of guarantees. The position of guarantors is a question with no easy answers, if guarantees are to retain their important role in promoting lending to individuals and small enterprises. Nevertheless, the mere fact of placing the issue on an international agenda is an important step.

Debt enforcement

The Recommendation takes up the effects of debt enforcement upon the over-indebted debtors and their families. The Recommendation attempts to strike a balance between debtors’ fundamental rights and the interests of creditors. Importantly, the Recommendation stresses the need to take the debtors’ interests into consideration.

While these goals do not seem very radical, the fact that they are taken up is itself significant. Until now, the international community has been one-sidedly interested only in the efficient enforcement of debts. The Council of Europe adopted as late as 2003 a recommendation to improve the efficiency of enforcement.[36] This 2003 recommendation can be seen as a part of many members’ transition to a market economy, with a central feature of securing functioning markets through more efficient legal mechanisms.

A Council of Europe study in 2005 collected information on the protection provided to debtors in the enforcement laws of the Member States. The general impression was of fairly similar patterns of protection. These laws contained provisions both on the property that debtors and their families were allowed to

35 E.g., Reifner 2009. The concept of responsible lending came up in the preparation of the Consumer Credit Directive. See Proposal for a Directive of the European Parliament and of the Council for the harmonisation of the laws, regulations and administrative provisions of the Member States concerning credit for consumers; art 8 and 9, COM(2002)443 final. The final text only uses the term “responsible practices,” and that only in the Introduction.

36 Council of Europe, Rec (2003)17.

retain (beneficium) and the part of salary or other recurring income that was protected.

National provisions on beneficium did not differ a great deal. Debtors were allowed to keep ordinary household items and personal possessions, as well as tools of the trade and objects related to studies. Although the provisions were similar, their practical application may have varied. In the countries of Western Europe, there seemed to be hesitation as to where to draw the line of reasonable protection – the issue whether a car should be a protected asset seems especially to cause controversy. In many countries in Eastern Europe, the beneficium covered a limited number of domestic animals, one cow or two goats or three sheep in Poland, for example, or a couple of beehives in Bulgaria. Even a small plot of land suitable for domestic needs could enjoy protection, and more often than not firewood or oil for heating was protected.[37]

There was greater national variation in the protection of salary. As is the case in Finland, it seemed to be quite common for the law to permit the garnishment of a third of an individual's salary. In order to cover a maintenance to child or spouse and taxes, up to two thirds of the salary could be garnished. Some countries, such as Belgium, Bulgaria, France, Latvia and Spain, used a staggered scale: the greater the income, the higher the percentage of garnishment. Some countries permitted garnishment of all income above a certain level. This group of countries, with high standards of living and of social security, included the Netherlands, Norway, Sweden and Switzerland. Garnishment of salary to cover private debts, excluding maintenance, was not possible in Greece and Denmark, although, apparently, in Denmark this alternative has been discussed.[38]

The study did not provide data to allow comparison of the severity of enforcement: to achieve this, it would have been necessary to survey the countries for the minimum incomes that are completely protected against enforcement and to compare them to the income and expenditure levels in each country. The general impression was that the enforcement of maintenance as well as taxes and other debts to public authorities may be quite severe. Therefore it is justified and even topical in the light of the current economic situation to pay attention to the balance between the interests of the debtor and those of the creditors. Further research and policy development in this area of law and social and market policy is merited.

---

37 Niemi-Kiesiläinen and Henrikson 2006, at 37.
38 Niemi-Kiesiläinen and Henrikson 2006, at 39.

Rehabilitation

The Council of Europe Recommendation is the first international document to urge member states to adopt debt adjustment procedures through which debtors can obtain a partial discharge of debts.[39] In this respect, the Recommendation is extremely cautious and clearly gives preference to alternative debt settlement procedures other than consumer insolvency proceedings. This attitude may be due to the composition of the working group responsible for the preparation of the Recommendation, which had strong representation from Belgium, France and the Netherlands, in other words, from the group of countries that have been the most vocal in emphasizing the social aspects of over-indebtedness and the connection between debt adjustment procedures and the prevention of over-indebtedness.[40]

The Recommendation urges member states to provide over-indebted individuals both advice and access to a debt adjustment procedure. Priority is given to the restructuring and payment of debts through a payment plant, while stating that there should be a possibility for the discharge of debt without completion of a payment plan where there is no reasonable alternative.[41] The Recommendation takes the approach that national legislations may adopt different solutions; it does not specify the desirable length of a payment plan other than to say that it should be reasonable both in terms of time and amount. This is realistic in the sense that the details of debt adjustment procedures vary greatly in the fifteen Member States that have legislated them.[42]

Nevertheless, the Recommendation draws attention to a couple of details, which have great importance. One such detail is that debt adjustment should cover all debts of the debtor, excluding those that are covered by special waivers specified in national law (a typical example is maintenance).[43] Second, the Rec-

---

39 Note also INSOL International 2001.

40 Members of the working group included Gerard Lankhorst, chairperson and representative of the Netherlands Ministry of Justice; Ella Neirink, a lawyer specializing in debt adjust, from Belgium; and Frederic Ferriere-Urvanowitz from the Central Bank of France. Other members were researchers Vesa Muttilainen from Finland and Victor Burac from the State University of Moldova. About the approach and legislation in the Netherlands, see Huls et al. 2003.

41 The pretty wording of the Recommendation is made less ambigious by item 38 of the backround memorandum, which states that "...discharge of debts can be used as an independent solution" and which refers to independence to perform a payment plan. European Committee on Legal Co-operation CDCJ(2007)23Final.

42 Niemi-Kiesiläinen and Henrikson 2006; Towards a common operational European definition 2008.

43 The possibility to exclude certain debts from the discharge in the American consumer bankruptcy is one of the main limitation of fresh start in the US. See Whitford 1997.

ommendation seeks to limit creditors' ability to hinder debt adjustment if such impediments would be unreasonable. In particular, the Recommendation emphasizes debtors' needs for appropriate advice and counselling, both during and after debt adjustment.

Conclusion

Individuals' debt problems have resurfaced in Europe, and so have laws relating to over-indebtedness. During or following the previous recession, several European countries adopted debt adjustment laws applicable to individual debtors. In retrospect, it may be fair say that the enactment of such laws in a time of steady economic progress would give legislators a better possibility to reflect on the issues of over-indebtedness; this timing also increases creditors' awareness and appreciation of the risks that may materialize in leaner times. Political pressure to enact laws like these is strongest in the midst of or after economic downturn, however.

The total impact of the current economic crisis on the households and individual debtors will be revealed in subsequent research. Already it is clear that the effects of the crisis crossed borders, not only as banks trembled but also at the level of individual debtors. In both respects, over-indebtedness is an international problem and the international community will have to approach it, in one way or another.

The European Union may have to reevaluate its policy concerning over-indebtedness after the ECJ judgement in *Raziejevsky*. After the judgment it is clear that over-indebtedness may constitute an obstacle to the free movement of persons. If member states enact laws concerning debt relief they need to take into consideration their effect on freedom of movement. The simplest way of solving this problem would be for countries like Sweden and Finland that have not included their consumer debt adjustment laws in the scope of the Insolvency Regulation do so by amending the Annex to that Regulation. Yet, interesting issues remain. Over-indebtedness is also an obstacle to freedom to movement when the country in question has no consumer insolvency law whatsoever. It is very difficult to envision how that obstacle could be challenged in jurisprudence. Rather, the European countries should develop a common policy concerning over-indebtedness.

References

Official documents

Brussels Convention on Jurisdiction and the Enforcement of Judgments in Civil and Commercial Matters 1968.

Council of Europe Committee of Ministers Recommendation Rec (2003)17 on enforcement.

Council of Europe Committee of Ministers Recommendation (2007)8E on Legal Solutions to Debt Problems.

Council of Europe Committee of Ministers Resolution Res (2002)12 establishing the European Commission for the efficiency of justice (CEPEJ).

Council of Europe Resolution No 1 on Seeking Legal Solutions to Debt Problems in a Credit Society, 26th Conference of European Ministers of Justice, MJU-26 (2005) Resol. 1 Final.

Council Regulation (EC) No 1346/2000 of 29 May 2000 on insolvency proceedings.

Council Regulation (EC) No 44/2001 of 22 December 2000 on jurisdiction and the recognition and enforcement of judgments in civil and commercial matters.

Directive 2008/48/EC on credit agreements for consumers and repealing Council Directive 87/102/EEC.

Government Bill 157/2008 to Parliament on the European Small Claims Procedure, on European Order for Payment Procedure, and on the Amendment of the Act on Payments to Courts and Certain Administrative Authorities.

Harmonization of Insolvency Law at EU Level: Note. European Parliament, Directorate-General for Internal Policies, Policy Department on Citizens' Rights and Consitutional Affairs 2010.

Lugano Convention on jurisdiction and the enforcement of judgments in civil and commercial matters (1988).

Model Law on Cross-Border Insolvency of the United Nations Commission on International Trade Law, adopted by the UN General Assembly 31.1.1998, A/RES/52/158.

Proposal for a Directive of the European Parliament and of the Council on the harmonisation of the laws, regulations and administrative provisions of the Member States concerning credit for consumers, COM(2002) 443 final.

Regulation (EC) No 805/2004 of the European Parliament and of the Council of 21 April 2004 creating a European Enforcement Order.

Regulation (EC) No 1896/2006 of the European parliament and of the Council of 12 December 2006 creating a European order for payment procedure.

Regulation (EC) No 861/2007 of July 2007 establishing a European Small Claims Procedure.

EU Consumer Policy strategy 2007–2013: Empowering consumers, enhancing their welfare, effectively protecting them. COM(2007) 99 final.

European Committee on Legal Co-operation CDCJ (2007) 23 Final, Draft Recommendation on Legal Solutions to Debt Problems and its Explanatory Memorandum.

World Bank, Insolvency and Creditor/Debtor Regimes Task Force. Working Group on the Treatment of the Insolvency of Natural Persons. INFORMAL DRAFT FOR DISCUSSION PURPOSES, Sept.2012. http://siteresources.worldbank.org/INTGILD/Resources/WBPersonalInsolvencyReportOct2012DRAFT.pdf visited 20.11.2012.

Literature

Braucher, Jean: Debtor Education in Bankruptcy: The Perspective of Interest Analysis. In: Niemi-Kiesiläinen, Johanna, Ramsay, Iain and Whitford, William C. (eds.): *Consumer Bankruptcy in Global Perspective*. Portland. Hart Publishing 2003: 319–342.

Carlsson, Bo and Hoff, David: Dealing with Insolvency and Indebted Individuals in Respect to Law and Morals. 2 *Socio-Legal Studies* 9 (2000): 295–319.

Ferguson Niall*: The ascent of money. A financial history of the world.* New York. Penguin Books 2008.

Fletcher, Ian F.: Historical Overview: The Drafting of the Regulation and its Precursors. In: Moss, Gabriel, Fletcher, Ian F. and Isaacs, Stuart (eds.): *The EC Regulation on Insolvency Proceedings. A commentary and Annotated Guide.* Oxford. Oxford University Press 2002: 1–14.

Franken, Sefa M.: The Political Economy of the EC Consumer Credit Directive. In: Niemi, Johanna, Ramsay, Iain and Whitford, William C. (eds.): *Consumer Credit, Debt and Bankruptcy: Comparative and International Perspectives.* Portland. Hart Publishing 2009: 129–152.

Gianni et al.: *Study of the Problem of Consumer Intebtedness: Statistical Aspects.* By Betti Gianni, Dourmashkin Neil, Rossi Maria Christina, Verma Vijay & Yin Yaping. Commission of European Union, 2001.

Green, Michael: New Labour: More Debt – The Political Response. In Niemi, Ramsay and Whitford (eds): *Consumer Credit, Debt & Bankrupcy. Comparative and International Perspectives.* Oxford and Portland. Hart Publishing 2009: 393-440.

Gross, Karen: Establishing Financial Literacy Programmes for Consumer Debtors: Complex Issues on the Platter. In: Niemi-Kiesiläinen, Johanna, Ramsay, Iain and Whitford, William C. (eds.): *Consumer Bankruptcy in Global Perspective.* Portland. Hart Publishing 2003: 343–360.

Huls, Nik, Jungmann, Nadja and Niemeijer, Bert: Can Voluntary Debt Settlement and Consumer Bankruptcy Coexist? The Development of Dutch Insolvency Law. In: Niemi-Kiesiläinen, Johanna, Ramsay, Iain and Whitford, William C. (eds.): *Consumer Bankruptcy in Global Perspective.* Portland. Hart Publishing 2003: 303–318.

Huls, Nik, Reifner, Udo and Bourgoinie, Thierry: *Overindebtedness of Consumers in the EC Member States: Facts and Search for Solutions.* Diegem, Louvain-la-Neuve. Kluwer Éditions Jurisdiques Belgique, Centre de Droit de la Consommation 1994.

INSOL International: *Consumer Debt Report. Report of Findings and Recommendations.* London 2001. Available at: http://www.insol.org/page/38/consumer-debt-report (7.6.2011).

Kelly-Louw, Michelle, Nehf, James P. and Rott, Peter (eds.): *The future of consumer credit regulation: Creative approaches to emerging problems.* Aldershot, England. Ashgate 2008.

Kilborn, Jason: *Comparative Consumer Bankruptcy*. Durham. Carolina Academic Press 2007.

Linna, Tuula: Europeanization of insolvency law. In A. Jokela, L. Ervo, & M. Gräns (Eds.), *Europeanization of procedural law.* Groningen: Europa Law Publishing: 151–196.

Mann, Bruce H.: *Republic of Debtors: Bankruptcy in the Age of American Independence.* Cambridge Massachusetts. Harvard University Press 2002.

Moss, Gabriel, Fletcher Ian F. and Isaacs Stuart: The EC Regulation on Insolvency Proceedings. A Commentary and Annotated Guide. 2 ed. Oxford University Press 2009.

Niemi, Johanna: Consumer Insolvency in the European Legal Context. 4 *Journal of Consumer Policy* 35 (2012): 443-459.

Niemi, Johanna, Ramsay, Iain and Whitford, William C. (eds.): *Consumer Credit, Debt and Bankruptcy: Comparative and International Perspectives.* Portland. Hart Publishing 2009.

Niemi-Kiesiläinen, Johanna: Consumer Bankruptcy in Comparison: Do We cure a Market Failure or a Social Problem? *1–2 Osgoode Hall Law Journal 37* (1999): 473–503.

Niemi-Kiesiläinen, Johanna: Collective or Individual? Constructions of Debtors and Creditors in Consumer Bankruptcy. In Niemi-Kiesiläinen, Ramsay & Whitford (eds): *Consumer Bankruptcy in Global Perspective*. Oxford. Hart Publishing 2003: 41-60.

Niemi-Kiesiläinen, Johanna and Henrikson, Ann-Sofie: *Legal Solutions to Debt Problems in Credit Societies: A Report to the Council of Europe.* Skrifter från Juridiska Institutionen 13, Umeå University 2006.

Niemi-Kiesiläinen, Johanna, Ramsay, Iain and Whitford, William C. (eds.): *Consumer Bankruptcy in Global Perspective*. Portland. Hart Publishing 2003.

Nylund, Anna: Europeiskt betalningsförläggande och småmålsförfarande. *Tidskrift utgiven av Juridiska Föreningen i Finland* 2008: 241–259.

Rajan, Raghuram G.: *Fault lines: how hidden fractures still threaten the world economy.* Princeton. Princeton University Press 2010.

Ramsay, Iain: Comparative Consumer Bankruptcy. *University of Illinois Las Review* 2007: 241-274.

Ramsay, Iain: Models of Consumer Bankruptcy: Implications for Research and Policy. 2 *Journal of Consumer Policy* (1997): 269–287.

Reifner, Udo: 'A Call to Arms' – For Regulation of Consumer Lending. In: Niemi, Johanna, Ramsay, Iain and Whitford, William C. (eds.): *Consumer Credit, Debt and Bankruptcy: Comparative and International Perspectives.* Oxford and Portland. Hart Publishing 2009: 105–128.

Reifner, Udo, Huls, Nick, Niemi-Kiesiläinen, Johanna and Springeneer, Helga: *Study on the Legislation relating to Consumer Overintebtedness in all European Union Member States.* 2003. Consumer Overindebtedness and Consumer Law in the European Union. Final Report. September 2003. Contract Reference No. B5-1000/02/000353. Available at:
http://www.ecri.eu/new/system/files/26+consumer_overindebtedness_consumer_law_eu.pdf

Reifner, Udo, Niemi-Kiesiläinen, Johanna, Huls Nick and Springeneer, Helga: *Overindebtedness in European Consumer Law. Principles from 15 European States.* Shriftenreihe des Instituts für Finanzdienstleistungen e.V. Band 15 Norderstedt: Books on Demand 2010.

Skeel, David A.: *Debt's dominion: a history of bankruptcy law in America.* Princeton University Press 2001.

Stiglitz, Joseph E.: *Freefall: America, Free Markets, and the Sinking of the World Economy.* London. Allen Lane 2010.

Sullivan, Teresa, Elizabeth Warren and Westbrook, Jay Lawrence: *As We Forgive Our Debtors: Bankruptcy and Consumer Credit in America.* New York. Oxford University Press 1989.

Sullivan, Teresa, Elizabeth Warren and Westbrook, Jay Lawrence: *The Fragile Middle Class.* New Haven. Yale University Press 2000.

Towards a common operational European definition of over-indebtedness. Observatoire del'Epargne Europeene, Centre for European Policy Studies & Personal Finance Research Centre. European Commission 2008.

Whitford, William C.: Changing Definitions of Fresh Start U.S. Bankruptcy Law. *Journal of Consumer Policy* (1997): 178-.

Wood, Philip R.: *Principles of International Insolvency.* Sweet & Maxwell. London. 2007.

Ziegel, Jacob S.: *Comparative Consumer Insolvency Regimes: A Canadian Perspective.* Oxford. Hart Publishing 2003.

Regulation and Self-regulation in the Fight against Over-indebtedness in the Netherlands: A Socio–legal and Economic Analysis

Nick Huls Nadja Jungmann

Introduction

The field of debt assistance is under pressure in the Netherlands. The numbers of people asking for help increases, while municipalities are faced with major cutbacks. Increasing applicants and decreasing budgets occur in a context of low effectiveness. On average, municipalities are able to help approximately 30 percent of all the applicants. In this situation, both the national and local governments are looking for ways to improve both effectiveness and efficiency.

One issue in this field is whether the increase in effectiveness and efficiency can or must be reached by self-regulation or regulation. In this paper we give in section 2 an overview of the law and economics and socio-legal theoretical literature. We then discuss in section 3 the history of regulation and self regulation in debt assistance provision. In the closing, section we formulate a few tentative conclusions.

Theoretical framework: general law and economics and socio-legal considerations

General consideration of self-regulation

Different definitions of self-regulation are used in the Dutch literature. The economists Baarsma *et al.* use a broad definition:

> Self-regulation means that social parties themselves take a certain degree of responsibility for setting up and/or implementing and/or enforcing the regulations.[1]

The civil lawyer Giesen similarly uses this description as a starting point and formulates the following definition:

> Alternative regulation means that social parties themselves take a certain degree of responsibility for setting up and/or implementing and/or enforcing the regulations, if necessary within a legal or judicial framework.[2]

1 Barbara Baarsma et al. 2003, at 13.
2 Ivo Giesen 2007, at 13.

These definitions show surprising similarities with the definition given by legal sociologist John Griffiths for the semi-autonomous social field (SASF), at whose center there is a group of people that jointly make rules and also enforce them.[3] In his sociological approach, which focuses on the social effect of the law, the point of departure is therefore not so much the government that sets regulations, but rather the social institutions, the work place, concrete activities and practices, etc. This is relevant for rule making because in this "bottom up approach," the primacy of the empirical reality is upheld, in which the central philosophy is "we all make rules." In this vision, government regulation and self-regulation constantly have an effect on each other.

In the literature, many forms of, reasons for and instruments of self-regulation are distinguished, ranging from quality marks and certification to codes of conduct and gentleman's agreements. In many analyses an emphatic distinction is made between types of self-regulation in which the government is, is not or is only partly involved. In the following sections we discuss a number of categorizations that are used in disciplines such as law and economics and socio-legal studies.

(i) Reasons for self-regulation

Roughly three reasons for self-regulation are distinguished in the literature:

- in order to avoid government regulation;
- in order to satisfy the intrinsic need in an industry or policy field;
- as a supplement to existing regulation.

(1) Self-regulation as a means of avoiding government regulation

The first form is self-regulation as an alternative to government regulation. Alternative is used in the sense that both government regulation and self-regulation are possible. It can be said that the motive behind this form of self-regulation must be comparable to the motive behind government regulation. In the economic approach self-regulation serves as alternative "in situations where in the absence of self-regulation, government regulation would be necessary, since there is a case of market failure or political motives."[4]

In this approach, self-regulation is a substitute for formal regulation, where the four known forms of market failure provide the reason for regulation: lack of competition, information asymmetry, negative external effects and public goods. There is also attention to political motives for the use of self-regulation, such as

3 John Griffiths and Heleen Weyers 2005, passim.

4 Barbara Baarsma et al. 2003, at 15.

to counter the unequal distribution of prosperity, paternalistic motives (to stimulate desirable behaviour and discourage undesirable behaviour) and to counter social imbalance (such as high unemployment in a particular sector).

The government's use of self-regulation as an instrument to realise political goals takes place under the label of "conditioned self-regulation." Self-regulation can also arise, for example, as the result of anticipating legislation, with the aim of preventing government intervention. The government can also force self-regulation by threatening legal regulation or subsidize initiatives of self-regulation. In the law and economics literature it is generally posited that self-regulation can serve as alternative to legislation in the case of regulatory failure. This last situation arises due to complexity, information problems, transaction costs and economic costs.

(2) Self-regulation as a means of providing for needs in a (policy) field

The second category of self-regulation involves those cases in which the motives for self-regulation are the same as those for government regulation, but in which the self-regulation in fact arises without a threat from the government. In such a case self-regulation is not seen as an alternative to legislation. This can arise if the problem is not serious enough to justify government intervention, but a need for intervention is felt in the social field of influence. Motives for this form of self-regulation by the relevant industry are, for example, the need to improve its image or to conduct business in a socially responsible manner. This category also includes self-regulation that arises in situations where the government lacks the knowledge necessary for regulation.

(3) Self-regulation can supplement existing regulation

A third category is self-regulation that has motives other than purely policy-related motives. Examples of this are self-regulation initiatives whose primary purpose is to lower transaction costs by making use of uniform general terms and conditions and alternative dispute settlement. This last category involves a supplement to laws or legal procedures that are already in place and not an alternative to legislation.[5] In practice, such initiatives are not always easy to distinguish from the second category.

5 Barbara Baarsma et al. 2003, at 14.

(ii) Advantages and disadvantages of self-regulation

Different advantages and disadvantages of self-regulation are mentioned in the general literature. Examples of advantages are:

- There is specific knowledge required for regulation and the sector is stronger than the government in this respect;
- Self-regulation is more flexible than legislation (which makes adjustments in the short term possible);
- The transaction costs are lower for both businesses and the public;
- There is greater willingness to comply;
- There is less of a burden on the government apparatus.

Disadvantages include:

- The industry or policy field abuses its information head-start on the government;
- The transaction costs are charged on to third parties;
- There is the risk of restricted competition;
- Enforceability is limited.

(iii) Costs of self-regulation

The Baardsma report states that the regulation costs and compliance costs are lower with self-regulation than legislation.[6] If 100 percent compliance is not necessary to promote public interests in an acceptable manner, self-regulation is a good alternative from a cost perspective, say the authors of the report, because the costs of creating and enforcing legislation are usually higher than the costs entailed by self-regulation.

This conclusion is also drawn in certain cases in the law and economics literature. Self-regulation can have a cost-saving effect both for society as a whole and the government in particular when the information needed for optimal standardisation and enforcement is present on the industry level but not on the government level. Another oft-cited cost argument is that with self-regulation costs can be internalized while with government regulation the costs of standardization and enforcement are at the taxpayers' expense.[7] This argument is not strong in those cases in which the supervisory and enforcement costs are charged directly to the market participants.

---

6 Barbara Baarsma et al. 2004, at 86-87.

7 Anthony Ogus 1995, at 98.

Self-regulation from a law and economics perspective

In the law and economics analysis of regulation and self-regulation, a distinction is traditionally made between the so-called "public interest" approach and the "private interest" approach. In the public interest approach, government action (or self-regulation) is primarily seen as a means of countering market failure and therefore increasing social prosperity. In this vision, government action (or self-regulation) is therefore regarded as an instrument whereby the government strives to increase social prosperity.

The private interest approach on the other hand assumes that the government does not, or does not only, aim to increase social prosperity, but rather enables the establishment of regulation or self-regulation that serves the private interests mainly of powerful lobby groups. Politicians seeking to maximize prosperity reportedly promulgate regulation that provides advantages to private lobby groups in exchange for support for, among other things, re-election. In the law and economics literature, such public interest arguments are weighed and it is indicated under what circumstances self-regulation can serve to increase prosperity. Legal economists identify a long list of advantages:

- With self-regulation, use can be made of the greater expertise and technical knowledge available within the professional group, consequently information costs for establishing standardisation can be lower.
- For the same reason, enforcement costs will be lower because in the case of self-regulation there is presumably stronger mutual trust. Moreover, it can be expected that companies will be more willing to comply with standards that have been reached in the context of self-regulation.
- Since self regulation usually requires less time-consuming decision making procedures, standards can not only be agreed on more easily, it is also easier to change them.
- The administrative costs of self-regulation are normally borne by the industry itself. The administrative costs can therefore be lower and the self-regulation can be financed by charging these costs on to the relevant companies without disadvantaging the public finances.

Despite these possible advantages of self-regulation, law and economic scholars see just as many disadvantages. These disadvantages are not just economic in nature, but are also noted by lawyers:

- Establishing standards via self-regulation lacks democratic legitimacy because the agencies that establish self-regulation cannot be called to account for the content of the self-regulation via the normal democratic control processes.

This is especially seen as a disadvantage when the standardisation that is established through self-regulation also affects the rights of third parties.
- Self-regulatory agencies do not have an impressive record when it comes to enforcement of the standards with respect to violators.
- The great danger of self-regulation is that the professional group can consequently end up engaging in anti-competitive practices in fact. Restricting the possibilities of advertising can limit price competition for instance and, more generally, there is the danger that self-regulation will be abused by the professional group to create restrictions on competition.

Self-regulation in a socio-legal perspective

In sociology of law, the emphasis is on the mutual influence of political actors and self-regulating groups. In a recent theme issue of *Recht der Werkelijkheid,*[8] the editors – with reference to E. Ullman-Margalit – cite three "standard generating basic patterns" that lie at the basis of the interaction between regulation and self-regulation:

- the prisoner's dilemma;
- the need for coordination;
- a situation of inequality that is seen as unacceptable.

The editors also devote attention to enforcement and the question of the extent to which self-regulation is "law in the making." From that perspective, one can view self-regulation as a leg up for government regulation. This last view fits in with the deregulation discussion that has dominated legal political regulation discourse since the nineteen eighties. If there is less confidence in the problem-solving ability of the government, businesses and lobby organizations have more interest in self-regulation.

The opposite also occurs now and again. In the 1992 legislative memo *Zicht op Wetgeving* (View on Legislation) from the Ministry of Justice, for the first time the government expresses its intention to pay more attention to the self-regulating ability of society. In this memo, which is still topical, the concept of "legally conditioned self-regulation" is also developed, whereby the legislator gives the framework within which most relevant parties can proceed with some freedom to regulate their conduct and in which the government has an important role in enforcement. A striking example of this approach is the concept of good credit lendership from article 16 of the Consumer Credit Act (WCK), which in

8 Heleen Weyers and Jolande Stamhuis 2003.

practice has been fleshed out by declaring the standards of the Honour Code of the Association of Finance Companies in the Netherlands (VFN) applicable to all credit lenders.

Worth mentioning also are the sociological studies from Van Waarden and De Vroom into the self regulation of manufacturers from the collective action perspective of Mancur Olson. Self-regulation is then a form of collective interest promotion by the industry. The industry's own rules are set up by the vanguard, which wants to distinguish itself from the unorganized. These latter are often labelled "cowboys," the less expert or quality-focused section of the industry. In this collective action approach, there is much attention to the problems that free riders can cause for the group as a whole.

The relationship between "insiders" and "outsiders" also plays a role in the establishment of so-called technical norms and standards for certain products. It emerges that large companies sometimes argue for high and therefore costly standards that are unaffordable for small businesses. The technical norms can therefore have the function of pushing competitors out of the market.

Central to the socio-legal analysis is the notion that the opposition between government and self-regulation cannot be made absolute. In a number of studies on negotiative legislating, Stoter and Huls[9] have shown that much legislation these days is not imposed unilaterally (top down) by the state on its subjects, but is created in an interactive process of give and take between the government on the one hand and the organized business sector on the other. In the context of garnering support, the government is often dependent on the self-regulating ability of organizations that know how to find their way to the government.

National government and self-regulation

To supplement to the socio-legal and law and economics approaches to self-regulation, we discuss two topics related to the position of the national government in self-regulation:

- The formal frameworks (where and how do policymakers and the legislator decide whether to use self-regulation as an instrument?);
- The degree to which self-regulation contributes in practice to the fulfilment of policy goals.

---

9 Nick Huls 1998; Suzan Stoter and Nick Huls 2003 and 2006.

(i) The Dutch policy and legislation process

All Dutch ministries are required to take the following steps before regulating:

- Collect knowledge of the relevant facts and circumstances regarding the subject in question;
- Determine as concretely and precisely as possible the policy objectives that are being aimed for;
- Investigate whether the objectives chosen can be achieved by means of the self regulating ability in the relevant sector or sectors or if government intervention is necessary;
- If government intervention is necessary, investigate whether the objectives chosen can be achieved by amending or making better use of existing instruments or, if this proves impossible, which other possibilities exist to this end.

The value of this set of tests and protocols is limited by, among other things, the time at which they are used and their relative value in light of the political rationality of choosing legislation as an instrument of policy implementation. Moreover, the element missing from these tests and protocols is an institutionalized feedback loop. There is no fixed standard for ex post evaluation to see whether the choice for a regulation instrument like self regulation has contributed to achieving the aim and whether the ex ante tests and protocols have helped in identifying the opportunities and threats that were inherent to the chosen instrument. That does not go to say that in reality no ex post evaluations take place, but that they are not in fact a fixed part of the policy cycle and therefore there is no automatic link between ex ante estimations and ex post evaluations.

(ii) The material frameworks: prerequisites for successful use

For a government considering the use of self-regulation as an instrument, the chances of success are important. It is not easy to estimate the degree of success and effectiveness of self-regulation ex ante, but that is needed of course in an instrumental view on self-regulation. In the literature we find three necessary, but not sufficient, conditions that the industry must satisfy in order to be able to self-regulate:

- there must be a certain level of knowledge present in the sector;
- there must be support within the sector;
- there must be an adequate degree of organization in the relevant industry or professional group.

These conditions can be translated into motives. Support presupposes interest: the self-interest of the business sector is cited as the main motive for self-regulation. Only if the industry expects it will gain something from self-regulation will it proceed to do it.[10] Self-interest can express itself in the attempt to avoid legal regulation: if restrictions must be introduced, rather by means of standards set up ourselves. The industry may also try to improve its reputation by ascribing idealistic motives to its standards, or introducing a quality mark function by attaching clear quality requirements to participation.

With regard to the necessary conditions for self-regulation as an instrument of government policy, Campbell has stated that it is necessary for the government to monitor in some way the institutions that establish standardization through self-regulation. This is called "audited self-regulation" and entails that whenever powers for standardization are transferred to a self-regulating institution, the government should still keep a finger on the pulse, for instance with regard to verifying the soundness of the regulation and compliance. In particular, in this literature the following prerequisites for self-regulation are mentioned:[11]

- The self-regulating institution must have both the expertise and the necessary motivation to perform the tasks delegated to it.
- The government must have information and expertise in order to actually be able to monitor the activities of the self-regulating institution.
- The prerequisites must be set down by legislation, and this legislation must also indicate that precise, clear standards can only be established via self-regulation.

Thus, according to this literature, self-regulation only generates social advantages when the government determines and maintains the preconditions under which the self-regulation functions. Positively formulated: if the government maintains control of the process, self-regulation can be a good instrument of government policy. Ogus also stresses that when controlled self-regulation is established in this way, it can play a useful role. He indicates that a means of doing this is by promoting competition between self-regulating institutions. A method to that effect that is also cited by Ogus is accreditation or certification. If there is competition in the relevant market, accreditation by a self-regulating institution can offer a sign to consumers that accredited services or products satisfy certain minimum quality requirements. If what is on offer is not limited to

10 MarinaVan Driel 1989, at 9.
11 Campbell 1999, at 719 et seq.

products or services that enjoy such accreditation from a single self regulating institution, accreditation (whereby also non-accredited products must remain on the market) could give information signals to consumers about distinct quality standards. In this way, conditioned self-regulation could realize policy goals and at the same time stimulate competition.[12]

Self-regulation played an important role in the development of the Dutch system of debt assistance

In the past decades, self-regulation played an important role in the Dutch system of debt assistance. Characteristic elements such as the division into a voluntary and legal trajectory and a three-year term for debt settlements can be directly ascribed to the self-regulation that took place. In this section, we describe how the most important acts of regulation by the government and self-regulation alternated with each other over the years. Looking back over the past 15 years, in the last section we ask whether the impact of regulation during that period was not significantly greater than the impact of self-regulation. Table 1 summarizes and briefly describes the most important acts of regulation and self-regulation.

Table 1: Years in which debt assistance regulation or self-regulation assistance took place

Year	Regulation or self-regulation	Adjustment
1896	Regulation	Bankruptcy Act is opened up for consumers
1939	Self-regulation	Municipal Credit banks offer a pragmatic solution for debt situations by introducing debt management credits
1979	Self-regulation	The Code of Conduct for Debt Settlement is introduced, thus providing a set of agreements between debt assistance organizations and creditors
1998	Regulation	Parliament calls for a legal debt settlement scheme in 1992 and in 1998 the WSNP becomes law.
2000	Self-regulation	By amending the Code of Conduct for Debt Settlement and standardizing the calculation of repayment capacity, the field tries to increase the effectiveness of the voluntary trajectory

12 This is further elaborated in Ogus 1995, at 102-107.

Year	Regulation or self-regulation	Adjustment
2008	Regulation and self-regulation	Amendment WSNP limiting admissibility in court and simplify procedure and self regulation by: • reaching various covenants between debt assistance organizations and creditors; • implementing demand-based way of working; • developing system certification; • setting up early warning system (National Debts Information System).
2009	Self-regulation	In the period 2006-2010, the NVVK (organisation that represents individual debt settlement organisations) agreed with certain groups of creditors (energy suppliers, landlords, etc.) on covenants that contain agreements and obligations to promote the cooperation between debt settlement organizations and the specific groups of creditors.
2012	Regulation	In 2007, the national government named itself responsible for the system and proposes a Municipal Debt Assistance Act (Wet gemeentelijke schuldhulpverlening). On the July 1, 2012 this act came into force. The act requires municipalities to offer debt relief. It is up to the municipalities to decide how to organize the implementation

1896 Regulation: Opening up the Bankruptcy Act to consumers

Debts are timeless. In order to offer natural persons a solution for the often hopeless situation in which they found themselves, in 1896 they were given the possibility of appealing to the Bankruptcy Act. Since the bankruptcies of natural persons yielded little for creditors in practice, most were quickly concluded "for lack of assets." The creditor could then write off its claims or wait for better times in which it could once again request the bankruptcy of the debtor. In retrospect, the opening up of the law had a counterproductive effect: it did not offer consumers the way out they needed but did give creditors an extra incentive to force payment. Many debtors regarded a bankruptcy as a disgrace and therefore paid as much as they could to avoid going to court. This was a case of the "bankruptcy of bankruptcy legislation."

1939 Self-regulation: Municipal credit banks offer a pragmatic solution for debt situations

Credit lending to private individuals slowly started to pick up in the Netherlands in the 1920. Credit was not used to buy consumer goods, but investments like tools or a sewing machine, for example, in order for the individual to earn something extra. Exorbitant interest rates were often charged for this credit. Partly under the influence of the 1929 economic crisis, a growing group of consumers faced irresolvable repayment problems. With the lack of a properly functioning bankruptcy act, more and more municipal credit banks offered a pragmatic solution in the form of debt settlement credits. The municipal bank issued a credit with which the debtor paid off his debt in one go. The credit bank charged a lower interest rate (and gave a longer repayment term), and consequently the debtor was, once again, able to honor his obligations.

In 1939, credit banks' umbrella organization proposed that the issuance of debt settlement credits as an answer to problematic debt situations be organized on a more structural basis. This is the first self-regulation of debt assistance.

1979 Self-regulation: The Code of Conduct for Debt Settlement lays the foundation for the current system of debt assistance

Despite this start, it took until the 1970s before debt assistance really became a core task of municipal credit banks (GKBs) in the Netherlands. In 1979, the credit banks' umbrella organisation and the commercial banks, who are the most important creditors, agreed upon a Code of Conduct for Debt Settlement, which contained the details for conducting debt settlements, such as repayment terms, repayment capacities and equality before the law of creditors. These entities viewed the Code of Conduct as necessary because debt assistance in the Netherlands had risen significantly in the 1970s. This rise can be explained by the increased use of consumer credit during that period and the number of households that were consequently facing financial problems and had turned to credit banks for help. The recession in which the Netherlands ended up at the end of the 1970s also reinforced the need for debt assistance.

The immediate reason for setting up a national code of conduct was the existence of large differences in the conditions that the GKBs set for the issuing of debt settlement credits. For example, similar debt settlements involved different interest rates and repayment terms. Requests for (partial) forgiveness of claims were also treated differently. When the number of debtors that asked for help was still limited, these differences were not a problem. The need for standardization arose when nationally operating creditors received debt settlement proposals that differed significantly from each other in terms of substance and complained about this to the individual credit banks.

The Code of Conduct for Debt Settlement is an important milestone in the development of the Dutch system of debt assistance. Its possibility to "buy off one's debts" was an important social innovation.[13] The "gentleman's agreement" between the regular commercial banks and credit banks initially gave a great boost to debt assistance. It created the foundation for the WSNP law that consists of a voluntary and a legal trajectory.

Although municipal credit banks had set up the Code of Conduct, in the years that followed it also became the central document that social services and social work institutions relied upon for offering debt assistance. In the 1980s, these organizations also started offering debt assistance in the Netherlands when they realized independent of each other that problematic debt situations got in the way of the help they offered. Thus, the social services and social work institutions retained a system initially developed through self-regulation.

The Code of Conduct for Debt Settlement played an important role in the standardization of implementation, but that this did not result in a uniformity of practice among these implementing organizations. The Code of Conduct contained agreements on the way in which most of the cases were handled, but at the same time offered discretionary latitude to deviate from these agreements. The agreement regarding the repayment term, for instance, was that "theoretically" a debt settlement would last 36 months.

1998: The new Act

In practice, the debt assistance organizations could offer a solution to about half of the debtors asking for help. The others had no other choice but to repay their debts, since even one hundred years after being opened up to consumers, the Bankruptcy Act still did not offer them any solution. This situation changed during discussion of the new legislation governing attachment. The House of Representatives passed a motion asking the government for a legal provision that offered debtors a debt-free future. Such a provision was requested precisely at this point because the new Act meant that recipients' benefits income could also be attached and their vulnerable position could mean that they could relatively often end up in a hopeless debt situation as a result. The moment of parliament-wide support was a "window of opportunity" to not only prevent the position of debtors from deteriorating, but in fact to ensure that for the future the position of debtors would improve.

In 1992, the state secretary at the time, Kosto, submitted the bill for the Debt Rescheduling (Natural Persons) Act (WSNP) to the House of Representatives. In this bill, the results of a study by Huls into the applicability of the Bankruptcy

---

13 See Nick Huls 1986

Reform Act to the Dutch system[14] and a study by the Mijnssen Commission into possibilities of amending the Bankruptcy Act could clearly be recognised. In the context of regulation and self-regulation it is important to note that with the legislative proposal for the WSNP, the government chose regulation that supplemented the existing system of self-regulation. With the WSNP, that became effective in 1998, the legislature wanted to design a regulation that would create an incentive for creditors to cooperate more often with voluntary debt settlements. [15] In the explanatory memorandum, the legislature mentions a number of elements from a legal debt settlement that in its view should lead to creditors cooperating more often with voluntary settlements. The hope was that the success rate in the voluntary trajectory would rise.

2000 Self-regulation: By adapting the Code of Conduct and standardizing the calculation of repayment capacity, the field tries to increase the effectiveness of the voluntary trajectory

Soon after the WSNP came into effect, it emerged that the effectiveness of the voluntary trajectory, which had functioned reasonably successfully until that point, did not increase but in fact declined due to the introduction. An insufficient policy theory from the legislature, strategic behavior by municipalities and creditors' bureaucratization of implementation were the most important causes.

Before the WSNP came into force, debt assistance agencies took an enormous amount of time to reach a voluntary debt settlement. In order to persuade creditors to cooperate, they would send letters, call creditors and offer tailor-made settlements. After the WSNP became law, the credit banks' umbrella organization (the NVVK) realized that the power to force a creditor to cooperate was the key to reaching a higher success rate. They amended the Code of Conduct in 2000 so that the work of debt assistance professionals would become less time consuming.

Characteristic of the amendments to the Code of Conduct is that the existing discretionary latitude was taken away, with the aim of further standardizing the implementation practice. With this change, the NVVK looked to reduce or even eliminate differences in implementation between voluntary and legal debt settlements so that as a result the WSNP would constitute a stronger incentive as a kind of "big stick." The old version of the Code of Conduct for example, stated that "theoretically" debt settlements should last 36 months. There were organisa-

14 Nick Huls 1992.

15 Explanatory memorandum to the WSNP, Parliamentary documents II, 1992/93, 22, 969, no. 3.

tions that deviated from this quite often. By including in the new Code of Conduct that debt settlements "always" lasted a maximum of 36 months, the implementation was equalized with the implementation practice of the WSNP.

Unintentionally, these changes to the Code of Conduct in 2000 caused the success rate to decrease. In 2004, the success rate dropped to a historical low of 9 percent.[16]

In addition to amending the Code of Conduct, the NVVK also tried to limit the counterproductive effect of the WSNP in other areas through self-regulation. Soon after the introduction of the WSNP it emerged, for example, that courts were stricter in their calculation of the repayment capacity than credit banks. As a result, creditors received a higher repayment in a legal debt settlement, thus making these settlements more attractive. This difference was later eliminated by making agreements with the judiciary on how the calculations were made.

2008 Regulation: A legislative proposal to amend the WSNP and self regulation by covenants, working in a demand-based way and guaranteeing quality in the voluntary trajectory

In 2001, the Ministry of Justice evaluated the impact of the WSNP and its effects on the voluntary trajectory.[17] The legal evaluation led to discussion on changing the WSNP, but not to a concrete legislative proposal. In 2008, the Ministry of Justice chose to change a number of sections of the WSNP.[18] An important reason for this was that in 2003 RECOFA, the professional organization of bankruptcy and debt settlement judges had written a letter to the Ministry of Justice to request that admission to the legal trajectory be restricted. The first-line judges said it was too easy for debtors to be admitted to the court and that courts were in danger of collapsing under the administrative burdens of the WSNP.

In addition to limiting admission to the courts, these amendments also:

- simplified the procedure for legal debt settlement so that the burden on the courts would decrease, thus;
- resulting in an increase in the success rate in the voluntary trajectory.

---

16 Nadja Jungmann 2006.
17 Nadja Jungmann, Bert Niemeijer and Marijke Ter Voert 2001.
18 Parliamentary documents II, 2004/05, 29 942, no. 3 (Legislative proposal for amendments to the WSNP).

In order to achieve a higher success rate, the legislation introduced three instruments:

• a compulsory debt settlement (art. 287a Fw (Bankruptcy Act));
• a moratorium art. 287b Fw;
• provisional relief (art. 287 lid 4).

In the event of compulsory debt settlement, the debtor can ask the judge to impose a debt settlement on creditors. If the judge awards the request, a debt settlement is established on a compulsory basis. The moratorium is an instrument by which creditors are forced to suspend their collection actions temporarily. It offers the debt assistance organization the time to start up or continue a proper voluntary trajectory, without being hindered by the collection measures of individual creditors. A moratorium can be sought whenever there is a threatening situation, such as an eviction, termination of the supply of gas, power or water, or termination or dissolution of health insurance. In addition, provisional relief can be applied for if the voluntary trajectory is (almost) completed. Provisional relief can prevent a creditor from getting an execution order for eviction or termination of utilities or health insurance just before a request for application of the WSNP is submitted.

The legal amendments to the WSNP took effect on January 1, 2008. In particular, the change to the admission requirements had major effects. The number of WSNP cases was approximately 40 percent lower in 2008 than in the previous year.

Figure 1 shows that this decrease indicates a break in the trend in the annual increases that had taken place since the law came into effect.

The year 2004 was not only dominated by the proposal to change the regulations under the WSNP. It was also characterized by a historical low in the success rate of the voluntary trajectory, 9 percent. All parties involved (debt assistance organizations, ministries, national politics and the judiciary) realized that something also had to happen in the voluntary trajectory. In addition to the proposed legislation, the field of debt assistance responded with several self-regulatory initiatives to increase the effectiveness of the voluntary trajectory, among others the conclusion of covenants with different creditors.

In the past years, the NVVK and municipalities concluded covenants on the national and local levels with important players, such as the Central Judicial Collection Agency, water supply companies, energy power companies, telephone companies (UPC), mail order companies and housing corporations. These covenants contain agreements on the terms and conditions under which the relevant creditors would cooperate on a debt settlement and sometimes also on prevention. For example, after just two months of non-payment, a power company passes on the name of a customer to debt assistance and if debt assistance then tries to reach a voluntary settlement, the power company always cooperates. These kinds of agreements are a form of self-regulation. It is not yet clear whether the covenants have contributed to a higher success rate.

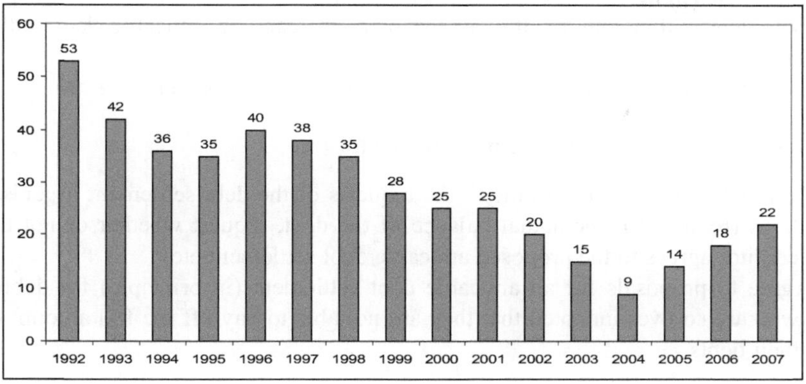

Figure 1: Number of debtors admitted to legal debt settlement between 1998-2007 (Jungmann 2006, NVVK 2008)

2010 Self-regulation: covenants between individual debt settlement organisations and specific groups of creditors to promote the cooperation

Between 2006 and 2011, the NVVK (the organization that represents individual debt settlement organizations) agreed to covenants with certain groups of creditors. The covenants contain agreements and obligations to promote the cooperation between debt settlement organisations and the specific groups of creditors. The aim of the covenants is twofold. First, the covenants are intended to improve cooperation between individual debt settlement organizations and groups of creditors. Without these sorts of covenants, individual creditors make in each file individual choices whether or not they are willing to cooperate with a voluntary debt settlement. Binding agreements for all creditors that belong to a group (energy suppliers, health insurance, etc) contributes to a higher success percentage since the creditors in the group are obliged to act in a certain way in specified circumstances. The second goal is to work together in acts of prevention.

During this period, the NVVK reached covenants with groups of creditors such as suppliers of water, energy and internet, the national agency that collects judicial debts, health insurance and the agency that provides social security benefits to the unemployed.

The covenants contain agreements for both individual debt settlement agencies and individual creditors. Debt settlement agencies must for example:

- Guarantee that the intake takes place within four weeks from the moment that someone applies for a debt settlement.
- Complete within four months all the work to reach an amicable debt settlement.
- Explain to creditors why there is no other option than a (part) remission.

In return creditors are (in principle) obliged to:

- Respond within a certain time to the requests of the debt settlement organisations (request for the actual balance of the debt, request whether or not the creditor agrees to the proposed amicable debt settlement etc)
- Agree to proposals for an amicable debt settlement (in principle) for debtor who are so over-indebted that they are not able to pay off the full amount of their debts.

2012 Regulation: debt assistance is a legal responsibility for municipalities

In the years after 2004, hard work was undertaken to increase the effectiveness of voluntary debt assistance. Considering the increases since then, it seems as thought he covenants and a new way of working by the debt assistance agencies introduced since 2006 actually had the envisioned effect (see Figure 2).

Figure 2: Success rates between 1992-2007
(Jungmann 2006, NVVK 2008)

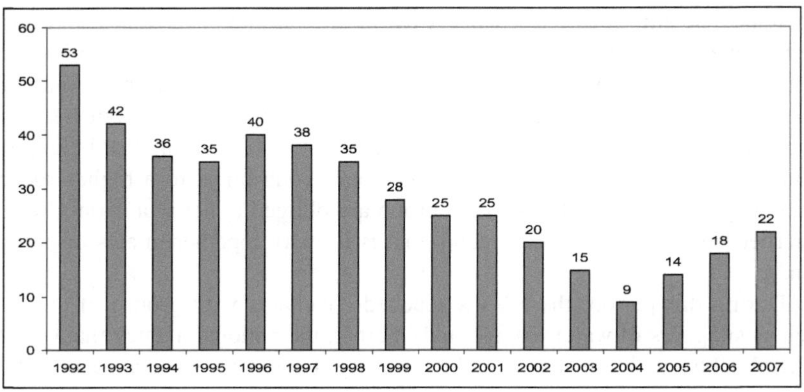

The national government regards a success rate of 20 percent to be insufficient and wrote to Parliament in autumn 2007 that it regarded itself as the party responsible for the whole system of debt assistance (voluntary and legal trajectory together) and would undertake investigation into the possibilities of increasing the effectiveness of the voluntary trajectory.[19] This represented its first decision to develop regulation related to the implementation of the voluntary trajectory. The investigation provided insight into the causes of the low success rate and an extensive set of recommendations to increase effectiveness.[20]

The Ministry of Social Affairs and Employment (SZW) considered the average effectiveness to be too low and wants to ensure that the amicable procedure in principle accessible to all residents. These two requirements represented the key motivation for the ministry to develop the Municipal Debt Assistance Act (Wet gemeentelijke schuldhulpverlening).[21] The proposal for the act was sent to parliament in February 2010. The act came into force on July 1, 2012.

The new law requires municipalities to offer:

- Integral debt assistance: the municipality is not only required to offer a solution to financial problems, but also a cohesive offer of assistance that includes support for other problems that caused the debts or that stand in the way of a sustainable solution.
- Preventative activities designed to prevent people from ending up in debt.
- An offer of aftercare to prevent people from becoming recidivist after the completion of the debt management plan (i.e., proactive counseling of people to ensure they do not incur new debts).

Municipalities can decide how to organize the implementation of the program. With an eye on democratic legitimacy, each year, municipal councils are required to establish a policy plan elaborating on the following elements:

- The objectives of the debt assistance program: the municipality has a certain degree of freedom to decide on the objective of the debt assistance programme, for example, that the assistance provided should result in a debt-free future for everyone. However, it is also appropriate for the debt assistance program to create a situation in which debts continue to exist, partially or ful-

19 Parliamentary documents II, 2007/08, 24,515, no. 124.
20 Nadja Jungmann et al. 2008.
21 Parliamentary Documents II, 2009-2010, 32,291 no. 1

ly, but no longer form any obstacle to participation in social life (working, attending school, etc).

- The method of implementation: the municipality can decide to carry out the program itself or hire an external party to provide the service (social institution, municipal bank or commercial party).
- Results to be achieved: the municipality must identify the results it intends to achieve with the debt assistance program. In terms of its profile, the municipality could, for example, identify the targeted result as its intent to enable residents to find their way to the debt assistance program independently or that it is sufficient if people with debts are made aware of the existence of the debt assistance program by other organizations (family doctors, social workers, etc.).
- Ensuring quality: the municipality must document how it guarantees that the debt assistance program is of the proper quality. Does it require the professionals assisting debtors to have certain education, or does it set other requirements?
- Prevention and aftercare: what is the municipality doing to prevent its citizens from incurring debts they cannot afford to repay or from falling back into debt after completing a voluntary debt management plan?
- Tailored work: how does the municipality ensure that everyone is provided with assistance that is appropriate to his/her own specific situation?

In addition to the above elements, the law also imposes a number of other requirements, including:

- Waiting times must not be longer than four weeks or, in case of a crisis such as a threatened eviction, no longer than three days.
- Following the intake, the municipality must let the debtor know how much time it will take before the debtor knows what solution the municipality is proposing. The municipality must adhere to the assessment provided.
- The municipality must offer integral debt assistance services, i.e., not only for the debts themselves, but also for problems that cause the debts to be incurred (e.g., addiction) or that represent an obstacle to solving the debt (e.g., rent that is too high).
- The municipality is in principle not permitted to exclude any group from the debt assistance program. The municipality can deviate from this in exceptional situations, for example, by stipulating that someone who previously received assistance no longer temporarily qualifies for assistance.

The new act would not oblige municipalities to meet specified quality demands in the event the ministry determines that the system of certification will provide a minimum level of quality.

Conclusion

In the field of debt assistance, self-regulation has played an important role for almost sixty years. The 1979 Code of Conduct for Debt Settlement was a success. Since then, however, for a long time there have been few improvements through regulation or self-regulation. The new initiatives seems to have had unclear, limited or no effects at all.

- Amendment of the Code of Conduct in 2000 had a counterproductive effect.
- Equating calculation of repayment capacity in the voluntary and legal trajectories prevented the success rate from falling further.
- The covenants between debt assistance organizations and creditors have created improvements.

The only piece of self-regulation that seems to have had any effect was the introduction beginning in 2006 of a new way of working. Because of a lack of national data, we are unable to assess the influence of the new work method. Some local studies by debt assistance agencies report impact and since the implementation the success rate really increased. When we look at government regulation, however, we see a different pattern.

These three moments of regulation all had visible effects:

- The opening up of the Bankruptcy Act in 1896 gave creditors an extra incentive to spur debtors to pay.
- The introduction of the WSNP in 1998 unintentionally led to a decrease in the success rate in the voluntary trajectory.
- The tightening up of the admission criteria of the WSNP as of 1 January 2008 led to a much stronger decline in the number of WSNP cases than foreseen.

The 2010 Act that is now pending in Parliament tries to strengthen the voluntary sector by imposing a duty of care on the municipalities. We interpret this proposal as a desperate attempt of the legislator to rescue the combination of informal and formal debt assistance.

We are not optimistic about the future of the self-regulatory mechanisms in the shadow of the WSNP law, however. The field of debt assistance is legalized to a great extent, the numbers of creditors in problematic debtors' files increase steadily, and the government is designing new legal preferences for itself. We believe that this two-tier system is ready for reconsideration.

References

Ayres, Iain and Braithwaite, John: Responsive Regulation - Transcending the Deregulation Debate. Oxford. Oxford University Press 1992.

Baarsma, Barbara et al.: Zelf doen? (inventory study of self regulatory instruments) SEO Report nr 664, Amsterdam. 2003.

Baarsma, Barbara, et al.: Goedkoop geregeld: een kosten baten analyse van regelgeving en zelfregulering, SEO rapport 720, Amsterdam. 2004.

Baldwin, R. and M. Cave: Understanding regulation. Theory, strategy, and practice. Oxford/New York. Oxford University Press 1999.

Campbell, A.J.: "Self-regulation and the media," Federal Communications Law Journal, vol. 51, 1999, 711-772.

Dorbeck-Jung Bärbel and Vrielink van Heffen, Mirjam Oude (red): "Op weg naar bruikbare zelfregulering", Special Issue on selfregulation. Recht der Werkelijkheid, 2006.

Driel, Marina van, Zelfregulering: hoog opspelen of thuisblijven. Deventer. Kluwer 1989

Giesen, Ivo: Alternatieve regelgeving en privaatrecht. Deventer. Kluwer 2007.

Griffiths John and Weyers, Heleen: De sociale werking van recht: een kennismaking met de rechtssociologie en rechtsantropologie. Nijmegen. Ars Aequi Libri 2005.

Gunningham, Neil, Grabosky, P. with Sinclair, Darren: Smart Regulation. Designing Environmental Policy. Oxford. OUP 1998.

Huls, Nick: Alternatives to personal bankruptcy, in Gunther Hormann (ed.) Consumer Credit and Consumer Insolvency. Perspectives for legal policy from Europe and the USA, ZERP, Bremen (1986) p. 289 – 310.

Huls, Nick: Towards a European Approach to overindebtedness of Consumers, 16 Journal Consumer Policy (1993), p. 215 – 234.

Huls, Nick: Onderhandelend wetgeven in de praktijk. Over ambtelijk activisme op middenniveau, Amsterdam University Press 1998.

Huls, Nick, Jungmann, Nadja and Niemeijer, Bert: Can Voluntary Debt Settlement and consumer bankruptcy co-exist? in Johanna Niemi- Kiesliainen, Iain Ramsay & William C. Whitford (Eds), Consumer Bankruptcy in global perspective, 303 -318, Hart Publishing 2003.

Huls, Nick and Jungmann, Nadja: Debt counselling in the shadow of the Courts: the Dutch experience, In : Johanna Niemi , Iain Ramsay & William C. Whitford (eds.), Consumer Credit, Debt & Bankruptcy. Comparative and international perspectives, Hart Publishing 2009, 419-439.

Jungmann, Nadja: De WSNP: Bedoelde en onbedoelde effecten op het minnelijk traject (PhD Thesis Leiden). Leiden: Leiden University Press 2006.

Jungmann Nadja et al.: Schulden? De gemeente helpt! Utrecht, Hiemstra & De Vries 2008.

Jungmann, Nadja: Wettelijke zorgplicht voor gemeenten, Kabinet werkt aan effectievere schuldhulpverlening. in: Wmo magazine, nr. 6, 2008, 16-20.

Jungmann, Nadja and H.D.L.M Schruer: Zorgplicht, grotere effectiviteit schuldhulpverlening. in: Sociaal Bestek, nr. 2, 2009, 26-31.

Ogus, Anthony: Regulation: Legal Form and Economic Theory. Oxford: Oxford University Press 1994.

Ogus, A.I.: "Rethinking self-regulation", Oxford Journal of Legal Studies, vol. 15, 1995, 97-108.
Olson, Mancur: The rise and decline of nations. Yale University Press 1982.
Stoter, Suzan en Nick Huls: Onderhandelend wetgeven. Een kwestie van geven en nemen. Sdu, Uitgevers, den Haag 2003.
Stoter, Suzan and Huls, Nick: Regeldruk: Een blinde vlek van onderhandelend wetgeven, Boom Juridische uitgevers, den Haag 2006.
Weatherill, Stephen (ed.): Better regulation, Oxford: Hart Publishing 2007
Weyers Heleen and J. Stamhuis (red): "Themanummer zelfregulering". Recht der Werkelijkheid 2003.

The New Swedish Debt Relief Act

Annina H. Persson[1]

Introduction

There are many signs that over-indebtedness has become a mounting problem in Swedish society. In 2008, there were 6,603 bankruptcies in Sweden, with 660 of these related to small individual traders and 334 to natural persons. By 2011, the number of bankruptcies had increased to 7,248, with 747 related to small individual traders and 321 to natural persons. Swedish debt relief proceedings have followed a similar trend. In 2008, there were 6,528 applications for debt relief; 4,376 of them were granted. In 2011, the number of applications for debt relief had increased to 8, 452, with 5, 943 of these granted. Debt advice also has increased over this period. In 2008, the number of cases brought to municipal budget and debt-counselors was 12,505. By comparison, in 2011, the numbers of cases to these counselors were approximately 46,000. Debt collection actions have also increased. In 2010, 391,168 persons were registered for a debt at the Swedish Enforcement Authority. By April 2012, the number had risen to 495,208 persons.

This increase in the number of persons who have payment difficulties is due mostly to the financial crisis and the financial turmoil in the world. In the wake of the economic downturn, the number of unemployed has also increased.[2] The prevailing recession, which among other things entails a sterner job market, also threatens to aggravate many people's private financial difficulties.

Another worrying factor is that every month, home mortgages increase by MSEK 13,000.[3] Lending has increased by 23% over the past three years. This rapid build-up of indebtedness has troubled the legislature, prompting it to appoint several Government commissions to assess the debt situation and propose new measures for curbing it. Proposal have been made to implement 1) stricter rules regarding credit assessment,[4] 2) a ceiling for certain interest rates, 3) an easing in the requirements for granting debt relief, 4) access to special state-

---

1 Professor of Private Law, Academy of Law, Psychology and Social Studies, Örebro University, Sweden and Centre for Banking and Finance, Royal Institute of Technology, Stockholm, Sweden.

2 Ekonomifakta, August 2012.

3 See for example SCB Finansmarknadsstatistik 2012, Dagens Industri, "Hushållen lånar mer", 2012-09-27, Jakobsson, Det är för billigt att låna, Svenska dagbladet, 2012-08-13.

4 Compare Section12 of the Consumer Credit Act (2010:1846) and the Directive 2008/48/EC of the European Parliament and of the Council of 23 April 2008 on credit agreements for consumers and repealing Council Directive 87/102/EEC.

financed social loans,[5] 5) stricter rules governing credit providers of so called sms-loans, 6) stricter regulation of a utility's ability to turn off electricity for non-payment without some kind of consent from the authorities, 7) new regulations on the trading of claims,[6] as well as 8) rules that make it possible for a debtor to protect his home from an executive procedure.

While these proposals have not yet gone into effect, earlier efforts have already been implemented. Financial education has been identified as a core subject in many schools, given that many young people appear ignorant of basic financial concepts. In a survey reported by Danske Bank in 2008, a number of young people were asked to define the financial concept of interest. The overwhelming majority were unable to answer.[7]

The Swedish Financial Supervisory Authority also has adopted a rule that new mortgage loans must not exceed 85 percent of the market value of the covered residential property.[8] The new rule looks to protect persons from over-indebtedness in the event of a drop in the real estate market.

In addition, the Debt Relief Act was amended in 2011 with the aim of making it easier to obtain debt relief. It is likely that this Act will be changed again in the near future,[9] as the legislature has appointed to two new commissions, one that will propose strategies for preventing over-indebtedness and one that will provide support for so called perpetual debtors.[10]

The new Debt Relief Act is outlined in part 4, below. However, firstly some of the problems with the old legislation are presented in parts 1 through 3.

The 1994 and 2006 Debt Relief Acts

Swedish lawmakers have discussed debt restructuring as an instrument for helping heavily indebted individuals since the end of the 1980s.[11] The Debt Relief Act (1994:334) entered into force on 1 July 1994 as a consequence of that debate,[12] and has been a subject of continuous monitoring and evaluation ever

5 See SOU 2008, at 82.
6 See Ds 2011, at 45 and SOU 2008, at 82 and FI Rapport:Handel med förfallna fordringar och inkasso 2006, at 3.
7 See www.danskebank.se/sv-se/Om-banken/Press/Pressmeddelanden/2008, 2008-02-08.
8 See FI Beslutspromemoria, Begränsning av lån mot säkerhet i bostadsfastighet eller bostadsrätt, FI Dnr 10-1533, 2010-07-08.
9 See Debt Relief Act (2006:548, amended SFS 2011:472).
10 See Directive 2012:31. Strategi för att motverka överskuldsättning and Directive 2012:30 Skuldsanering för evighetsgäldenärer.
11 See Directive 1988:52. *Utredningen av vissa konkursrättsliga frågor.*
12 See SOU 1990:74, proposition 1993/94:123.

since it came into force.[13] The main points of criticism have been that debt restructuring cases take too long to process and that the allocation of roles between the authorities involved has been unclear. Following a review of the legislation and the presentation of legislative proposals, a new Debt Relief Act (2006:548) was passed, effective from 1 January 2007.[14]

The 2006 Debt Relief Act was only as a step towards a more efficient way of dealing with the over-indebtedness problems of individual persons. Soon after the new amendments were implemented, events showed that the Debt Relief Act of 2006 was insufficient. One problem concerned over-indebted entrepreneurs with personal liability for the debts of their businesses. The act applied exclusively to private persons, but a business proprietor who was a natural person could obtain debt relief, if the conditions laid down in Section 5 of the Act were met.[15] Under Section 5, so long as other requirements in the act were fulfilled, a business proprietor could be granted debt relief if there was special reasons for doing so, having regard to the limited extent and simple character of the business activity. However, it was found that no debtor had ever been granted debt relief under that section.[16] Under Swedish law, natural persons remain liable for debts outstanding after a bankruptcy. An active entrepreneur debarred from the possibility of applying for debt relief was therefore in great danger of over-indebtedness. For many an entrepreneur who was declared bankrupt, failure spelled private financial disaster. He was to contend with a heavy burden of debt, which precluded new entrepreneurial activity for a long time. On account of this and other problems, changes to the Debt Relief Act were enacted and became effective from 1 July 2011.[17] Now a business proprietor may be granted debt relief if the economic conditions in the business are easy to investigate. The objective of this legislation is to create for entrepreneurs a system of debt write-downs enabling them to get back into business quickly.

The 2011 Debt Relief Act

Debt relief has a number of purposes, the main one being rehabilitation. People who are heavily indebted must be given the chance of solving their fi-

---

13 See, e.g., Konsumentverket (Swedish Consumer Agency) report: Utvärdering av skuldsaneringslagen, 1995/96:34, Riksskatteverket (National Tax Board) report, Rapport från skuldsaneringsprojektet december 2001, (RSV Rapport 2002:5), and SOU 2000:29, at 197. Cf. Directive 2002:139

14 See Directive 2002:139, SOU 2004:81 and proposition 2005/06:124.

15 Cf. Section 5 of the Debt Relief Act. See proposition 2005/06:124, at 78.

16 See Hellners and Mellqvist, 2007, at 104.

17 See Directive 2007:29 Samordnat insolvensförfarande, SOU 2008:82, proposition 2010/11:31.

nancial problems and in this way of leading more adequate and socially useful lives.[18] This rehabilitative purpose, however, has to be balanced against creditors' rightful interests in asserting their financial claims.

Debt relief is designed to make even-handed provision for these somewhat contradictory interests. The Act also has a preventive purpose, in the sense of making credit less readily available so that fewer people become over-indebted. A third purpose of debt restructuring is to favor the creditor collective in the sense of debtors coming to pay at least part of what is owing. Through debt relief the debtor usually pays more than would otherwise have been the case. If both the debtor and his creditors benefit, society will be spared a great deal of expense in various fields. It is also important that the debt relief system should not impair general payment morale[19] and that it should be constructed so as to gain the confidence of the general public.[20]

To meet these three ends, the Act builds on three basic principles, namely (1) that the institution is general, i.e., debt relief should in principle include all the debtor's liabilities, (2) that the claims included in a debt relief proceeding are all to be treated equally, and (3) that the institution is to be definitive in character.[21]

Debt relief procedure is concentrated in a single proceeding by the Enforcement Authority. Accordingly, a debtor can approach the Enforcement Authority directly, without first having attempted to make an arrangement with his creditors. Section 2 of the Debt Restructuring Act requires the Enforcement Authority both to examine and reconsider an application for debt relief. The intention here is for the Authority to be able to grant debt relief despite one or more creditors objecting to the proposal. In this way, the district courts are allotted a purely judicial role. A different role is also allotted to municipal budget and debt restructuring counselors, namely that of helping to prevent over-indebtedness and also that of helping persons in debt to find a solution to their problems. The Swedish Consumer Agency is the co-ordinating central authority for municipal budget and debt relief advisory services. Thus, the main responsibility for drawing up the debt relief scheme devolves on the Enforcement Authority (Section 19 of the Debt Restructuring Act, cf. Section 9), which is required in various ways actively to assist the investigation of the matter, although the proposal must be endorsed by the debtor as well.

Under Section 4 of the Debt Relief Act, debt relief can be granted to a natural person domiciled in Sweden if he is insolvent and so indebted that he cannot be presumed capable of paying off his debts within the foreseeable future (this is

---

18 See proposition 1993/94:123, at 73; SOU 2004:81, at 56.

19 See proposition 1993/94:123, at 77; SOU 2004:81, at 56.

20 See proposition 1993/94:123, at 95.

21 See proposition 1993/94:123, at 76; SOU 2004:81, at 57.

the "qualified insolvency requirement") and if, having regard to the debtor's personal and financial circumstances, it is reasonable that debt restructuring be granted to him (the "general equity requirement"). It should be noted that the two requirements in Section 4 of the Debt Relief Act are cumulative; both have to be satisfied in order for debt relief to be granted. In assessment of the general equity requirement, special consideration must be paid to the circumstances surrounding the occurrence of the debts, the efforts which the debtor has made to discharge his obligations and reach unaided a settlement with his creditors, and the manner in which the debtor has assisted with the conduct of the debt relief proceedings. The two material requirements – the qualified insolvency requirement and the general equity requirement – are deliberately couched in general terms. For this reason, case law has an important bearing on more detailed decision-making as to whether debt relief can be granted.[22]

The grant of an application for debt relief means that the debtor will have to subsist for a certain period – usually five years – on limited financial resources, with any surplus being distributed among his creditors.[23] Distribution conforms to a payment plan drawn up when debt relief is granted, unless the debtor is incapable of paying. In that case no payment plan is drawn up and the debtor is directly exempted from liability for the debts restructured. Under Section 37 of the Debt Relief Act, a debt relief order can be enforced without having acquired force of law. Thus, even if the decision is appealed, the debtor is obliged to comply with the payment plan decided on, and accordingly the plan starts to run from the time of the introductory decision.[24]

Nor may the debtor be the subject of a trading prohibition under the Trading Prohibition Act (1986:436) or have been granted debt relief previously, unless exceptional reasons are at hand, (Section 6 of the Debt Relief Act).[25]

---

22 See further Mellqvist, SvJT 1998, at 134; Persson, JT 2003-04, at 910; Persson, JT 2004-05, at 157, Persson, JT 2003-04, at 125 and NJA 2010, at 496 and Persson, JT 2010-2011, at 912, NJA 2011, at 957 and RH 2010:59.

23 A shorter period may, however, apply in special cases, e.g. if the debtor is an elderly person or is suffering from a life-threatening illness, or if it was already apparent at the time of debt relief being granted that, owing to impaired financial circumstances, the debtor would be unable to pay anything at all. When reviewing a restructuring order, however, the payment plan may not be prolonged by more than 7 years (Section 26 of the Debt Relief Act). See Hovrätten för Övre Norrland, ÖÄ270-05, beslut 2005-06-03, in which an 82-year-old man was granted debt relief with a three-year payment plan. See also NJA 2003 C 6, in which debt relief was granted to a man suffering from severe obesity and hypertension, and HD Ö 559-06 beslut 2006-03-21, in which HD (the Supreme Court) ruled that the court of appeal had been in error when it refused leave to appeal in a debt relief case involving a man with heart disease. See SOU 2004:81, at 137 and 234, proposition 2005/06:124, at 52. Cf. proposition 1993/94:123, at 108 and NJA 1998, at 15.

24 See proposition 2005/06:124, at 56, SOU 2004:81, at 242, 281, and 271.

25 See RH 2011:41.

The Swedish Enforcement Authority and its duties

The KFM is an autonomous national authority with nationwide coverage, headed by a Director-General. KFM's activities are divided into a number of branches: enforcement of payment and other liabilities under the Enforcement Code (1981:774) and other statutory instruments, debt collection under the Collection of State Claims Act (1993:891), summary process (payment injunctions and enforcement assistance), debt relief, bankruptcy supervision and wage guarantees in connection with bankruptcy and company reconstruction.[26] The Authority's activities cover the whole country and its organizational structure is geared to its various branches of activities, instead of conforming to geographic boundaries. The bulk of the KFM's activities involve enforcement actions under the Enforcement Code and debt collection under the Collection of State Claims Act.

Although all enforcement activities under the Enforcement Code in Sweden devolve on KFM, as a first resort, a creditor with an outstanding claim can approach a private enterprise engaging in permit-regulated debt collection activity (*inkassoverksamhet),*[27] that is debt collection on behalf of a third party. The debt collection company can take a collection measure, such as threatening the debtor with legal or executory action if the debt remains unsettled. If the debtor does not pay, the debt collection company may take legal action by applying to KFM for a payment injunction or filing judicial proceedings against the debtor as a first step towards applying to KFM for attachment.

Once KFM receives a payment injunction application, a special "summary process" follows. KFM sends the respondent an injunction demanding payment of the claim. The respondent, who is served with the injunction, can comment on the content of the injunction and possibly dispute it within a specified time. If the respondent objects to the claim, for example, by denying that anything owed, the case will, at the applicant's request, be referred to the district court for further processing. If the respondent/debtor does not object to the claim, the applicant's request will be upheld in a decision by KFM. KFM will then enforce the decision or any judgement returned if the case has gone to a district court. A payment injunction can only be applied for if the claim concerns money, has fallen due for payment, and is amenable to out-of-court settlement.

---

26 See Förordning (2007:781) med instruktion för kronofogdemyndigheten (Ordinance containing standing instructions for the Swedish Enforcement Authority), amended SFS 2011:1550.

27 See the Debt Collection Act (1974:182), amended SFS 2009:415.

As previously mentioned, debt relief procedures are concentrated within KFM. The Authority examines debt relief cases under powers conferred by Section 2 of the Debt Relief Act. It also reviews debt relief orders. The decision to vest an administrative authority with extensive decision-making authority over matters of debt relief has not been entirely uncontroversial.[28] Is it not contrary to Art. 6 of the European Convention on Human Rights[29] for an administrative authority to be the tribunal of first instance examining a dispute concerning a person's civil rights, with the courts only examining the question of appeal? The Swedish legal position, however, is that this is not at variance with the rules of the European Convention,[30] in that the individual can always appeal the Authority's decision to a district court, where he is entitled to a fair trial. The stipulations in Art. 6:1 of the Convention presuppose the possibility of judicial recourse and a court having sufficient competence for a complete assessment of civil rights. This requirement is not always met by a court reviewing an administrative authority's decision, because the court's competence may be limited to examining the legality of the administrative decision but not include the discretionary assessments and actual circumstances on which the administrative authority based its initial decision.[31] Since the rules have been framed to permit individual debtors to appeal from a KFM's decision to a district court, without any need for a review dispensation, and to require district courts to retry the case to its full extent, they have not been considered to be at variance with Art. 6 of the European Convention.

A debt relief application is made out on a special form provided by KFM and has to be signed by the debtor personally. The initial examination of the matter by KFM involves examining the content of the application and any need for elucidation or further particulars, the point being that the debtor risks having the application refused if he fails to complete it properly. Before KFM can take a stand in the matter of debt relief, further examination of the debtor's application is needed. The Authority is responsible for this investigation being carried out as thoroughly as possible. To this end, it may obtain particulars concerning the debtor from other authorities. When sufficient data have been collected, a debt-relief scheme is drafted. The draft is sent to all creditors for comment. KFM then carries out its final examination of the matter. If the debtor is granted debt relief, the decision is announced in the official bulletin "Post-och inrikes-tidningar". Alternatively, KFM can make a debt relief order against the wishes of one or more creditors.

---

28 See SOU 2004:81, at 216-223.

29 The European Convention of 4 November 1950 for the Protection of Human Rights and Fundamental Freedoms.

30 See SOU 2004:81, at 222; proposition 2005/06:124, at 33.

31 See Danelius, 2007, at 174.

A person applying for debt relief can of course engage a legal representative. Given the way in which debt relief cases are drafted by KFM and the slim chances of lawyers being paid for their services by the clients, it is rare for a debtor to be represented by a qualified lawyer in a debt relief case, and Section 10 (1) (3) of the Legal Aid Act (1996:1619) rules out the possibility of legal aid in matters of debt relief. Although legal aid counsel cannot represent the debtor, the debtor can obtain support and assistance from a budget and debt counselor in connection with the application during the handling process and, moreover, for the duration of the payment plan thereafter. The services of debt and budget counselors are paid for with public funding. It should be added, however, that the demand for budget and debt counselors greatly exceeds supply.

The main amendments in the 2011 Debt Relief Act

The basic objective of the new legislation is to create for entrepreneurs a system for writing down debts that enables them to get back into business quickly, while at the same time giving all severely over-indebted persons better opportunities for debt relief than under former legislation.[32]

The Act retains qualified insolvency as a prerequisite for the granting of debt restructuring (Section 4 of the Debt Relief Act). However, the former provisions required special attention to be paid to the age of the debts when assessing what is equitable has now been completely discarded (Section 4 (2) of the Debt Relief Act).[33] This is not to say that the age of the debts is of no interest in the assessment of what is fair and reasonable, but the issue should be toned down and nuanced. If a person has been heavily in debt for a long time on account of debts incurred previously, this should be counted in their favor. Normally the need for financial rehabilitation can then be considered to be very real. The change also implies that, contrary to former practices, individual new debts will not invariably stand in the way of a debt restructuring.

The Government refrained from introducing several of the proposals suggested by the Commission. The Government argued that the Act was changed as late as 2007 and on this basis thought that it was appropriate to defer the impact of the new changes before introduction of these additional proposals.[34]

The Commission had proposed a considerable change in the substance of the requirement, compared with the provisions now in force. Instead of a person being judged so debt-ridden as to be incapable of paying their debts within the foreseeable future, which in practice has been taken to mean a period of between

32 See proposition 2010/11:31 at 10-16.

33 See proposition 2010/11:31 at 22-23.

34 See proposition 2010/11:31, at 19.

10 and 12 years, the proposal required a presumption of the debtor being judged incapable of settling his debts within the next few years. On this point, it would refer to a space of up to 5 years.[35] The Government did not accept this proposal.

Another proposal was to reduce the present payment scheme from 5 to 3 years, in order to enhance people's readiness to apply for debt relief.[36] The Government also rejected this proposal.

In the assessment of what is fair and reasonable, existing rules require consideration of the efforts the debtor has made to honor his obligations (Section 4 (2)). The Commission proposed a new wording of the statutory text regarding the debtor's conduct toward his creditors.[37] This new wording in the proposed statutory text was to be construed against the background of the expression "the debtor's efforts" linguistically suggesting that it is only the debtor's active, actual attempts at repayment that can be taken into account when contemplating debt relief, which may not pay heed to the prevailing image of apathetic perpetual debtors. The new wording made clear that passive behavior due to some form of paralysis and not forming part of a disloyal strategy for withholding funds should at least not be counted against the debtor in the assessment of what is fair and reasonable. This proposal was also rejected by the Government.

During the research preceding the drafting of a new Debt Relief Act, the issue was addressed of whether severely indebted and still active entrepreneurs whose activity is neither slight nor of a simple nature should be given opportunities for debt restructuring.[38] This was partly ruled out for several different reasons, and active entrepreneurs wishing to remain in business are in general referred to company reconstruction or a freestanding settlement with creditors.[39]

Conclusion

Most of the authorities and organizations in the consultation process favor the amendments to the Debt Relief Act. It is a good thing that debt restructuring will be granted more rapidly now that the "age of debts" requirement is no longer to be expressly factored into the general assessment of what is fair and reasonable. Under precedent that has developed since the Act came into force, a person with payment arrears has had to wait several years before an application can be granted, after which, assuming the application was granted, the process

35 See SOU 2008:82, at 129, 263.

36 See SOU 2008:82, at 135, 266

37 See SOU 2008:82, at 265.

38 See proposition 2010/11:31, at 10 and 22.

39 The final report has been submitted on the 28 of January 2010. See SOU 2010:2, Ett samlat insolvensförfarande - förslag till ny lag. See also Directive 2007:29, Directive 2008:77 and Directive 2009:41. See also SOU 2008:82, at 117.

had to continue for another 5 years or so; as a result, the elimination of debt may take between 10 and 15 years altogether. The amendment in the law means that an over-indebted person will now be able to obtain debt relief more rapidly. A change of this kind will also improve the chances of the debtor paying at least part of what is owed, since he will not need to have been in debt for many years.

Nonetheless, the Government restrained from introducing several of the Commission's more controversial proposals, especially those that the banks objected to vociferously. It was argued that even minor amendments to the Debt Relief Act had heavily impacted the number of applications for debt relief. For example, amendments enacted in 2007, which eliminated the "own attempt" requirements regarding the debtor's duty to endeavor to reach settlements with his creditors, led to a doubling of the number of debt relief applications, from 3,600 to over 7,000 annually.[40] Critics argued that if the new proposed changes would be introduced, the number of debt restructuring applications might rise from 7,000 to 26,000 per annum, an increase of several hundred percent, by the Commission's own projections. In light of that fact and that 60 percent of all debt relief applications generally are granted,[41] it was argued that the proposed change in what is termed the qualified insolvency requirement could result in even moderately debt-ridden persons being granted debt relief. As a consequence, it was argued, people who ought to have been granted credit would be refused access, due to the banks having to increase their safety margin when creditworthiness assessments deteriorate and the risk of claims being written down increased. The banks were therefore very much afraid of debt relief becoming excessively available, with repercussions for consumers' access to credit. An opening up of debt relief procedure to the extent proposed by the Commission, argued these opponents, posed a risk that the benefit of entrepreneurs and private individuals being able to quickly get back on their feet will be negated by suppliers and creditors raising prices and demanding payment in advance or some other security to offset the greater risk of their claims being written down. The concern is that credit may grow harder to come by.

Critics also argue that the Commission's report was devoid of empirical material shedding light on these potential adverse consequences. Many questions were not answered, for example: Was there a danger of good payment behavior in Sweden drastically deteriorating? Would the grant of credit to private persons become a blunter and more expensive instrument with an inferior national economic outcome, leading to a stagnation of entrepreneurial activity and private consumption?

---

40 See SOU 2008:82, at 21, 249, 271.

41 See Kronofogden, Allt fler får skuldsanering, Press release from Kronofogden, 2009-02-20.

To summarize, the Debt Relief Act was changed in 2011, aiming to make it easier to be granted debt relief. However, it is likely that the Act will be changed again in the near future.[42] As already mentioned, the legislature has appointed two new commissions, one that will propose strategies for preventing over-indebtedness and one that will provide support to so called perpetual debtors,[43] due to an increase in the number of over- indebted persons.

The Commissions' task will be to strike a balance between two interests. People should not find themselves subject to long-term over-indebtedness, which is expensive both to the community and to creditors. At the same time, debt relief should not be abused by persons with normal debt burdens, which in turn would be detrimental to entrepreneurial activity and consumption. How the new Debt Relief Act will be constructed in order to meet these ends remains to be seen.

References

Ds (Departementsserien) 2009:67. Ny konsumentkreditlag.
Ds 2011:45 Preskription av betalningsansvar för styrelseledamöter med flera.
Directive 1988:52. Utredningen av vissa konkursrättsliga frågor.
Directive 2002:139. Översyn av skuldsaneringslagen.
Directive 2007:29. Samordnat insolvensförfarande.
Directive 2008:77. Tilläggsdirektiv till 2077 års insolvensutredning (JU 2007:05).
Directive 2009:41. Tilläggsdirektiv till 2077 års insolvensutredning (JU 2007:05).
Directive 2012:31. Strategi för att motverka överskuldsättning
Directive 2012:30 Skuldsanering för evighetsgäldenärer.

Proposition 1993/94:123. Skuldsaneringslag.
Proposition 2005/06:124. Ett enklare och snabbare skuldsaneringsförfarande.
Proposition 2010/11:31. Bättre möjlighet till skuldsanering.

SOU (Statens offentliga utredningar)1990:74. Förslag till skuldsaneringslag.
SOU (Statens offentliga utredningar) 2000:29. Starka konsumenter i en gränslös värld.
SOU (Statens offentliga utredningar) 2004:81. Ett steg mot ett enklare och snabbare skuldsaneringsförfarande.
SOU (Statens offentliga utredningar) 2008:82. Vägen tillbaka för överskuldsatta.
SOU (Statens offentliga utredningar) 2010:2. Ett samlat insolvensförfarande - förslag till ny lag.

Danelius, Hans, Mänskliga rättigheter i europeisk praxis. En kommentar till Europakonventionen om de mänskliga rättigheterna, 3rd ed., 2007. Stockholm. Norstedts Juridik.
FI (Finansinspektionens) Rapport, Handel med förfallna fordringar och inkasso, 2006:3.

---

42 See Debt Relief Law (2006: 548, amended 2011:472).

43 See Direktiv 2012:31. Strategi för att motverka överskuldsättning and Direktiv 2012:30 Skuldsanering för evighetsgäldenärer.

FI (Finansinspektionens) Beslutspromemoria, Begränsning av lån mot säkerhet i bostadsfastighet eller bostadrätt, FI Dnr 10-1533, 2010-07-08.

Hellners, Trygve & Mellqvist, Mikael, Skuldsaneringslagen. En kommentar till 2006 års lag, 2007. Stockholm. Norstedts Juridik.

Konsumentverket (Swedish Consumer Agency) report: Utvärdering av skuldsaneringslagen, 1995/96:34.

Konsumentverkets PM 2003:26, En samordnad uppföljning av skuldsaneringsprocessen.

Kronofogden, Allt fler får skuldsanering, Press release from Kronofogden, 2009-02-20.

Kronofogden, Rekordmånga ansökningar om obetalda skulder till Kronofogden, Press release from Kronofogden, 2009-02-23.

Mellqvist, Mikael, Praxis i skuldsaneringsärenden, Svensk Juristtidning (SvJT) 1998 p. 134-151.

Persson, Annina H., Förutsättningar för att bevilja skuldsanering, Juridisk Tidskrift (JT) 2003-04 p. 910-918.

Persson, Annina H., Hur behandlas en okänd och tvistig fordran i ett skuldsaneringsärende, Juridisk Tidskrift (JT) 2004-05 p. 157-163.

Persson, Annina H., Allmänna villkor för skuldsanering uppfyllda? Juridisk Tidskrift (JT) 2003-04 p. 125-132.

Persson, Annina H., När är en gäldenär kvalificerat insolvent? Juridisk Tidskrift nr 4, 2010-2011, p. 912-916..

Riksskatteverket (National Tax Board) report Rapport från skuldsaneringsprojektet december 2001, (RSV Rapport 2002:5)

Court cases

NJA 1998 p. 15. (NJA= Nytt Juridiskt Arkiv avdelning 1)
NJA 2003 C 6 (NJA= Nytt Juridiskt Arkiv avdelning 1)
NJA 2010 p. 496 (NJA= Nytt Juridiskt Arkiv avdelning 1)
NJA 2011 p. 957 (NJA= Nytt Juridiskt Arkiv avdelning 1)
RH 2010:59 (RH =Rättsfall från hovrätterna)
RH 2011:41(RH = Rättsfall från hovrätterna)
Hovrätten för Övre Norrland, ÖÄ270-05, beslut 2005-06-03.
Högsta domstolen (HD) Ö 559-06 beslut 2006-03-21

Fourteen Years of Consumer Bankruptcy in Austria

Georg E. Kodek

Introduction

This chapter attempts an overview of the Austrian rules on consumer bankruptcy and of the empirical data available, however scarce, in this field. The situation in Austria is different from many other countries in that consumer bankruptcy was only introduced relatively late, in 1993. Also, Austria has a highly developed social security system. Nonetheless, evidence gained in Austria may produce insights in the effects, if any, of a social welfare system on consumer bankruptcy.

Empirical information available

Empirical research in bankruptcy law is still in its infancy in Austria.[1] In the first edition of my book on Austrian consumer bankruptcy, which was published in 2002,[2] I provided some empirical data, trying to collect what little information was available at that time.[3] Of course one of the difficulties in trying to do empirical research in this field (like in any other) is obtaining reliable data. While by no means complete, fortunately there are several sources that offer valuable insights into consumer over-indebtedness.

---

1 Austria is a small country of approximately 8 million inhabitants. According to the Austrian Ministry of Justice, some 80,000 households in Austria are over-indebted. This figure was used in the legislative history of the 1993 reform and has been widely used since. However, this figure is probably a very conservative estimate; some authors suggest that the actual number is much higher, assuming that there are as many as 200,000 over-indebted individuals in Austria.

2 Kodek 2002. A new edition is scheduled to be published in 2013. The author has accompanied the reform both as a judge at the first instance and appellate levels, as a lecturer at the Austrian Judicial Training Center and as a professor at the Vienna Law School and the WU – the Vienna University of Economics and Business Administration.

3 I would like to thank all persons and institutions who have provided me with statistical data on consumer bankruptcy. First and foremost, I extend my sincere gratitude to the Arbeitsgemeinschaft Schuldnerberatungen, and in particular to its managing director Dr. Grohs, for regularly providing me with these statistics. Unless otherwise indicated, the figures presented in this paper are based on information furnished by the Arbeitsgemeinschaft Schuldnerberatungen.

First, some statistics concerning bankruptcy proceedings are published in the official Insolvency Database ("*Insolvenzdatei*"). This database shows the opening and disposition of all bankruptcy cases and also provides additional information as to dates of hearings, terms of a payment plan, etc. The Insolvency Database does not provide any information as to the occupation of the debtor, as to the amount of debts or the number of creditors and – most importantly – as to whether or not the payment plan is fulfilled. The reason for this is that the payment plan is paid, usually by way of installments, after the bankruptcy proceeding has been closed. Therefore, the courts have no information about the situation of the debtor after the proceeding has been closed.

Additional valuable information can be gained from annual statistical reports published by the Arbeitsgemeinschaft Schuldnerberatungen, a platform for all consumer debtor advisor organizations. These reports are in part based on an analysis of the official Insolvency Database and in part on information provided by debt counseling organizations. Therefore, some of the data in these reports relate solely to debtors represented by an official debt counseling institution since sufficient information is not available on other debtors. While 71 percent of all debtors file bankruptcy petitions with the assistance of an official debt counseling institution, so that the information gained from these institutions should provide a sufficiently large sample, it appears that some kinds of debtors, particularly debtors who are or were formerly self-employed, generally do not contact these institutions, instead preferring to be represented by a lawyer or instituting a proceeding on their own. This is important to note since a large number of debtors in Austrian consumer bankruptcy proceedings are debtors who formerly had their own business. The situation of these debtors is not adequately portrayed by the data collected by debt counseling institutions.

An ambitious empirical analysis of Austrian consumer bankruptcy law was undertaken in 2004, which resulted in a publication ("Der Privatkonkurs auf dem Prüfstand" – hereinafter referred to as the "Prüfstand-Study"). This study provided valuable insights because it included data from new sources. The Prüfstand Study gathered information from the official Insolvency Data Base. In addition, it relied on data gained from all judicial discharge proceedings where the Arbeitsgemeinschaft Schuldnerberatungen was appointed trustee. The information generated in this way was supplemented by 1,560 questionnaires and by related Computer Assisted Telephone Interviews (CAT). Unfortunately, only 176 properly filled out questionnaires were returned. Finally, it considered anecdotal evidence available from various lawyers, debt counselors, judges and other court personnel.

The starting point: Austrian bankruptcy law prior to 1993

While bankruptcy law in Austria has a long history, with the origins of modern bankruptcy procedure going back well into the nineteenth century,[4] traditionally bankruptcy proceedings in Austria were not attractive for consumers. The reason for this is quite simple. As a rule, Austrian bankruptcy proceedings do not end with a discharge of the debtor. Rather, creditors are still entitled to claim the remainder of their unpaid claims.

While for a long time there have been procedures available under Austrian law and resulting in a discharge, these, likewise, were not attractive for consumers. Depending on the type of procedure used, the debtor had to pay a quota between 20 and 40 percent. In composition proceedings ("*Ausgleich*"), a proceeding that a debtor can institute in order to avoid bankruptcy proceedings, a discharge is possible if the majority of the creditors accept a plan. Under the law, the plan has to offer to pay at least 40 percent of the debtor's obligations over two years. Alternatively, a discharge is possible by way of a plan in an ordinary bankruptcy proceeding ("*Zwangsausgleich*"). This requires a minimum quota of 20 percent to be paid within five years. In light of the fact that the average debtor owes some €70,000, a quota requirement of 20 or even 40 percent made it extremely difficult if not impossible for most individual debtors to achieve a discharge. Additionally, the relatively high cost of the proceedings of approximately €3,000 constituted an insurmountable obstacle for many consumers, there being no legal aid available to cover these costs.

The 1993 Reform

The difficulties posed to consumers by traditional bankruptcy proceedings led to a reform of Austrian bankruptcy law in 1993. The reform brought a package of changes that made it easier for individuals to file for bankruptcy and obtain a discharge. While this reform is generally referred to, both in the media and in academic writings, as "Privatkonkurs," it should be pointed out that the new rules apply to all individuals, regardless of whether they are self-employed or consumers. The only difference is that the procedure for consumers was even more simplified, dispensing in large measure with the requirement to appoint an administrator and removing the proceeding from the superior courts to local district courts.

While this reform in several respects used the German "Insolvenzordnung" as a model, it avoided some of the difficulties of the German law by providing

4 An enlightening portrait the early origins of modern Austrian bankruptcy law is provided by Demelius 1976, at 13.

for simpler rules. Most importantly, two new types of discharge were introduced. In addition to the procedures briefly described above, a debtor can now propose a payment plan ("Zahlungsplan"), which is, roughly speaking, a more flexible version of the traditional plan ("Zwangsausgleich"). Under the new scheme, there is no fixed minimum quota. Rather, the quota offered by the debtor has to be adequate in light of his means. This is specified by the statute to mean that a debtor has to offer over a five year period at least that part of his income that could be attached by way of a garnishee order. In other words, the debtor has to be prepared to live on minimum income for at least five years. The maximum payment period for such a plan is seven years. Also, all property subject to execution, such as a house, stereo equipment, etc., has to be sold before the plan is voted on.[5] The plan requires approval by a majority of creditors and can be amended later if the debtor's financial situation deteriorates through no fault of his own.

If the creditors do not accept the payment plan, despite its adequacy at law, the debtor can obtain a discharge without creditor approval by order of the court. If the debtor's income exceeds the amounts exempt from enforcement proceedings, he has to assign this "excess" income to a court appointed trustee for seven years. If the debtor manages to pay at least 10 percent of his obligations during this period, he is entitled to a mandatory discharge. Otherwise, the court can grant a discretionary discharge, taking into account a variety of factors. Unfortunately, Austrian courts are relatively strict here, following a 1998 decision of the Austrian Supreme Court, which held that a disabled debtor who could offer only a quota of 1.24 percent was not eligible for judicial discharge proceedings.[6] Alternatively, the court can extend the proceeding for an additional three years; if the debtor manages to pay 10 percent of his obligations during this extended term, he is entitled to a discharge. According to a recent Austrian Supreme Court decision, there is no discretional discharge available in such extended proceedings, however.[7]

The 1993 reforms also made additional changes to Austrian bankruptcy law, which resulted in bankruptcy proceedings becoming more accessible to consumers. Notably, a kind of legal aid was introduced for "promising debtors" who already were able to present a realistic payment plan together with the petition

5 This is an important difference to the traditional plan ("Zwangsausgleich"). Therefore, if a debtor owns a house or other property he wants to keep, this can only achieved by way of a Zwangsausgleich, for which, however, there are higher quota requirements.

6 Austrian Supreme Court judgment of August 7, 1999, 8 Ob 342/98. More recently, Austrian lower courts seem to have become more generous. See Grohs et al. 2008.

7 Austrian Supreme Court judgment of August 3, 2006, 8 Ob 84/06w.

for opening the proceedings. Under the new scheme, the federal government advances the costs of the proceeding (such as the fee of the administrator or trustee). Also, a number of reforms reduced the cost of all consumer bankruptcy proceedings. Most importantly, while the appointment of an administrator was mandatory before the reform, this appointment now is only required in exceptional circumstances. In addition, the introduction of a government-run web platform and insolvency database enable consumers to avoid the cost of various mandatory publications in newspapers. Also, the costs of a bailiff seizing or selling property are now borne by the government instead of the debtor.

Other changes concern the traditional plan ("Zwangsausgleich"). The reform attempted to achieve greater flexibility for consumers in this context, requiring a 30 percent quota to be paid within five years (instead of the normal two years) for consumer bankruptcies.

Although the reform met with severe opposition both from tabloid newspapers and the banking industry, it was approved unanimously by the Austrian Parliament. The reform took effect on January 1, 1995. Generally, the new scheme works quite well. One important factor, which greatly contributed to the success of the reform, was the implementation of a network of debt counseling institutions to assist debtors in filing bankruptcy petitions and, in some instances, also represent debtors during the proceeding. In 2008, 47,525 persons contacted a debt counseling agency at least once.

Applications and openings of proceedings

Consumer bankruptcy filings have increased continuously over the past years; in some years, consumer bankruptcy filings increased at a pace of double-digit increase over the previous year. Correspondingly, the number of bankruptcy proceedings that were actually opened increased. This figure is somewhat smaller, because not every application successfully opens a proceeding. For example, in 2008, roughly 88 percent of all applications led to an opening of a bankruptcy proceeding by the court. A variety of reasons explain why 12 percent of the filings were not opened in this year, including defects in the application that the debtor failed to amend, lack of jurisdiction of the court, and other factors.

The 2004 Prüfstand Study yielded valuable data as to what debtors expect from bankruptcy proceedings.[8] Not surprisingly, the expectation of a discharge was ranked very highly. An even higher priority was given to the expectation

8 See Prüfstand-study 2008, at 38.

that enforcement proceedings instituted by creditors would end. This is an indication that ongoing enforcement proceedings are considered more troublesome by many debtors than the existence of debts, as such. Similar emphasis was given to a hope that the bankruptcy would enable better planning of income and expenses and to relief from psychological problems resulting from the over-indebtedness. Other factors mentioned, although less frequently, include an expectation of a more stable job situation and the desire to protect family members from potential conflicts associated with the collection of these "debts."

Tables A, B and C, below, encourage further scrutiny of the difference between filing rates and openings over time and across Austria. There are regional differences in the "success rate" of applications that cannot be explained by ordinary statistical fluctuation margins. Thus, in Vienna, the success rate was 94 percent (3,406 openings compared to 3,606 applications), while in Upper Austria the rate was only 81 percent (1,070 openings compared to 1,317 applications).

Table 1A: Overview 1995–2008

	Openings	**Change form previous year**	**Applications**	**Change from previous year**
1995	776		917	
1996	1,248	61 %	1,458	59 %
1997	1,639	31 %	1,960	34 %
1998	2,071	25 %	2,478	26 %
1999	2,614	26 %	3,049	23 %
2000	2,823	8 %	3,460	13 %
2001	3,021	7 %	3,644	5 %
2002	3,202	5 %	3,768	3 %
2003	3,720	13 %	4,462	15 %
2004	4,676	20 %	5,636	21 %
2005	5,349	12 %	6,523	14 %
2006	6,296	13 %	7,509	12 %

2007	7,388	14 %	8,717	14 %
2008	8,599	13 %	9,703	9 %

(Source: author, based on information furnished by asb)

Table 1B: Regional statistics on applications 2005–2008

	2005	**2006**	**2007**	**2008**
Burgenland	169 -- 2.6 %	148 – 2.0%	179 – 2.1%	196 – 2.0%
Carinthia	668 – 10.2%	832 – 11.1%	645 – 7.4%	737 – 7.6%
Lower Austria	732 – 11.2%	777 – 10.3%	962 – 11%	989 –10.2%
Upper Austria	1,157 –17.7%	1,174 – 15.6%	1,330–15.3%	1,317--13.6%
Salzburg	466 – 7.1%	450 – 6%	484 – 5.6%	479 – 4.9%
Styria	572 – 8.8%	610 – 8.1%	721 – 8.3%	816 – 8.4%
Tyrol	733 – 11.3%	804 –10.7%	957 – 11%	872 – 9%
Vorarlberg	541 – 8.3%	472 – 6.3%	605 – 6.9%	691 – 7.1%
Vienna	1,480--22.7%	2,242–29.9%	2,834–32.5%	3,606 – 37.2%
Total	6,523 – 100%	7,509 – 100%	8,717 – 100%	9,703 – 100%
Change from previous year	13.6%	11.6%	13.6%	8.9%

(Table: author, based on information furnished by asb)

Table 1C: Regional statistics 2005–2008 on openings of proceedings

	2005	**2006**	**2007**	**2008**
Burgenland	130 – 2.4%	124 – 2.0%	136 – 1.8%	164 – 1.9%
Carinthia	633 – 11.8%	731 – 11.6%	594 – 8.0%	700 – 8.1%
Lower Austria	555 – 10.4%	649 – 10.3%	753 – 10.2%	830 – 9.7%
Upper Austria	827 – 15.5%	884 – 14.0%	1,053 – 14.3%	1,070 – 12.4%
Salzburg	424 – 7.9%	366 – 5.8%	421 – 5.7%	432 – 5.0%
Styria	393 – 7.3%	425 – 6.8%	519 – 7.0%	622 – 7.2%
Tyrol	640 – 12.0%	643 – 10.2%	761 – 10.3%	759 – 8.8%

Vorarlberg	455 – 8.5%	396 – 6.3%	523 – 7.1%	616 – 7.2%
Vienna	1,292 – 24.2%	2,078 – 33.0%	2.628 – 35.6%	3,406 – 39.6%
Total	5,349 – 100%	6,296 – 100%	7,388 – 100%	8,599 – 100%
Change from previous year	11.9%	13.4%	14.4%	13.4%

(*Source: author, based on information furnished by asb*)

Debt situation[9]

The following section provides some information as to the average amount of debt per debtor. The information is provided for all of Austria's nine states for the years 2004 to 2008. To put this into a wider perspective, the nationwide figures for 1998 to2003 are also provided.

Table 2A: Overview 1998-2003

	1998	**1999**	**2000**	**2001**	**2002**	**2003**
Average	70,622	73,943	78,621	74,064	70,058	65,797
change from previous year	1.82 %	4.70 %	6.33 %	–5.80 %	- 5.41 %	- 6.08 %

(Source: author, based on information furnished by asb)

9 These data again are from the Prüfstand Study 2008, at 34 et seq. The figures provided there are based on the information provided by 155 debtors in questionnaires. Additional data were provided by the Arbeitsgemeinschaft Schuldnerberatungen. Beginning in 2001, debts exceeding €726.728 (10 million ATS) are not used for calculating the average in order to avoid a distortion of the statistics. This was necessary because of a proceeding where the debtor (who had defrauded a bank) had debts in the amount of 5 billion ATS (€363 million).

Table 2B: Regional statistics 2004-2008

	2004	2005	2006	2007	2008
Burgenland	89,170	85,000	88,000	95,188	88,568
Carinthia	58,414	61,172	56,973	62,188	59,990
Lower Austria	73,101	70,171	66,532	75,114	79,598
Upper Austria	56,279	55,917	57,251	56,607	54,972
Salzburg	65,516	58,075	62,245	65,243	63,862
Styria	58,712	62,893	61,231	63,734	68,871
Tyrol	63,640	69,690	64,061	68,283	73,694
Vorarlberg	69,416	70,602	72,547	73,157	73,130
Vienna	47,375	63,007	60,833	56,824	57,853
Average	60,665	63,547	63,565	64,555	66,942
change from previous year	-7.80 %	4.75 %	0.03 %	1.56 %	3.70 %

(Source: author, based on information furnished by asb)

These data show that, in 2008, the median amount of debt was €40,000. Interestingly, among debtors who succeed in obtaining approval of a payment plan, the percentage of debtors with debt between €10,000 and 50,000 is lower (31.0 percent) than in judicial discharge proceedings (43.4 percent).[10] If one assumes that statistically there is a correlation between level of income and debts, with people with higher income also having greater debt, this may be in indication that debtors with lower income have greater difficulty in obtaining approval of their payment plans.

Not only the total amount of the debt, but also the number of creditors is significant, because the higher the number of creditors the more difficult it is typically to get approval for a plan or obtain a discharge. According to the Prüfstand Study of 2004,[11] of those debtors who obtained a payment plan, 35.4 percent had between 2 and 5 creditors, 29.1 percent between 6 and 10 creditors and 28.5 percent 11 to 20 creditors. Only 6.3 percent had more than 20 creditors. Such a high number of creditors is typical for debtors who formerly had their own business. In judicial discharge proceedings, 42.5 percent of all debtors had

10 ASB Prüfstand-study 2004, at 35.
11 ASB Prüfstand-study 2004, at 37.

between 2 to 5 creditors, 28.6 percent between 6 and 10 creditors, 21.8 percent between 11 and 20 creditors and 6.9 percent more than 20 creditors. Interestingly, in those judicial discharge proceedings that do not lead to a discharge, only women have more than 20 creditors (55.6 percent). A possible explanation for this could be a certain behavior of consumption of women with average or below-average income, with a larger number of creditors making it more difficult to maintain control.[12]

Reasons for over-indebtedness

Unfortunately, empirical evidence of the reasons for over-indebtedness is scarce generally and no different in Austria. The official Insolvency Data base does not contain information on the reasons for over-indebtedness of debtors. The only evidence available is the information provided by debtors to debt counseling institutions.

In most countries, consumers overwhelmingly blame their over-indebtedness on the same "the big three" reasons: unemployment, sickness, and separation or divorce. In light of Austria's highly developed social welfare system, it would be interesting to find out whether the availability of social benefits has an impact on consumer bankruptcies.[13] Unfortunately, the available data do not support any conclusions as to such a connection (or the absence thereof). For example, "unemployment or reduction of income" was treated as a single category in the study. Therefore, this category comprises debtors who have suffered a loss of income for whatever reason, be it sickness or change of work (e.g., less overtime work). Precise data on the influence of sickness on the situation of debtors is only available for payment plans. Here, sickness is given as a reason for non-fulfillment of payment plans by 25 percent of the debtors who did not fulfill their plan.[14]

Relatively few debtors (6.7 percent) indicate divorce or separation as a reason for their over-indebtedness. Noteworthy is the relative high percentage of debtors (21.5 percent) who were formerly self-employed. Also, 18.2 percent of the debtors admit that their over-indebtedness is a result of their spending habits ("Umgang mit Geld"). This is significant because there is some controversy about the relationship between spending habits and consumer bankruptcies, although Iain Ramsay has pointed out correctly that "expenditure in excess of in-

12 ASB Prüfstand-study 2004, at 71.
13 On this, see Kilborn 2008.
14 ASB Prüfstand-study 2004, at 58.

come" is a limited indicator since it provides little guidance as to what caused the expenditure to be in excess of income.[15]

The following table shows the reasons given by debtors for their over-indebtedness in 2008:[16]

Table 3

Former business	21.5 %
Unemployment or deterioration of income	19.3 %
Spending habits	18.2 %
Suretyship / guarantees	8.7 %
Separation or divorce	6.7 %
Expenses for housing and furniture	7.5 %
Other	15.1 %

(Source: asb Konkurs- und Eckdatenreport 2008, at 27)

Out of court settlements

In theory, a debtor can always re-negotiate his debts with creditors out of court and obtain an extension in the term of the obligation or a reduction of the principal amount. In practice, this is extremely difficult because a workout agreement of this nature generally requires all or substantially all of the creditors' consent. Particularly in cases with several creditors, it is extremely difficult to obtain a consensus among all or substantially all of the debtor's creditors.

The 1993 reform should have made things easier here because creditors know that the debtor can also obtain a discharge in a court proceeding by a court decision without an approval from the creditors. Anecdotal evidence suggests that the reform did indeed strengthen the position of debtors in this respect, but mostly in cases where there is only one major creditor. Cases with several creditors are still extremely difficult to settle out of court, and a number of debt counseling institutions outright refuse to even attempt such a settlement, instead preferring to file immediately for bankruptcy.

15 See Ramsay 2009.
16 See asb Konkurs- und Eckdatenreport 2008, at 27.

Naturally, there are no precise data available on out-of-court settlements. Of those clients who are represented by an officially recognized debt counseling institution, roughly 1,800 to 2,000 enter into out-of-court settlement negotiations every year. The failure rate of such out-of-court settlements seems to be high. According to the Prüfstand Study, the failure rate is somewhere near 80 percent. Also, the available data suggests that the rate of out-of-court-settlements seems to be declining. Explanation of this disappointing figure is difficult. There is no clear explanation why the success rate is so much lower compared to the one of payment plans in court proceedings.

A possible explanation would be that, of the debtors examined more closely by the study, only those who did not see a sufficiently promising perspective in court proceedings even attempted out-of-court settlements. If this is true, the low success rate would be explained by the more difficult situation (or at least, attitude) of the debtors.

It has to be pointed out, in addition, that this success rate only concerns a relatively small sample of debtors and may not represent the actual situation for all debtors. Particularly, in cases with only one creditor, often the debtor does not contact a debt counseling institution, but prefers to negotiate with the bank on his own or with the assistance of a lawyer. Therefore, the empirical information gained from debt counseling institutions may not apply to all debtors equally. In cases with only one creditor, based on my own experience, I do not see a difference between the success of out-of-court-settlements compared to court proceedings.

Table 4A: Overview 2000-2006

	2000 **Total**	**2001** **Total**	**2002** **Total**	**2003** **Total**	**2004** **Total**	**2005** **Total**	**2006** **Total**
approved by creditors	527 – 37.0%	538 – 37.0%	490 – 32.2%	53 – 29.9%	559 – 26.7%	512 – 25.7%	420 – 20.1%
refused by creditors	896 – 63.0%	915 – 63.0%	1,031 – 67.8%	1,263 – 70.1%	1,535 – 73.3%	1,478 – 74.3%	1,674 – 79.9%

(Source: author, based on information furnished by asb)

Table 4B: Regional statistics for 2007 and 2008

	2007				**2008**			
	approved by creditors		refused by creditors		approved by creditors		refused by creditors	
Burgenland	10	9.8%	92	90.2	3	2.4%	122	97.6%
Carinthia	27	14.9%	154	85.1%	24	18.8%	104	82.3%
Lower Austria	38	18.8%	154	80.2%	32	16.0%	168	84.0%
Upper Austria	148	34.3%	283	65.7%	166	37.4%	278	62.6%
Salzburg	20	31.3%	44	68.8%	11	18.3%	49	81.7%
Styria	34	21.4%	125	78.6%	32	18.5	141	81.5%
Tyrol	49	46.2%	57	53.8%	27	35.1%	50	64.9%
Vorarlberg	32	31.4%	70	68.6%	31	27.7%	81	72.3%
Vienna	46	8.6%	489	91.4%	31	6.7%	434	93.3%
Total	**404**	**21.6%**	**1,468**	**78.4%**	**357**	**20.0%**	**1,427**	**80.0%**

(Source: author, based on information furnished by asb)

Appointment of an administrator

Traditionally, Austrian bankruptcy proceedings always involved a court-appointed administrator. Under the 1993 reform, administrators are only appointed in exceptional cases. This is a measure introduced in order to make the proceedings cheaper. The statistics show that courts were originally quite skeptical about the new concept of a "debtor in possession." Thus, in the years immediately after the reform, administrators were appointed in 55.08 and 40.08 percent, respectively, of all cases. However, this figure declined steadily during the following years. Now, an administrator is only appointed in 14.2 percent of all consumer bankruptcy cases, which shows that generally courts give effect to the legislature's intentions.

A closer look, however, reveals extreme disparities between individual states. Thus, in Vienna, an administrator is appointed only in 3.6 percent of all cases. A possible explanation for this low figure is that generally debtors in Vienna live in rented apartments and do not own houses or condominiums so that there is little a court-appointed administrator could contribute to the proceeding. On the other hand, while practice in most states is similar to the nation-wide average, in Upper Austria there is a tendency in the opposite direction. There, the debtor-in-possession is almost the exception rather than the rule, with an administrator being appointed in more than 60 percent of all cases. That number used to be even higher in previous years, where it reached 91.08 in 2000 and 82.95 percent in 2001, at a time when the nation-wide average was already as low as 28.62 and 25.65 percent, respectively. This figure is more difficult to explain. The attitude of a well-known judge of the Court of Appeals in Linz, Upper Austria, who seems to have been skeptical of consumer bankruptcy in general and of the concept of "debtor in possession" in particular and who apparently was involved in the training of judges and other court personnel, may have contributed to this high figure.

Table 5A: Overview 1995–2008

	1995	**1996**	**1997**	**1998**	**1999**	**2000**	**2001**
Debtor in possession	44.92%	59.92%	58.92%	69.90%	69.80%	71.38%	74.35%
adminstrator	55.08%	40.08%	41.08%	30.10%	30.20%	28.62%	25.65%

	2002	**2003**	**2004**	**2005**	**2006**	**2007**	**2008**
Debtor in possession	73.83%	74.38%	76.96%	77.9%	82.4%	83.0%	85.8%
adminstrator	26.17%	25.62%	23.04%	22.1%	17.6%	17.0%	14.2%

(Source: author, based on information furnished by asb)

Table 5B: Regional information 2007 and 2008

	debtor in possession		adminstrator		debtor in possession		adminstrator	
	2007				**2008**			
Burgenland	114	83.8%	22	16.2 %	133	81.1 %	31	18.9 %
Carinthia	552	92.9 %	42	7.1 %	668	95.4 %	32	4.6 %
Lower Austria	579	79.3 %	156	20.7 %	657	79.2 %	173	20.8 %
Upper Austria	391	37.1 %	662	62.9 %	405	37.9 %	665	62.1 %
Salzburg	376	89.3 %	45	10.7 %	402	93.1 %	30	6.9 %
Styria	427	82.3 %	92	17.7 %	525	84.4 %	97	15.6 %
Tyrol	682	89.6 %	79	10.4 %	713	93.9 %	46	6.1 %
Vorarlberg	498	95.2 %	25	4.8 %	591	95.9 %	25	4.1 %
Vienna	2,498	95.1%	130	4.9 %	3,283	96.4 %	123	3.6 %
Total	6,135	83.0 %	1253	17.0 %	7,377	85.8 %	1,222	14.2 %

(Source: author, based on information furnished by asb)

Interestingly, in proceedings in which an administrator is appointed, payment plans are approved more often than in "debtor in possession" proceedings in which an administrator is not appointed.[17] While for several years this impression was largely based on anecdotal evidence, the 2004 Prüfstand Study confirmed this assumption: Between 1995 and 2004, the percentage of proceedings with a payment plan was 77.8 percent in proceedings with an administrator, compared to only 69.2 percent in "debtor in possession" proceedings.[18]

Result of proceedings

The payment plan, newly introduced by the 1993 reform, is now by far the most popular form of discharge. In 2008, more than two thirds of all proceedings were disposed of by way of a payment plan. This development is in contrast to the situation in the first years after the reform entered into force. At that time, debtors and creditors also relatively frequently resorted to the traditional plan ("*Zwangsausgleich*") with its stricter quota requirements. In later years, a kind

17 Kodek 2002, at 85.
18 ASB Prüfstand-study 2004, at 43.

of "learning curve" developed which reduced the use of the traditional instrument of discharge to an infinitesimal 0.4 percent.

Table 6

	1995	**1996**	**1997**	**1998**	**1999**	**2000**	**2001**
payment plan (*Zahlungsplan*)	57.49 %	62.85 %	65.32 %	66.30 %	66.20 %	68.05 %	70.33 %
judicial discharge proceeding (*Abschöpfungsverfahren*)	21.46 %	22.98 %	24.85 %	25.90 %	27.30 %	26.47 %	25.51 %
plan (Zwangsausgleich)	14.98 %	11.33 %	7.81 %	4.70 %	3.60 %	2.97 %	2.04 %

	2002	**2003**	**2004**	**2005**	**2006**	**2007**	**2008**
payment plan (*Zahlungsplan*)	71.72 %	72.29 %	73.6 %	71.7 %	73.2 %	72.5 %	66.7 %
Judicial discharge proceeding (*Abschöpfungs-Verfahren*)	24.97 %	24.39 %	23.0 %	25.7 %	24.6 %	25.6 %	31.0 %
Plan (Zwangs-Ausgleich")	1.74 %	1.33 %	1.2 %	0.8 %	0.7 %	0.4 %	0.4 %

(Source: author, based on information furnished by asb)

Difficulties after payment plan

While unfortunately data is difficult to obtain on this issue, since debtors are reluctant to talk about their experiences, many debtors seem to encounter difficulties despite having obtained a discharge by a payment plan with approval of the creditors. The Prüfstand Study managed to obtain a small sample of 18 responses by debtors.[19] Five of them reported that they were unable to obtain credit and to open a bank account. Ten of them indicated that the bank would not permit them to overdraw their account. Nine, i.e., half of the debtors inter-

19 Multiple answers were possible.

viewed, had difficulties obtaining a mobile phone. Seven debtors reported that they were treated like a "criminal."

This is a matter of some concern, because it seems to indicate that at least in a significant number of cases the discharge obtained in a consumer bankruptcy may not provide a "fresh start" as intended by the legislature. On the other hand, no debtor seems to have encountered difficulties with utilities, such as electricity or gas. This may have to do with the fact that utilities, in large measure, are state-owned in Austria and so more willing to give effect to the legislature's intent in this regard.

Difficulties after discharge proceedings

Similar difficulties are reported by debtors who obtained their discharge, not by a payment plan, but rather by court decision.[20] They reported that they had been "black listed" and had difficulty obtaining credit. Likewise, they had difficulties obtaining permission by the bank to overdraw their account or getting a mobile phone. Again, state-owned utilities, such as electricity or gas, seem not to cause problems to former debtors.

Failure of the plan or discharge proceedings

Since the fulfillment of the payment plan is not monitored by the court, but rather takes place after the bankruptcy proceedings are closed, no precise empirical information is available as to the success rate of payment plans. It is widely assumed that at least 10 percent of these plans fail. The only information available from the Insolvency Data Base (*Insolvenzdatei*) is that in 5 percent of all payment plans there are entries to the effect that the plan was void or that it was superseded by a new plan. From the debtors examined more closely by the Prüfstand Study, 91 percent of all female debtors fulfilled their payment plan, compared to only 81 percent of male debtors. The reasons mostly given for failure to fulfill the payment plan are unemployment, illness, new debts, family problems, and motivational problems. It should be noted that the success rate of payment plans in consumer bankruptcies seems to compare favorably with the success rate of plans in business cases, where 83 percent are fulfilled.[21]

As to discharge proceedings ("*Abschöpfungsverfahren*"),[22] approximately 15.4 percent of all debtors get a discharge before expiration of the full seven

20 See again the Prüfstand-study 2008, at 48.
21 See Klikovits, 2004.
22 ASB Prüfstand-study 2004, at 65.

year period, either because they manage to pay 50 percent (in which case they are entitled to a discharge after three years) or because they take up a new loan and negotiate a settlement with their creditors. An additional 54.3 percent of the debtors get a discharge after 7 years because they managed to pay 10 percent of their debts. Moreover, 4.6 percent of the debtors obtain an equitable discharge after 7 years. In another 4.6 percent of the cases, the court ordered an extension of the proceeding; 3.4 percent of the debtors died during the proceeding.

On the other hand, approximately 15 to 20 percent of the debtors failed to obtain a discharge, mostly because they did not reach the required quota of 10 percent or because they violated their duties during the proceeding. Interestingly, the single most important factor explaining debtors' failure to obtain a discharge is a failure to reach the 10 percent minimum quota in case of men (38.5 percent) and the incurring of new debts (33.3 percent) by women.[23] The explanations given by debtors for this failure are similar to the reasons given for non-fulfillment of the payment plan.

Further details

The average duration of the proceeding in consumer bankruptcies is 4.1 months, with considerable variations from state to state. The regional figures range from 102 to 137 days. Note that this only concerns the actual bankruptcy proceeding where the debtor is divested and an administrator may be appointed. This figure does not include the payment period of a payment plan adopted during the proceeding. Neither does it include the duration (ordinarily seven years) of a judicial discharge proceeding in cases in which the creditors refused to accept the payment plan proposed by the debtor.

Nonetheless, in light of the fact that the statutory time period for creditors to lodge their claims is 30 to 60 days, the 4.1 months figure is quite impressive. It means that the debtor will know after a relatively short time whether a payment plan is accepted by the creditors and whether he is admitted by the court to a discharge proceeding. Also, keeping the actual bankruptcy proceeding short results in a reduction of costs since an administrator, if at all, is only appointed during bankruptcy proceedings and not for the subsequent stages such as payment period of a payment plan or a discharge proceeding.

It is also interesting to note that 47.7 percent of all debtors were 20 to 40 years old in 2008. The largest group (16.9 percent) is between 41 and 45. Almost two thirds (62.1 percent) of all debtors in bankruptcy proceedings are male and only 37.9 percent female. Since this number is based on bankruptcy filings, it may not accurately reflect the actual number of over-indebted women.

---

23 ASB-Prüfstand-study 2004, at 68.

Of all the persons who contacted a debt counseling institution in 2008 (regardless of whether they actually filed a bankruptcy petition), the median income was €1,060 per month, and the average income was €1,131.

Finally, it should be noted that 27.76 percent of all debtors who contacted a debt counseling agency for the first time in 2008 were unemployed in 2008. While this is an increase from the previous year (32.75 percent), this figure compares favorably to earlier years where it was as high as 36.91 percent (2005). Regardless of this fluctuation, the relatively high number of unemployed debtors clearly is a matter of concern since a discharge is evidently much more difficult to obtain if the debtor is without stable income. This is clearly demonstrated by the comparatively smaller number of filings by unemployed debtors. Of all debtors who successfully instituted consumer bankruptcy proceedings, only 15.2 percent were unemployed. Apparently, a large number of unemployed debtors do not institute proceedings because, in light of the 10 percent minimum quota requirement, their chances to obtain a discharge are slim at best. Equally disturbing is the fact that 43.4 percent of the female debtors and 32.6 percent of the male debtors do not have a high school education.

Further reform

While an important step in the right direction, the 1993 reform clearly was not the last reform of Austrian consumer bankruptcy law. The reform generally works quite well, but it seems that it failed to reach a large percentage of all over-indebted persons. There are approximately 1,140,000 individual enforcement proceedings in Austria every year. While this of course does not imply that 15 percent of the Austrian population are subject to enforcement proceedings (rather, the relatively high figure is explained by multiple filings by the same or different creditors against a single debtor), it shows that there is a significant number of over-indebted persons in Austria who – for whatever reason – have not availed themselves of the advantages of consumer bankruptcy.

Whether the reasons for this phenomenon are passivity on part of certain debtors or slim perspectives for obtaining a discharge for certain debtors (or a combination of both) or whether there are other reasons is not quite clear.

In light of these shortcomings, for several years there have been discussions about a further reform of consumer bankruptcy law. Unfortunately, this reform has been halted with priority given to the reform of business bankruptcy.[24]

---

24 The reform of business bankruptcy law proceeded to an official draft of the Ministry of Justice which was circulated widely, but was ultimately not enacted because of political resistance. The main reason for this resistance is that the draft reduced the avoidance (Article 13 European Insolvency Regulation) of certain payments to banks, but not of tax

One suggestion is that the court should be given wider discretion for granting a discharge. A more ambitious proposal[25] is to provide for some form of "convergence" of individual enforcement proceedings and bankruptcy proceedings if the debtor is over-indebted. Under this proposal, the court could open bankruptcy proceedings ex officio in certain cases. The exact prerequisites for such an ex officio opening of proceedings, as the reform proposal in general, have been and remain the subject of controversy. One proposal would be that the court should be given the power to open bankruptcy proceedings ex officio in cases where the debtor has not paid his debts for more than one year. This reform would relieve courts and bailiffs from hundreds of thousands of enforcement proceedings that do not lead to any result due to the debtor's lack of means, a reform that could save valuable resources. Also, it would spare the debtor the costs of several enforcement proceedings. In spite of these possible advantages, the Ministry of Justice is somewhat skeptical due to fears that, at least initially, such a reform could bring too much strain on the bankruptcy courts and might require additional resources there. With the number of over-indebted consumers rising every year, there is some hope at least that the Ministry will reconsider its position.

References

ASB Konkurs- und Eckdatenreport, published annually

ASB Schuldnerberatungen GmbH: Der Privatkonkurs auf dem Prüfstand. Wien: 2004.

Demelius, Ernst: Konkurs im alten Wien, Festschrift für Reimer, Otto 13. Salzburg: Pustet 1976.

Gabriel, Tamara Kathrein,, Georg, Mohr, Franz and Pirker-Hörmann, Beate: Verschuldung – Individuelle und sozialstaatliche Verantwortung. Wien: Verlag Österreich 2008.

Grohs, Hans W., Hauer, Harald, Jürgens, Susanne and Maly, Alexander A.: Das Abschöpfungsverfahren und die Praxis der Billigkeitsentscheidungen nach § 213 KO im "Privatkonkurs". Wien: LexisNexis, Zeitschrift für Insolvenzrecht und Kreditsicherung („ZIK") 2008, 46.

Kilborn, Jason J.: Comparative Cause and Effect: Consumer Insolvency and the Eroding Safety Net. Columbia Journal of European Law Vol 14, No 3, 2008.

Klikovits, Alexander: Der Zwangsausgleich – eine österreichische Erfolgsstory. Wien: LexisNexis, Zeitschrift für Insolvenzrecht und Kreditsicherung („ZIK") 2004, 12.

Kodek, Georg E.: Handbuch Privatkonkurs. Die Sonderbestimmungen für das Konkursverfahren natürlicher Personen. Wien: Manz 2002.

---

payments and payments to social security institutions. Eventually, the reform entered into force in July 2010, with works on the consumer bankruptcy reform being halted until then.

25 See Kodek 2002, 802 et seq.

Konecny, Andreas: Zur Neugestaltung der Durchsetzung von Geldforderungen, Gedenkschrift Halûk Konuralp (2009) II 281. Ankara: Yetkin Yayinlari.

Konecny, Andreas: Lebenslang im Schuldturm? Zum Streit um die Erleichterung der Restschuldbefreiung, in Potz, Richard (ed.): Armut und Recht. Wien: Manz 2010.

Konecny, Andreas: Möglichkeiten erleichterter Restschuldbefreiung für natürliche Personen, Jahrbuch für Konsumentenschutz 2009.

Mohr, Franz: Privatkonkurs, 2nd ed. Wien: Manz 2007.

Ramsay, Iain: "Wannabe Wags and Credit Crunch Binges": The Construction of Over-Indebtedness in the UK. In Niemi, Johanna, Ramsay, Iain & Whitford, William C. (eds.): Consumer Credit, Debt and Bankruptcy: Comparative and International Perspectives. Oxford: Hart Publishing 2009.

South African Homeowners Are Not Protected against Various Interest Rates Hikes

Michelle Kelly-Louw[*]

Introduction

There have been numerous interest rate hikes in South Africa between June 2006 and December 2008 that have had a detrimental financial effect, particularly on low-income homeowners. This coupled with the worldwide financial crisis have lead to an increase in the debt levels and many consumers have since lost their mortgaged homes, while others are still struggling to keep their homes. Although the South African National Credit Act[1] was implemented in June 2006 to protect the consumer, it did little to curb the negative effect that the rising interest rates have had.

In terms of the National Credit Act, a credit provider may only conclude a credit agreement with a consumer after he has made a proper financial assessment and concludes that the consumer will be able to satisfy all his obligations under all his credit agreements.[2] The affordability assessment made by the credit provider will depend on the prevailing interest rates at the time.[3] Therefore, the determination of loans allowed to be made to a consumer is based on financial data available at the time at which such a determination is made.

There has been a failure to consider what happens if the interest rate increases radically after the credit agreement is concluded, however, causing the

---

* This contribution is based on Kelly-Louw, Michelle: The South African National Credit Act Fails to Protect Homeowners Against Various Interest Rates Hikes. US-China Law Review, Vol 6, No 12, 2009, at12–24, and parts thereof have been republished here with the permission of that journal's editorial staff.

1 34 of 2005 (hereinafter "the National Credit Act" or "the Act").

2 See sections 80–82 of the Act. In this chapter, words in the singular also mean in the plural and vice versa, and words in the masculine also mean in the feminine and neuter.

3 Interest rates are defined by the South African Reserve Bank as follow (see the South African Reserve Bank Research Department: Information Division "Interest Rates and How They Work" 8th Fact Sheet (available at <http:www.reservebank.co.za> (click on "About us > Fact Sheet") (accessed 2 November 2009) (hereinafter "the Reserve Bank Fact Sheet") at 2):

> Interest rates are prices for loanable funds – prices of funds invested, lent out or borrowed for various periods of time. The supplier or lender of funds normally wants to earn an income and the user or borrower will generally be prepared to pay for the right to use the accumulated funds.

consumer to be unlikely to be in a position to satisfy his obligations under the agreement. The increase in interest rates may also cause the consumer to become over-indebted and, in the end, he may even end up, for example, losing his mortgaged home.[4] If the consumer involved is one from the middle-class or high-income group, he will be able to cut back on his living costs, sell his home, and then buy a cheaper home in a poorer area. So at least that type of consumer will still be able to afford to buy and own a home. But what about the low-income consumer, who just managed to comply with the installments on his housing loan?[5] This low-income consumer cannot lower his living standard any further and will possibly never be able to buy/own his own home again. This situation is not negligently or intentionally caused by the low-income consumer and seems to be unfair.

Due to the various interest rate hikes and the prevailing high interest rates many consumers (not only from the low-income group) have lost their mortgaged homes.[6] The South African Government provides free housing or housing subsidies to certain members of the public – mainly the unemployed, those who have never previously owned homes and the poorest of the poor.[7] While the rest of the low-income consumers whose homes have been foreclosed upon, generally, do not qualify for such assistance and, in the end, it is this group that is left homeless.

In this chapter it is shown that the South African National Credit Act has failed to take into its purview cases such as these. As a consequence there is no sort of consumer protection available for the low-income homeowner who becomes over-indebted because of the constant rising interest rates on his mortgage loan. This chapter will also investigate whether or not the South African Government has a responsibility to protect low-income consumers against increases of the interest rate that are causing them to lose their mortgaged homes.

---

4 Section 1 of the Act defines "mortgage" as a pledge of immovable property that serves as security for a mortgage agreement and "mortgage agreement" as a credit agreement that is secured by a pledge of immovable property.

5 The Home Loan and Mortgage Disclosure Act 63 of 2000 defines a housing loan as a loan or advance by a financial institution to a person for purposes of constructing, purchasing, renovating or improving in any way such person's home with the security of a registered mortgage bond or any other form of accepted security (see section 1).

6 See also Watson 2008, at 5; Anon 10 December 2008; Alliance Group October 2007; Mohamed August 2008; and Theobald April 2009, at 4.

7 See <http://www.housing.gov.za> (accessed 2 November 2009).

Reckless lending and over-indebtedness

It has been said that over-indebtedness results from reckless lending and borrowing,[8] low levels of awareness, and a lack of enforcement. Also that over-indebtedness occurs when a consumer can no longer service all his debts or where the level of debt servicing is depleting the household income and consumption.[9] In my view, over-indebtedness can also occur where the interest rates increase drastically after the conclusion of a credit agreement.

One of the objectives of the National Credit Act[10] is to encourage responsible borrowing, the avoidance of over-indebtedness and reckless lending, and to provide for a consistent and harmonized system of debt restructuring, enforcement and judgment. The Act specifically prohibits a credit provider from entering into a reckless credit agreement with a prospective consumer and also heavily penalizes the credit provider that does enter into such an agreement.[11]

In order to assist a credit provider in determining whether a consumer is creditworthy, the Act has incorporated and defined the concepts of "over-indebtedness" and "reckless lending," in particular in sections 79, 80 and 81.

Credit is lent recklessly if *either*

- the credit provider took *no steps to assess* the proposed consumer's general understanding and appreciation of the risks and costs of the proposed credit agreement, and his rights and obligations under the agreement; debt repayment history for credit agreements; or his existing financial means, prospects and obligations[12] (that is, an assessment of whether a consumer could

---

8 The view has been expressed that the dominant cause of the current worldwide financial crisis was excessive borrowing (see Anon April 2009, at 1).

9 See the Department of Trade and Industry August 2004, at 3; and Kelly-Louw 2008, at 218.

10 For more on the Act, see Renke, Roestoff and Haupt 2007; Kelly-Louw 2008; Kelly-Louw 2009, at 175–198; Otto 2006; Campbell and Logan 2008; Scholtz 2008; and Scott 2009, at 167–197.

11 The provisions dealing with reckless lending and over-indebtedness apply only if the consumer involved is a natural person (see sections 1, 6(a) and 78(1) of the Act).

12 Section 78(3) clearly provides that "financial means, prospects and obligations" in this context, with respect to a consumer or prospective consumer, include the following:
• income, or any right to receive income, regardless of the source, frequency or regularity of that income, other than income that the consumer or prospective consumer receives, has a right to receive, or holds in trust for another person; and
• the financial means, prospects and obligations of any other adult person within the consumer's immediate family or household, to the extent that the consumer, or prospective consumer, and that other person customarily share their respective financial means; and mutually bear their respective financial obligations; and

make the repayments); or, lastly, whether there was a reasonable basis to conclude that any commercial purpose may prove to be successful, if the consumer has such a purpose for applying for the credit;

or

- *after having conducted such an assessment*, the credit provider still entered into the credit agreement with the consumer despite the fact that the preponderance of information available to the credit provider indicated that the consumer did not generally understand or appreciate his risks, costs or obligations under the proposed credit agreement, or that entering into that credit agreement would make the consumer over-indebted.[13]

The Act provides that whenever a credit agreement is being considered in any court proceedings, the court may declare the credit agreement reckless. If a court declares that a credit agreement is reckless the court may make an order:

- setting aside all or part of the consumer's obligations under that agreement, as the court determines may be just and reasonable in the circumstances; or
- suspending the force and effect of that credit agreement, and it may then issue an order suspending its force and effect until a date determined by the court, and restructuring the consumer's obligations under any other credit agreements, in accordance with the Act.[14]

The Act also provides that, if a court declares that a credit agreement is reckless, because entering into the agreement made the consumer over-indebted, the court

- must further consider whether the consumer is over-indebted *at the time of these court proceedings*; and
- if the court concludes that the consumer is over-indebted, the court may make an order suspending the force and effect of that credit agreement until a date

---

if the consumer has or had a commercial purpose for applying for or entering into a particular credit agreement, the reasonably estimated future revenue flow from that business purpose.

13 See section 80(1) read with section 81(2) of the Act. Observe, however, that the provisions for reckless lending do not apply to a school loan, student loan, and an emergency loan, provided the necessary information is reported to the South African National Credit Regulator: see section 78(2) of the Act, read with reg 23 (see Regulation Gazette No 8477, R489 in Government Gazette 28864 of 31 May 2006, (hereinafter "the Regulations").

14 See section 83(1)–(2) of the Act.

determined by the court; and restructuring the consumer's obligations under any other credit agreements, in accordance with the Act.[15]

However, before making such an order, the court must consider the consumer's current means and ability to pay his current financial obligations that existed at the time the agreement was made, as well as the expected date when any such obligation under a credit agreement will be fully satisfied, assuming the consumer makes all required payments in accordance with any proposed order.[16]

In addition to the above, section 85 provides for further specific powers of the court. It provides that despite any provision of law or agreement to the contrary, in any court proceedings in which a credit agreement is being considered, if it is alleged that the consumer under a credit agreement is over-indebted, the court may:

- refer the matter directly to a debt counselor with a request that the counselor evaluate the consumer's circumstances and make a report to the court; or
- declare that the consumer is over-indebted, and make any order contemplated in section 87 (for example, declare the credit agreement(s) reckless) to relieve the consumer's over-indebtedness.[17]

The Act also determines the effect of the suspension of a credit agreement.[18] It provides that during the period that the force and effect of a credit agreement is suspended, the consumer is not required to make any payment required under the agreement; no interest, fee or other charge under the agreement may be charged to the consumer; and the credit provider's rights under the agreement, or under any law in respect of that agreement, are unenforceable, despite any law to the contrary. Furthermore, the Act also provides that after the suspension of the force and effect of a credit agreement has ended, all the respective rights and obligations of the credit provider and the consumer under that agreement are revived, and are fully enforceable except to the extent that a court may order otherwise.

The Act provides for debt re-organization (debt restructuring) and debt counseling in cases of over-indebtedness. An over-indebted consumer may apply to a debt counselor (a natural person registered with the South African Na-

15 See section 83(1) and (3) of the Act.

16 See section 83(4) of the Act.

17 See also Standard Bank SA Ltd v Hales & Another 2009 (3) SA 315 (D) ([2009] 2 All SA 416 (D)); Standard Bank of South Africa Ltd v Panayiotts 2009 (3) SA 363 (W); and Ex parte Ford and Two Similar Cases 2009 (3) SA 376 (WCC).

18 See section 84 of the Act.

tional Credit Regulator and offering a service of debt counseling[19]) directly for a review of his debt or to a court so that it can refer the matter to a debt counselor. Debt counselors are therefore appointed either by over-indebted consumers or by courts.[20] Over-indebtedness is defined as follows:[21]

> A consumer is over-indebted if the preponderance of available information *at the time a determination is made* indicates that the particular consumer is or will be unable to satisfy in a timely manner all the obligations under all the credit agreements to which the consumer is a party, having regard to that consumer's–
>
> (*a*) financial means, prospects and obligations;[22] and
>
> (*b*) probable propensity to satisfy in a timely manner all the obligations under all the credit agreements to which the consumer is a party, as indicated by the consumer's history of debt repayment.

If a debt counselor has to decide whether a consumer is over-indebted, he must take these matters into consideration and must also further consider whether the consumer's total monthly debt payments exceed the balance derived by deducting his minimum living expenses from his net income. The counselor must calculate the net income by deducting from the gross income of the consumer, statutory and other deductions that are made as a condition of employment. The minimum living expenses are based upon a budget supplied by the consumer, and adjusted by the debt counselor with reference to the guidelines issued by the South African National Credit Regulator.[23] The debt counselor must also determine whether or not any credit agreement concluded by the consumer is reckless and must make the appropriate recommendation to a relevant court. The precise procedure that a debt counselor must follow when he reviews the debt of a consumer is set out in the Act and the Regulations.[24]

Where a credit provider makes a proper financial assessment and finds that the low-income consumer will be able to satisfy in a timely manner all his obligations under all his credit agreements he will probably conclude the agreement with the consumer. Obviously the affordability assessment made by the credit provider will depend on the prevailing interest rates at the time. Without doubt, the credit provider would also have made some provision for possible increases in the applicable interest rate. This low-income group, being high-risk, usually

---

19 See section 46 of the Act and reg 10 of the Regulations.

20 See, for example, sections 83(3)(b)(ii), 86(a) and 86(1) of the Act.

21 See section 79(1) of the Act (emphasis and footnote by author).

22 For a definition of what is meant by "financial means, prospects and obligations," see section 78(3) of the Act as quoted above in note 12.

23 See reg 24(7) of the Regulations.

24 See sections 86–87 of the Act and regs 23–26 of the Regulations. See also First Rand Bank Ltd v Smith (unreported, case no 24206/08 of 31 October 2008 (W)).

pays much more than the prime lending rate (often close to the maximum allowable interest rates).[25] Therefore, any fluctuation in the interest rate normally influences this group immediately.[26] It is not always possible to correctly predict how interest rates will increase in future. Also, if credit providers take a too stringent approach regarding possible interest rate increases in future, it might cause this low-income group to be marginalized, making it impossible for them to ever obtain a housing loan. So when the interest rates increases dramatically after the conclusion of a housing loan, the low-income consumer often defaults by not being able to pay the new increased installments due in terms of the loan.[27] Clearly this credit agreement does not constitute reckless lending on the part of the credit provider, since the consumer was initially able to afford the credit.

Although the provisions of over-indebtedness and the mechanisms of debt review/restructuring are at the disposal of a consumer, they might not adequately protect the low-income consumer described here. Even if the debts of the consumer were to be successfully restructured part of the restructuring could still entail that the mortgaged home should be sold. Of course, it might also be possible, due to the small income received by the consumer, that it might not even be possible at all to restructure his debts to the satisfaction of a court and/or the credit providers. If this turns out to be the case, the consumer will have no other option but to consider the sequestration of his estate as a possibility out of his debt trap. Sequestration will naturally have the effect that all the assets of the consumer, including his mortgaged home, be realized and sold, therefore, leaving the consumer homeless. Currently in South Africa there is no legislative protection for the family home in insolvency proceedings.

Interest rates

In recent years, high interest rates have been one of the major reasons why South Africans, particularly the low-income group, have lost their mortgaged homes.[28] Therefore, a brief discussion of how the interest rates are determined and regulated is required for purposes of this chapter. A look at how the prime lending rate has varied since June 2006 is also necessary.

The National Credit Act is prescriptive of the type of fees or charges that a credit provider may charge a consumer. In terms of the Act, a credit agreement may not require payment by the consumer of any money or other consideration

---

25 See discussion in section 3, below.
26 See also Watson 2008, at 5.
27 Ibid.
28 See Watson 2008, at 5.

except the principal debt, an initiation fee, service fees, interest, the cost of credit insurance, default administration charges and collection costs. The Act stipulates that there are certain maximums for interest and other costs of credit that may be charged on the different credit agreements.[29] Chapter 5 of the Regulations[30] compliments the Act and specifically provides for the maximum allowable interest rates[31] and other costs of credit (that is, service fees[32] and initiation fees[33]) that may be charged on the different credit agreements.

In terms of the Regulations to the Act, the maximum "interest rate" which a credit provider may charge a consumer for a credit agreement is calculated according to a formula where the reference rate ("RR") is the ruling South African Reserve Bank Repurchase Rate[34] as at the time that the credit agreement is entered into. The Reserve Bank Repurchase Rate is the interest rate (price) at which the South African Reserve Bank lends cash to commercial South African banks. The South African Reserve Bank acts as banker for the commercial banks. Banks experience a cash shortfall or a need for liquidity daily and their lender of last instance is the Reserve Bank. The Repurchase Rate is determined by the Reserve Bank at each meeting of its Monetary Policy Committee and is expressed as an interest rate per annum.[35] In the Regulations to the Act there are different types of credit agreements (for example, mortgage agreements, credit facilities, and development credit agreements) to which different maximum interest rates[36] and initiation fees apply.[37] For instance, the maximum interest rate that may be charged for a mortgage agreement is the Reserve Bank Repurchase Rate (for example, 7 percent)[38] x 2.2 + 5 percent per annum (equals 20.4 percent per annum).[39] The different interest rates that apply to the different type of credit

29 See sections 100–106 of the Act.
30 See regs 39–48 of the Regulations.
31 See reg 42(1).
32 See reg 44.
33 See reg 42(2).
34 As at 5 November 2009, this rate was 7 percent (see <http://www.reservebank.co.za> (accessed 5 November 2009)).
35 See Reserve Bank Fact Sheet, at 3. A formal system, called the repurchase transaction system, is in place to guide the process through which commercial banks borrow from the Reserve Bank. This system of borrowing and lending involves the temporary sale of a financial asset by the borrower (that is, a commercial bank) in exchange for the needed cash from the lender (that is, the Reserve Bank). In such a transaction, there is an express agreement that the borrower must repurchase the financial asset at an agreed future date (see Reserve Bank Fact Sheet, at 3).
36 See reg 42(1).
37 See reg 42(2).
38 See <http://www.reservebank.co.za> (accessed 5 November 2009).
39 See reg 42(1)(Table A). This was the maximum interest rate as at 5 November 2009.

agreements are rather complicated to understand and a comprehensive discussion of them falls beyond the scope of this chapter.

Although the maximum interest rates that may be charged by credit providers are capped, the rate is still linked to the South African Reserve Bank Repurchase Rate that is not capped and often fluctuates as clearly seen over the last couple of years. Commercial banks use this Repurchase Rate to determine their prime rate or prime lending rate that is slightly higher than the Reserve Bank Repurchase Rate allowing them a profit margin. If the Repurchase Rate increases, banks have to pay more for repurchase funds, and therefore, they have to increase their prime rate or prime lending rate.[40] "Prime rate" or "prime lending rate" is a term applied in certain countries (such as South Africa) to a reference interest rate used by commercial banks. The term originally indicated the rate of interest at which commercial banks lent to preferential customers, that is, those with high credibility, though this is no longer always the case. Some variable interest rates may be expressed as a percentage above or below prime rate.[41] The low-income group usually pays much more than the prime lending rate, because they are considered to carry a higher risk for defaulting and their credit rating is often lower.[42] Therefore, any fluctuation in the Reserve Bank Repurchase Rate and prime lending interest rate will influence this group immediately, and have a more detrimental effect on them than on the other income groups.[43]

Currently, the difference between the Reserve Bank Repurchase Rate and the commercial banks' prime lending rate is 3.5 percent. In a recent press release the former Reserve Bank Governor (Mr. Tito Mboweni at the time) stated that the difference between these two rates was too high and South African commercial banks should make it smaller by lowering their prime lending interest rates.[44] This might be difficult to do as commercial banks are already lending money to many preferential customers (that is, those with high credibility) at a rate far below the prime lending rate (often at a rate indicated as prime minus two). This has the effect that in many instances the difference between the Reserve Bank Repurchase Rate and banks' prime lending rate is only 1.5 percent. Unquestionably the banks should be allowed to make a profit on the money they advance to consumers as they bear the loss for default by the consumers. Even if the difference between these two interest rates were to be made smaller, the interest rate for the low-income consumers will still be much higher than the prime lending rate and will be close to or equal to the maximum allowable inter-

---

40 See the Reserve Bank Fact Sheet, at 3.

41 See <http://en.wikipedia.org/wiki/Prime_lending_rate> (accessed 2 November 2009).

42 See the Reserve Bank Fact Sheet, at 2.

43 See also Watson 2008, at 5; Futuse 2007; and Loos 2008.

44 See Van Tonder May 2009, at 8.

est rate that is linked to the Reserve Bank Repurchase Rate and not the prime lending rate (as explained above).

Furthermore, even if the commercial banks were to lower the difference between these two rates, other credit providers (for example, micro-lenders), who do not work with a prime lending rate, but with the maximum interest rates prescribed by the National Credit Act and its Regulations (and linked to the Reserve Bank Repurchase Rate), will not be influenced by a lower prime lending rate. Accordingly, this suggested solution by the Reserve Bank will not result in these credit providers lending to consumers at lower interest rates. As this type of credit provider (for example, micro-lenders) often focuses on supplying finance to the low-income group, these consumers will not benefit if the commercial banks were to lower their prime lending rate *ratio* to the Reserve Bank's Repurchase Rate. Therefore, it remains that it is the Reserve Bank Repurchase Rate that plays a pivotal role for consumers to be able to keep their mortgage homes and it is this rate that needs to be lowered. With the aforementioned statement made by the former Reserve Bank Governor the impression is created that the South African Reserve Bank (and by implication the government) is trying to shift their responsibility of lowering the interest rates, necessitated by the current financial crisis, to that of the commercial banks.

The Act expressly states in section 105 that the South African Minister of Trade and Industry, after consulting the National Credit Regulator, may prescribe a method for calculating a maximum rate of interest and other non-interest costs of credit (for example, service fees and initiation fees) for the different type of credit agreements.[45] However, before the Minister may prescribe the maximum interest rates and other costs of credit, he must consider amongst other things:[46]

- the need to make credit available to (1) historically disadvantaged persons; (2) low-income persons and communities; and (3) remote, isolated or low density populations and communities;[47]
- the conditions prevailing in the credit market, including the costs of credit and the optimal functioning of the consumer credit market; and
- the social impact on low-income consumers.

Before the Act there was no express statutory duty on the South African Government (that is, the Minister of Trade and Industry and/or the Reserve Bank) to consider how an increase in the interest rates would affect the low-

---

45 See section 105(1) of the Act.
46 See section 105(2) of the Act.
47 See section 105(2)(a), read with section 13(a) of the Act.

income consumers, or whether there was a need to make credit available to historically disadvantaged persons, low-income persons and communities and remote, isolated or low density populations and communities. It is also not clear whether any of these factors set out in section 105 of the Act were taken into consideration when the existing method for calculating a maximum rate of interest was drafted and determined. There are no documents in the public domain as to how these existing methods for calculating a maximum rate of interest applicable to the different types of credit were determined. It is clear that the responsibility for prescribing workable interest rates that are sustainable in the current financial and credit market lies with the Minister of Trade and Industry. As the current prescribed maximum rates are all linked to the Reserve Bank Repurchase Rate, it is argued that the South African Reserve Bank should also have a social responsibility to take these said factors (for example, how interest rates would affect the low-income consumers) into consideration before making decisions regarding increases in the Repurchase Rate. The Reserve Bank should not only focus on the existing factors like the supply and demand for funds and inflation.[48] Looking at the history of the Reserve Bank Repurchase Rate and that of the prime lending rates of banks, particularly during the period June 2006 to June 2008,[49] it seems that the policymakers did not carefully consider what the impact of such high rates would be on the low-income consumers.

Although it is possible for commercial banks to conclude mortgage agreements with a fixed interest rate that will prevail for the full duration of the agreement, they are often reluctant to do so. Consumers are also hesitant to conclude housing loans with fixed interest rates. Consumers often hope that their current interest rates will go down in the future. However, when these rates suddenly and rapidly rise after conclusion of the mortgage agreement (as seen during June 2006 to December 2008), the consumers who have waited too long for the rates to come down again might in the end no longer be in a financial position to request the bank to cap his interest rate at the prevailing rate. In practice, banks generally opt for a variable interest rate that is often linked to the fluctuating prime lending rate.

In the past, it was a contentious issue as to whether or not a credit provider had the right to vary unilaterally the original rate of interest payable in terms of a loan (for example, mortgage agreement) where the rate was linked to the fluctuating prime lending rate. The issue was, however, eventually settled by the South African Supreme Court of Appeal in *NBS Boland Bank Ltd v One Berg River Drive CC and Others; Deeb and Another v ABSA Bank Ltd; Friedman v*

48 For a full discussion of all the factors the Reserve Bank takes into consideration before determining their Repurchasing Rate, see Reserve Bank Fact Sheet.

49 See Figure 1, below.

Standard Bank of SA Ltd.[50] In all three these of cases, the relevant question was whether a clause in a mortgage bond conferring upon the bondholder the right to vary the original rate of interest payable in terms of the mortgage was valid.[51] Today, however, the National Credit Act specifically allows for a variable interest rate.[52] Section 103(4) specifically provides that a credit agreement may provide for the interest rate to vary during the term of the agreement only if the variation is by fixed relationship to a reference rate stipulated in the agreement, which reference rate must be the same as that used by that credit provider in respect of any similar credit agreements currently issued by it. This means that it is valid, for example, if a customer's mortgage agreement stipulates that his interest rate during the term of the agreement will be two percent above the prime lending rate. Of course, the variable interest must always fall within the prescribed maximums allowed in the Act and the Regulations.[53]

As already mentioned, it is also necessary to look at the recent history of the prime lending interest rates between June 2006 and August 2009. The increases and decreases are shown in the graph below.

Figure 1 demonstrates that there were ten increases in the South African prime lending rate between the period June 2006 and June 2008.[54] What effect this has had on the middle- to low-income consumer can be explained by way of the following example.[55] Say a consumer concluded a mortgage loan for ZAR 500,000 on June 1, 2006 at the prevailing prime lending rate at the time, which was 10.5 percent, his initial monthly cost over a twenty-year period was about ZAR 4,992. However, then two years later (that is, on June 1, 2008), due to the rise in the prime lending interest rate to 15.5 percent, his new monthly cost is ZAR 6,769. In this example, the ten increases in the prime lending rate over a two-year period have meant a monthly cost increase of ZAR 1,777. Therefore, the monthly cost of servicing such a mortgage has increased with 36 percent in two years, possibly placing the consumer in a position where he can no longer satisfy in a timely manner the obligations under his mortgage agreement.

50 1999 (4) SA 928 (SCA). For more on this, see Lawack-Davids 2001; and McLennan 2000.

51 See also Investec Bank (Pty) Ltd v GVN Properties CC 1999 (3) SA 490 (W).

52 Section 104(1)(b) of the Act also provides that a credit provider may not unilaterally increase the rate of interest applicable to a credit agreement, except with respect to an agreement with a variable interest rate. The National Credit Act also prescribe the exact notice periods that should be given to consumers when there are increases and decreases of their interest rates (see section 104(2)–(3)).

53 See sections 100(1)(c), 101(1)(d) and 105(1) of the Act.

54 See Figure 1, above.

55 Example taken from Anon September 2008, at 1.

Figure 1: History of the Prime Lending Interest Rates from June 2006 to 31 August 2009[56]

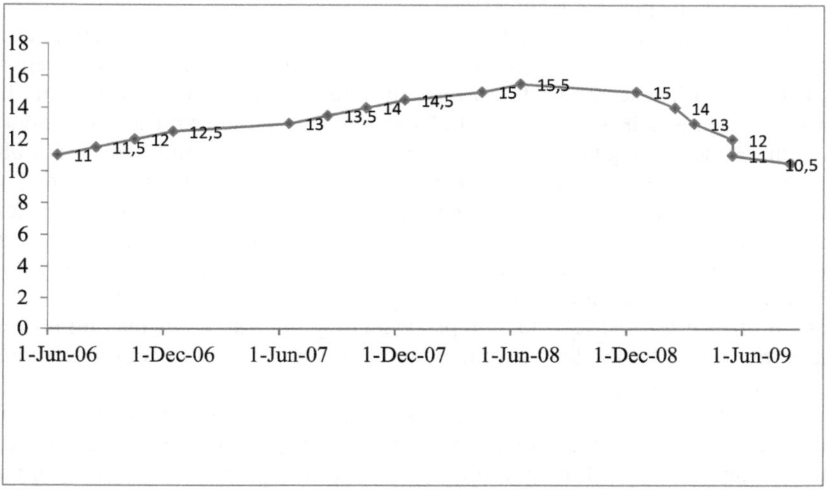

The National Credit Act came into operation in three phases since June 1, 2006.[57] When studying the history of the prime lending rate it is interesting to note that the interest rates were only increased drastically when the Act came into operation in June 2006. With the Act already having the unintended consequence of closing access to finance,[58] particularly for the low-income group,[59] it is not clear why the South African Government also saw it fit to increase the interest rates. In doing so, the Government not only closed access to finance even further, but also caused possible over-indebtedness for the low-income group who had already concluded housing loans when the interest rates were still low. However, whether there has, in fact, been a correlation between the coming into operation of the Act and the various increases in the interest rate by the government remains unclear. Of course, it is not only the increase in interest rates over the last couple of years that are to be blamed for causing over-indebtedness. The continuing rise in inflation, which is driven primarily by high food and energy

56 Information obtained from <http://www.absa.co.za/absacoza/content.jsp?/Home/Rates-&-Fees/Prime-Rates/Absa-Prime-Rates> (accessed 2 November 2009).

57 See Proc 22 in Government Gazette 28824 of 11 May 2006.

58 See Anon March 2009, at 2; Klopper 2009, at 16; Visser 2009; and Van Zyl & Van Rooyen 2009.

59 See also the report prepared for FinMark Trust, South Africa, November 2006.

prices,[60] and increases in municipal rates and taxes[61] also worsened the erosion of consumers' disposable incomes.[62]

When the rest of the world (for example, the United States of America, China, Canada, and the United Kingdom) was lowering their reserve bank repurchasing and prime lending interest rates in order to deal with the worldwide financial crisis, South Africa was initially still increasing their rates.[63] The South African prime lending rate only came down for the first time in December 2008. South African interest rates have always been fairly high compared to the rest of the world. This is often blamed on the fact that South Africa has a high inflation rate.[64] As 85 percent of the South African population falls into the low-income group, having an unrealistically high interest rate does not make sense to the layman. With the Act already having the unintended consequence of closing access to finance for many,[65] the high prime lending interest rate is making it even more impossible for the low-income group to obtain credit or to continue paying their existing housing loans.[66]

Currently there is no legislative protection for a consumer against various increases in the interest rate applicable to his credit agreement as long as the rate falls within the ambit of the prescribed maximums. But there are a few informal alternative protective measures at the disposal of a consumer that is experiencing financial difficulty in paying his housing loan, because of subsequent increases in his interest rate. For instance, he can approach the bondholder (bank) and request that the term on his housing loan is extended from 20 to 30 years. This, however, depends on the willingness of the bank and will only be a short-term benefit and in the long run he will be liable for additional interest over the

---

60 See Styan 2009; and Van Tonder October 2009.

61 See Van Vuuren 2009, at 8.

62 See Anon September 2008, at 1; and Anon March 2009, at 2.

63 See Anon November 2008.

64 See the Reserve Bank Fact Sheet, at 2 and 4. Another reason for this, as explained by the South African Reserve Bank, is apparently because South Africa has a small, open economy the domestic interest rates are inevitably affected by events in other countries. They point out that if interest rates increase in one country, that country becomes relatively more attractive to international investors than other countries (assuming that the risk associated with investing in that country has not changed) and interest rates in these countries will tend to respond if outflows of capital are to be averted. Therefore, South African interest rates have become increasingly more sensitive to developments in both developed and emerging financial markets (see the Reserve Bank Fact Sheet, at 4). Hopefully, this is not the sole driving force, behind the Reserve Bank's reasoning when they determine their Repurchase Rate, and that they do, in fact, also take other factors into consideration, such as what the impact of high rates will be on all domestic consumers, but especially the low-income consumers.

65 See Klopper 2009, at 16.

66 See also Anon March 2009, at 2.

extended period of the loan and the credit will be more expensive. Furthermore, he can also request the bank to fix his interest rate on the loan for a certain period, for example, 12, 18, 24 or 36 months. This will allow the monthly installment to stay the same during the fixed period despite any increases in the prime lending rate. However, it might also happen that by the time the consumer request a fixed rate from the bank that the existing rate might already have escalated to such a high rate that he will not be able to service his loan at this fixed rate. Where a consumer has defaulted, a bank might also be willing to allow a consumer to pay his arrears off over a stipulated period. But it is unlikely that a low-income consumer who is already cash-strapped will be able to pay the current installment and also carry an additional installment to pay off the arrears. A bank might also be willing to allow a consumer to pay a reduced installment or to suspend payment for a specified period, but this will solely depend on the willingness of the bank to accommodate a specific consumer.[67]

Sometimes a bank might even request a consumer to voluntarily surrender his mortgaged home to the bank so that they can sell it and recover the shortfall from the consumer without having taken legal action against the consumer. The bank might even try to assist a consumer in selling his home to enable him to repay his loan amount. Both these options have the effect of the consumer losing his home. Of course, the consumer may also apply to a debt counselor for debt review, but this option will solely depend on whether his debts can, in fact, be workably restructured and he can actually repay a newly structured installment.

Conclusion

As high interest rates have been one of the main reasons why so many South Africans, particularly the middle- and low-income group, have lost their mortgaged homes, the South African Government (as well as the South African Reserve Bank), needs to pay attention to this fact and should take some responsibility for their role in causing this situation.

The National Credit Act expressly states that the South African Minister of Trade and Industry, after consulting the National Credit Regulator, may prescribe a method for calculating a maximum rate of interest and other non-interest costs of credit for different types of credit agreements.[68] However, before the Minister may prescribe the maximum interest rates and other costs of credit, he must, amongst other things, consider[69] the need to make credit availa-

67 See Anon September 2008, at 2; and Anon March 2009, at 3.

68 See section 105(1) of the Act.

69 See section 105(2) of the Act.

ble to historically disadvantaged persons, low-income persons;[70] the conditions prevailing in the credit market (that is, the costs of credit and the optimal functioning of the consumer credit market); and the social impact on low-income consumers.

Before the National Credit Act, there was no express statutory duty on the South African Government to take any of these factors into consideration. It is also unclear whether any of these factors were taken into consideration when the existing method for calculating a maximum rate of interest, as prescribed in the National Credit Act and the Regulations, was set.

The responsibility for prescribing workable maximum interest rates that are sustainable in the current financial and credit market lies with the Minister. However, as the current prescribed maximum rates are all linked to the Reserve Bank Repurchase Rate, it is argued that the South African Reserve Bank also has a social responsibility to take these factors into consideration together with their usual factors, such as the supply and demand for funds and inflation,[71] before they increase their Repurchase Rate. Looking at the history of the Reserve Bank Repurchase Rate and that of the prime lending rates of banks, particularly during the period June 2006 to December 2008,[72] it seems that the South African Government did not carefully consider the impact such high rates would have on consumers, particularly the low-income group. In my view, the South African Government has a social responsibility (especially if one also takes section 26 of the South African Constitution into consideration)[73] to protect low-income consumers against rapid and repeated increases in the interest rates on their mortgage agreements that could cause them to lose their mortgaged homes.

The National Credit Act prescribes the maximum allowable interest rates, but it does not govern how the South African Reserve Bank determines its Repurchase Rate, which, in the end, plays a pivotal role in how the maximum interest rates are determined. Therefore, the protection provided in the National Credit Act, in this regard, means nothing to a consumer who once complied with the Act and his bank's credit assessment criteria but then defaulted because he

---

70 See section 105(2)(a), read with section 13(a) of the Act.

71 For a full discussion of all the factors the Reserve Bank takes into consideration before determining their Repurchasing Rate, see Reserve Bank Fact Sheet.

72 See Figure 1, above.

73 Section 26 of the Constitution of the Republic of South Africa of 1996, which deals with a person's right to housing, reads as follows:

(1) Everyone has the right to have access to adequate housing.

(2) The state must take reasonable legislative and other measures, within its available resource to achieve the progressive realization of this right.

(3) No one may be evicted from their home, or have their home demolished, without an order of court made after considering all the relevant circumstances. No legislation may permit arbitrary evictions.

could no longer pay his installments on his existing home loan, simply because his interest rate was rapidly increased after the loan was grante.

References

Alliance Group: Recent Interest Rate Hike Will Increase Bank Foreclosures. eProp Commercial Property News, 12 October 2007 (available at <http://www.eprop.co.za> (accessed 2 November 2009)).

Anon: Interest Rates Down 100bps. News24.com, 10 December 2008 (available at <http://www.news24.com> (accessed 2 November 2009)).

Anon: It's Time to Sit Tight, be Conservative and Patient. Enrich (Newsletter for Transnet Retirement Fund Members) April 2009, 1.

Anon: Manage Your Home Loan Effectively. Standard Bank's Home Loans Newsletter, March 2009, 3.

Anon: No Respite for Residential Property. Standard Bank's Home Loans Newsletter, September 2008, 1.

Anon: Residential Property Market Under Strain, but there is Light at the End of the Tunnel. Standard Bank's Home Loans Newsletter, March 2009, 2.

Anon: SA Consumers Need an Immediate Rate Cut. November 2008 (available at <http://www.ooba.co.za/site/press-centre/oobabond%20news%20archive>) (accessed 2 November 2009)).

Anon: Tips to Help you Manage your Home Loan. Standard Bank's Home Loans Newsletter, September 2008, 2.

Campbell, Nicky & Logan, Stephen: The Credit Guide. Cape Town: Juta & Co Ltd 2008.

Department of Trade and Industry: Consumer Credit Law Reform: Policy Framework for Consumer Credit. August 2004.

FinMark Trust, South Africa: Report prepared by Goodwin-Groen, RP (with input from Kelly-Louw, M): The National Credit Act and Its Regulations in the Context of Access to Finance in South Africa. November 2006 (available at http://www.finmarktrust.org.za (accessed 2 November 2009)).

Futuse, Bongolethu: High Rates Batter Homeowners. Fin24.com, 9 December 2007 (available at <http://www.fin24.com/articles> (accessed 2 November 2009)).

Kelly-Louw, Michelle: Prevention of Overindebtedness and Mechanisms for Resolving Overindebtedness of South African Consumers, Chapter 9, 175–198 in Niemi, Johanna, Ramsay, Iain & Whitford, William C. (eds): Consumer Credit, Debt and Bankruptcy: Comparative and International Perspectives. Oxford: Hart Publishing 2009.

Kelly-Louw, Michelle: The Prevention and Alleviation of Consumer Over-indebtedness. South African Mercantile Law Journal Vol 20, 2008, 200.

Kelly-Louw, Michelle: The South African National Credit Act Fails to Protect Homeowners Against Various Interest Rates Hikes. US-China Law Review Vol 6, No 12, 2009, 12.

Klopper, Elma: Dis Nog Huisie Verby vir Gretige Kopers. Rapport Newspaper (GeldSake24), 3 May 2009, 16.

Lawack-Davids, VA: The Mortgagee's Power to Unilaterally Increase the Interest Rate. *Obiter Vol 22, 2001,* 200.

Loos, Johan: Latest Interest Rate Hike – Effect on the Property Market, 24 April 2008 (available at <http://coolgroup.co.za/latest-interest-rate-hike-in-south-africa/> (accessed 2 November 2009)).

McLennan, JS: Unilateral Determination of Contractual Performance: the Interest-rate Controversy Solved – but what next? South African Mercantile Law Journal Vol 12, 2000, 485.

Mohamed, Seeraj: High Interest Rates and the Carry Trade. 28 August 2008 (available at <http://www.polity.org.za> (accessed 2 November 2009)).

Otto, JM: The National Credit Act Explained. Durban: LexisNexis Butterworths 2006.

Renke, S, Roestoff, M & Haupt, FS: The National Credit Act: New Parameters for the Granting of Credit in South Africa' Obiter Vol 28, 2007, 229.

Scholtz, JW (ed) et al: Guide to the National Credit Act. Durban: LexisNexis (loose leaf) 2008.

Scott, J (ed) et al: The Law of Commerce in South Africa. Cape Town: Oxford University Press 2009.

South African Reserve Bank Research Department: Information Division. Interest Rates and How They Work, 8th Fact Sheet (available at <http:www.reservebank.co.za> (click on 'About us > Fact Sheet') (accessed 2 November 2009) ("the Reserve Bank Fact Sheet").

Styan, James-Brent: "Oorlog" Dreig oor Eskom se Kragpryse. Rapport Newspaper (Sake-Rapport), 5 April 2009, 1.

Theobald, Stuart: When Banks Struggle, Expect More Fees. Sunday Times Newspaper (Business Times), 26 April 2009, 4.

Van Tonder, Johann: Eskom-verhogings sal SA se Ekonomie Martel. Rapport Newspaper (Sake24), 11 October 2009, 5.

Van Tonder, J: Tam Ekonomie Noop Daling van Presentasiepunt. Rapport Newspaper (GeldSake24), 24 May 2009, 8.

Van Vuuren, Marthinus: Skuldmonster Sluk Al hoe Meer In. Rapport Newspaper, 24 May 2009, 8.

Van Zyl, Adri and Van Rooyen, David: Manual: Staat Kan nie aan Banke Voorskryf. Rapport Newspaper (Sake-Rapport), 15 February 2009, 6.

Visser, Jaco: Reserwebank Raas met Banke oor Uitleenkriteria. Beeld Newspaper (Sake24), 7 May 2009, 1.

Watson, Letitia: Rentekoers Groot Kopseer vir Kliënte van Mikroleners. Rapport Newspaper (Sake-Rapport), 25 May 2008, 5.

Cases

Ex parte Ford and Two Similar Cases 2009 (3) SA 376 (WCC).

First Rand Bank Ltd v Smith (unreported, case no 24206/08 of 31 October 2008 (W)).

Investec Bank (Pty) Ltd v GVN Properties CC 1999 (3) SA 490 (W).

NBS Boland Bank Ltd v One Berg River Drive CC and Others; Deeb and Another v ABSA Bank Ltd; Friedman v Standard Bank of SA Ltd 1999 (4) SA 928 (SCA).

Standard Bank SA Ltd v Hales & Another 2009 (3) SA 315 (D) ([2009] 2 All SA 416 (D)).

Standard Bank of South Africa Ltd v Panayiotts 2009 (3) SA 363 (W).

Acts, Regulations and Government Gazettes

Constitution of the Republic of South Africa of 1996 (Act 108 of 1996).

Home Loan and Mortgage Disclosure Act 63 of 2000.

National Credit Act 34 of 2005.

Proc 22 in Government Gazette 28824 of 11 May 2006.

Regulation Gazette No 8477, R489 in Government Gazette 28864 of 31 May 2006.

Websites

http://www.absa.co.za/absacoza/content.jsp?/Home/Rates-&-Fees/Prime-Rates/Absa-Prime-Rates

http://www.housing.gov.za

http://en.wikipedia.org/wiki/Prime_lending_rate

Punishing the Lender for Who's Sake? Impacts of the New Case Law and Follow-ups to the 2006 Reform of the Consumer Credit Regulation in Japan

Souichirou Kozuka

Introduction: Japan's experiment with the consumer credit law

Since 2006, Japan has been engaged in a social experiment involving its consumer credit law. This was started by a Supreme Court decision. The decision deprived moneylenders of virtually all of the privileges they previously had enjoyed under the governing Moneylenders' Control Law, a law that had provided special rules to the earlier Interest Rate Restrictions Law (IRRL). The Supreme Court's 2006 decision pushed the Diet to enact regulatory reforms reinstating the interest rate cap and strengthening the IRRL. Moreover, as a result of the Court's decision, excess interest that moneylenders had received in the past became unfounded, paving the way for borrowers' claims for recovery of excess interest paid in unjust enrichment.

The effects of this sequence of events have been enormous. Though the principal part of the regulatory reform was implemented in June 2010, the effects on moneylenders were immediate. Even the largest lenders have recorded large deficits, two of them becoming insolvent. Many small and medium size lenders have quit the business. On the other hand, many borrowers are reported to have been relieved that they no longer need to borrow to repay their loans. At first glance, the judiciary has been successful in protecting the interests of the over-indebted.

It is easy to see that this will not be the end of the story. This apparent success has occurred by punishing lenders retrospectively and is not relevant to future borrowers. The true challenge is whether those who would have resorted to moneylenders' high interest rates can be financed appropriately in the new regime. In an attempt to ensure the availability of finance to such people, the government has established the headquarters to combat against over-indebtedness and published the policy package. It is, though, still early to see whether the proposed policies will be effective.

This experiment in Japan provides lessons to countries that take over-indebted consumers' problems seriously. The recovery of excess interest can be seen as a wealth transfer from lenders to borrowers, which has some commonalities with the bankruptcy discharge. The anticipated need for a finance mechanism after the reform is fully in force may indicate that discussing bankruptcy law or regulation of lenders is not enough. Finally, the policy package stresses the need for empirical research of over-indebtedness, echoing similar attempts in other countries.

Having thus identified the usefulness of sharing the Japanese experience with other parts of the world, this chapter describes what has taken place in Japan since 2006. Following a brief introduction of previous regulation in this Part 1, Part 2 describes the court decisions that permitted recovery of excess interest beginning in 2006. Next, Part 3 examines the impacts of recovery suits under this case law, referring to some statistical data. Finally, Part 4 considers the Japanese government's policy response, with special attention to the problems that may arise when bringing the proposed policies into practice. A brief analysis of what has and has not been done follows as a conclusion in Part 5.

Recovery of excess interest: The aftermath of a Supreme Court decision

Regulation before 2006[1]

Interest rate regulation has existed in Japan since 1877, only ten years after modernization. In fact, the proliferation of loan sharks was followed by reinstatement of interest regulation under the pre-modern Tokugawa government, after a decade of freedom of contract.[2] Since 1954, the Interest Rate Restrictions Law (IRRL)[3] set the highest permissible annual interest rate at 20 percent for principal less than ¥100,000, 18 percent for principal between ¥100,000 and ¥1 million, and 15 percent for principal of ¥1 million or more. Agreements on interest in excess of these caps are null and void. The case law in the 1960s established that the payment of excess interest under the IRRL was converted into repayment of the principal, and that the borrower was entitled to recover any residual amount when the total amount he paid was larger than the sum of the interest allowed under the IRRL and the principal.[4]

However, the IRRL had a loophole. Debtors could not reclaim the payment of excess interest as long as payments were made "voluntarily." The Moneylenders' Control Law[5] (MCL), enacted in 1983, further extended this privilege to registered lenders; it regarded payments in excess of the cap under the IRRL to be valid if payment was made voluntarily and the registered lender complied

1 For further details of the previous regulation, see Kozuka and Nottage 2008, at 215-220.

2 Pardieck 2008, at 537-538.

3 Interest Rate Restrictions Law (Risoku Seigen Hô), law no.100 of 1954, art.1.

4 Supreme Court, 18 November 1964, Minshû vol.18, no.9, at 1868; Supreme Court 13 November 1968, Minshû vol.22, no.12, at 2526. See Matsumoto (2007), at 327-329, Pardieck 2008, at 546-548.

5 Moneylenders Control Law (Kashikingyo no Kisei tô ni Kansuru Hôritsu), law no.32 of 1983 (to be without effect by 18 June 2010).

with several procedural requirements, such as the delivery of the contract details upon conclusion of the loan agreement and the issuance of a receipt each time the borrower made a payment.

Still, a complying lender was not able to set the interest rate as high as they wished. The third regulation by the Capital Funding Law (CFL),[6] dating back in 1954, sanctioned lenders demanding an "extremely high" rate of interest and imposed, various other regulations aimed at suppressing fraudulent financial transactions. Since 2000, the CFL set this cap at 29.2 percent, higher than the cap in the IRRL. Prior to 2000, it was 40 percent.

There are two lines of thought with regard to interest rate regulation. Legislators have sympathized with the argument that simply applying a cap on interest rates does not result in the optimal arrangement, thus exempting voluntary payment in the IRRL. The judiciary, on the other hand, viewed such an exemption as allowing lenders to evade regulation, and rendered the exemption almost meaningless by adopting an interpretation that seemed to be contrary to a simple reading of the text. The legislature reversed this case law by introducing the Moneylenders Control Law and providing a clearer basis for retention of excess interest by lenders under certain conditions. Lenders complying with the requirements of the Moneylenders Control Law enjoyed this privilege and requested the maximum interest rate that was not penalized. The interest between the IRRL cap and the penalized rate under the Capital Funding Law was called the "grey zone" (Figure 1).

Figure 1: Interest rate regulation before 2006

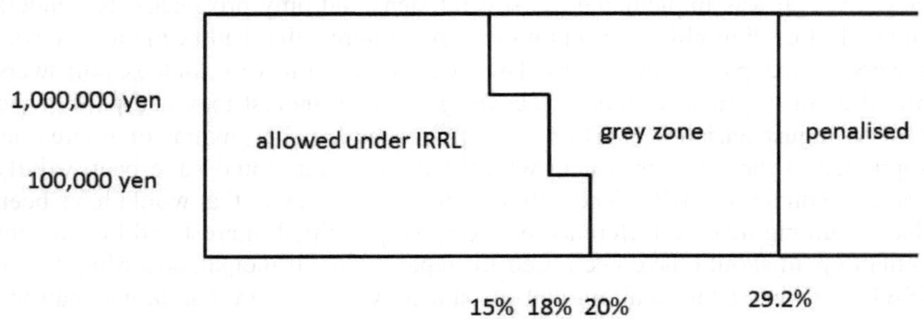

6 Capital Funding Law (Shusshi no Ukeire, Azukarikin oyobi Kinri tô no Torishimari ni kansuru Hôritsu), law no.195 of 1954.

Supreme Court decision of 2006

In the 2000s, courts took their turn, overriding legislative intent and compromising lenders' positions.[7] In case after case, the requirements of the Moneylenders' Control Law were interpreted more and more strictly, so that the registered lenders' ability to retain interest in the grey zone became narrower and narrower. Finally, in 2006, the Supreme Court decided that repayment was not "voluntary" if there was an acceleration clause in the loan agreement, because such a clause imposes psychological pressure on the debtor to make repayment.[8] As an acceleration clause is nothing unusual in a loan agreement, this decision virtually eliminated the privilege under the MCL. The same decision also voided the Ministerial Order that had allowed a simplified statement in the receipt as going beyond the mandate of the statutory provision. As a result, many moneylenders that had relied on the Ministerial Order were deprived of this basis for retaining grey zone interest.

In reaction, the Diet changed its policy and discarded the concept of grey zone interest. The MCL has been totally reformed and renamed as the Moneylenders Law. It no longer derogates from the interest rate cap in the IRRL and provides many other strengthened regulations, most notably prohibiting "excessive lending", which it defines as extending a loan when the outstanding amount of the debt exceeds one third of the annual income of the borrower. The amended regulation went into force on 18 June 2010.[9]

Besides triggering this reform, the Supreme Court decision of 2006 brought great benefit to existing over-indebted borrowers, as well as to those who used to be over-indebted. Since case law applies retrospectively, unlike the new regulation, which was implemented in several steps and only prospectively, lenders suddenly lost their ability to retain grey zone interest that had been paid by borrowers in the past. Advised by lawyers, many borrowers and ex-borrowers raised claims against lenders to recover grey zone interest they had paid in the past as unjust enrichment. Borrowers first compare the amount of interest as stipulated in the loan agreement with the amount that could have been validly agreed to under the IRRL. Then, they work out the amount that would have been due, assuming that the difference between the permitted interest and the amount actually paid should have been used for repaying the principal, according to the 1964 decision. If the total amount of paid grey zone interest is larger than the sum of the principal and interest payable under the IRRL, the borrower requests the difference (excess payment; *kabarai* in Japanese) to be disgorged and re-

---

7 See Kozuka and Nottage 2008, at 221-223.

8 Supreme Court, 13 January 2006, Minshû vol.60, no.1, at1. See Pardieck 2008, at 566-567; Kozuka 2009, at 88.

9 The background and the policy reasons for this reform are discussed in detail in Kozuka and Nottage 2009.

turned to the borrower. (See Table as a hypothetical case for calculating the excess payment.)

Dates	Principal	Agreed interest	Re-payment	Outstanding amount	Interest under IRRL	Balance under IRRL	Excess payment	Interest on excess payment	Events
15.1.2001	500,000			500,000		500,000			Initial loan
15.2.2001		12,315	25,000	487,315	7,644	482,644			Starts repayment
15.3.2001		10,841	25,000	473,156	6,664	464,308			
15.4.2001		11,654	25,000	459,810	7,098	446,406			
15.5.2001		10,960	25,000	445,770	6,604	428,011			
15.6.2001		10,979	25,000	431,749	6,543	409,554			
15.7.2001		10,291	25,000	417,040	6,059	390,613			
15.8.2001		10,272	25,000	402,312	5,972	371,585			
15.9.2001		9,909	25,000	387,221	5,681	352,266			
15.10.2001		9,230	25,000	371,451	5,212	332,477			
15.11.2001		9,149	25,000	355,600	5,083	312,560			
15.12.2002		8,476	25,000	339,076	4,624	292,184			
15.1.2002		8,351	25,000	322,427	4,467	271,651			
15.2.2002		7,941	25,000	305,368	4,153	250,804			
15.3.2002		6,793	25,000	287,162	3,463	229,267			
15.4.2002		7,073	25,000	269,235	3,505	207,772			
15.5.2002		6,417	25,000	250 652	3,074	185,846			
15.6.2002		6,174	25,000	231,826	2,841	163,687			
15.7.2002		5,526	25,000	212,351	2,422	141,109			
15.8.2002		5,230	25,000	192,582	2,157	118,266			
15.9.2002		4,743	25,000	172,325	1,808	95,074			
15.10.2002		4,107	25,000	151,432	1,407	71,480			
15.11.2002		3,730	25,000	130,162	1,093	47,573			
15.12.2002		3,102	25,000	108,265	704	23,277			
15.1.2003		2,667	25,000	85,931	356	-1,367	1,367	0	Continues to pay because there was apparent outstanding debt
15.2.2003		2,116	25,000	63,048	0	-26,373	26,373	6	Excess payment starts accruing interest
15.3.2003		1,403	25,000	39,450	0	-51,474	51,474	101	
15.4.2003		972	25,000	15,422	0	-76,693	76,693	219	
15.5.2003		368	15,790	0	0	-92,798	92,798	315	Complete repayment
15.6.2005		0	0	0	0	-93,179	93,179	381	
15.7.2003		0	0	0	0	-93,562	93,562	383	
15.8.2003		0	0	0	0	-93,947	93,947	385	

15.9.2003	100,000	0		100,000		6,053			New loan/ Excess payment can be utilized as repayment
15.10.2003		2,384	20,000	82,383	90	-13,857	13,857		
15.11.2003		2,029	20,000	64,412	0	-33,916	33,916	59	
15.12.2003		1,535	20,000	45,948	0	-54,055	54,055	139	
15.1.2004		1,132	20,000	27,079	0	-74,285	74,285	230	
15.2.2004		667	20,000	7,746	0	-94,600	94,600	315	
15.3.2004		178	7,925	0	0	-102,901	102,901	376	Complete repayment of the second loan

In this hypothetical case, the borrower makes loans on the revolving facility agreement with the lender. The agreed interest is at 29% per annum, which is in the "grey zone." The interest cap under the IRRL is 18% per annum. Under the latter rate, the initial debt is paid out on 2003/01/15, but the borrower did not realize it and continued to pay. When the apparent outstanding debt was completely repaid on 2003/5/15, there existed ¥92,798 of excess payment ("kabarai"). This amount can be treated as the repayment on the spot when the second loan is extended on 2003/9/15. The result is that most of the repayments made for the second loan became excess payment. If this borrower makes a recovery claim in March 2009, five years after all the transactions were over, he is entitled to ¥131,331, including the statutory interest of yearly 5 percent as the unjust enrichment of the lender.

Case law after 2006

Even after 2006, the judiciary continued supporting borrowers' claims for recovery of excess interest. First, a Supreme Court decision in 2007 held that lenders receiving grey zone interest were presumed to have done so "in bad faith," since lenders must have been aware that they were not entitled to the payment if any one of the requirements was missing.[10] As a result, lenders subject to recovery claims are required to return the excess payment plus interest calculated at the statutory interest rate of five percent per annum.[11]

With regard to the not unusual case in which the borrower took loans repeatedly from the same lender, the Supreme Court held that the excess payment for the previous loan can be converted into repayment of the later loan only when there is an agreement to that extent.[12] Despite the restrictive phrasing, in fact the Court affirmed the implied existence of such an agreement in the case of a revolving loan[13] and sequential loans,[14] denying it only when there are two or more base contracts.[15] Since interest accrues as compound interest, the borrower benefits if the excess payment from the previous loan can be utilized to reduce the amount of the principal for the later loan rather than simply returned at the time the recovery claim is made.

10 Supreme Court, 13 July 2007, Minshû vol.61, no.5, at 1980.
11 See the Civil Code (Mimpô), art.704.
12 Supreme Court, 7 June 2007, Minshû vo.61, no.4, at1537.
13 Id.
14 Supreme Court, 19 July 2007, Minshû vol.61, no.5, at 2175.
15 Supreme Court, 18 January 2008, Minshû vol.62, no.1, at 28.

The Supreme Court subsequently held in a series of decisions that, where an agreement of "conversion into repayment for later loans" was found, the prescription for the recovery claim for excess payment did not commence to run until the whole transaction was terminated and no additional loans could be extended.[16] This means that a lender having offered a revolving credit facility can be subject to claims for recovery of excess payments made decades ago, if the base agreement for the revolving facility had remained current. On the other hand, the statutory interest on the excess payment to be returned to the borrower started accruing at the time the relevant excess payment was made, even if the loan was based on a revolving facility agreement.[17]

Changes in the consumer credit market

Since 2006, the Japanese consumer credit market has changed significantly due both to recovery claims under the new case law and to regulatory reforms, in particular the prohibition against excessive lending. While the former has had an impact on the current earnings of lenders, the latter affected lenders' behavior even in advance of the implementation of the law in 2010.

The scale of recovery claims

According to data from an industry organization,[18] the total amount of the excess payment returned to borrowers reached ¥293.6 billion in 2006 and ¥525.9 billion in 2007. In addition, the amount that has been converted into repayment of the principal marked ¥259.9 billion in 2006 and ¥425.2 billion in 2007, respectively. Together, nearly ¥1 trillion was transferred from lenders to borrowers in 2007. Even in 2010, four years after the initial Supreme Court decision, the number of outstanding recovery claims remains between 50,000 and 60,000.[19]

The data on recovery claims against four largest nonbank lenders (the "Big Four") shows that 58 percent of the claims were made by lawyers and 33 percent by judicial scriveners.[20] This may indicate that legal experts use recovery of ex-

16 Supreme Court, 22 January 2009, Minshû vol.63, no.1, at 247; Supreme Court, 3 March 2009, Hanrei Jihô no.2048, at 9; Supreme Court, 6 March 2009, Hanrei Jihô, no.2048, at 12.

17 Supreme Court, 17 July 2009, Hanrei Jihô no.2048, at14.

18 Nihon Kashikingyo Kyokai 2009, at 86.

19 Material no.3 submitted by the Japan Moneylenders Association to the Follow-up Hearing on the Amended Moneylenders Law held on June 27, 2011, at10, (dated June 27, 2011).

20 Nihon Kashikingyo Kyokai 2009, at 88.

cess payment as a substitute for debt adjustment or bankruptcy with discharge. The difference between debt adjustment and recovery of excess interest is that the latter benefits the borrowers' other creditors as the proceeds of the recovery are available for repayment of these creditors' claims. For example, it has been reported that the return of excess payment to borrowers has enabled local governments to collect tax claims, which over-indebted borrowers often fail to pay.[21] In this sense, recovery claims are a kind of simplified debt adjustment in which the nonbank lender is subordinated to other creditors.

Lenders' performance

Since 2006, the performance of nonbank lenders has deteriorated rapidly. The largest nonbank lender, Takefuji Corporation, earned ¥425.4 billion in fiscal year 2001. In 2007 and 2008, its earnings were ¥270.5 billion and ¥186.3 billion, respectively. Earnings for fiscal year 2009 were reported to be ¥120.2 billion, a 35.5 percent decline from the same period in the previous year.[22] The amount was almost a quarter of the earnings in 2001. In September 2010, the company became insolvent and filed for corporate reorganization.

The situation is more or less the same with other nonbank lenders. As a result, one of the Big Four lenders, Aiful Corporation, sought out-of-court rescheduling in September 2009, which was agreed to by its creditors on December 24 of the same year.[23]

Obviously, downward pressure on lenders' performance derives partly from the need to meet the growing number of recovery claims. However, the actual payout to borrowers is not the only cause of their financial troubles. Another factor is that lenders were required as a practical matter to lower the interest rate they charged new borrowers, even before the amendment eliminating the grey zone interest came into force. No reasonable lender would extend a loan at an interest rate higher than the limit set in the IRRL, even before the effective date of the new regulation, when it is easily foreseen to be subject to a recovery claim under the Supreme Court's case law. Further, the major lenders also started to prepare for the prohibition on excessive lending even before the effective date of this provision in June 2010, and became quite defensive about extending loans. The remarkable decline in lenders' earnings is the result of all these factors.

---

21 Minutes of the 4th meeting of the Experts Meeting to Combat Over-indebtedness, at 20 (dated March 2, 2007).

22 See the Financial statements of Takefuji Corp., available on its website < http://www.takefuji.co.jp/corp/fncldt/index.html > (in Japanese).

23 See the press release of Aiful Corp., available on its website < http://www.ir-aiful.com/data/current/newsobj-1704-datafile.pdf > (in Japanese).

The number of registered lenders decreased

Under these adverse business circumstances, smaller lenders have chosen to quit the business. The number of registered lenders is rapidly decreasing. In April 2011, registered lenders numbered 2,560, a more than 80 percent reduction from the 14,236 lenders that had been registered in March 2006.[24] It appears that small- and medium-sized lenders cannot survive without grey zone interest.

The decline in registered lenders does not appear to have caused an increase in illegal lenders. According to statistics collected by the Financial Services Agency (FSA), 14,942 complaints were lodged with regulators about unregistered lenders in 2007; 14,243 in 2008. These numbers represent about half of the complaints registered in 2003, 26,231, which marked the highest number of complaints in recent years. [25] The bar association confirms that consultation about illegal lending has been decreasing from its peak in 2003.[26] The prediction that stricter regulation would lead to the proliferation of illegal lenders[27] has not come true.

The impact on the borrowers

The effects of the new case law and regulation on borrowers are not straightforward. On one hand, many existing borrowers have benefited from recovery claims. They have been relieved from taking a new loan to pay the interest to the existent loan, which was a commonplace situation before the reform.[28] Many of them were paid out in cash. Perhaps as a result of these recovery claims, the number of borrowers with multiple debts is decreasing. The number of borrowers with five or more debts dropped from 1.71 million in March 2005 to 1.18 million in March 2006 and then to 0.73 million in March 2009.[29] Comparing these numbers with 2.3 million quoted by the Financial Services Agency as the number of such debtors before the reform,[30] we may evaluate that the reform has been successful in decreasing over-indebted borrowers.

---

24 Material no.7 submitted by the Financial Services Agency to the Follow-up Hearing on the Amended Moneylenders Law held on June 27, 2011, at 9, (dated June 27, 2011).

25 Kin'yucho 2009, 23. The numbers in the intermediate years are: 17,022 in 2004, 20,364 in 2005, and 19,075 in 2006.

26 Minutes of the 13th meeting of the Experts Meeting to Combat Over-indebtedness, at15 (dated May 19, 2009).

27 See Kozuka and Nottage 2008, at 224.

28 For the situation of debtots before the reform, see Kozuka and Nottage 2008, at 211-212.

29 Material no.3 submitted to the 14th meeting of the Experts Meeting to Combat Over-indebtedness, at 35, (June 17, 2009).

30 'Kashikingyôhô tô no Kaisei ni Tsuite' (About the amendments to the Moneylenders Law), at 5, available on the website of the FSA <http://www.fsa.go.jp/policy/kashikin/02.pdf >. Though this brochure does not specify

On the other hand, new borrowers are being screened more and more severely. The industry organization of nonbank lenders reports that only 26.8 percent of new loan applications were granted in March 2008, which is a sharp decline from the 42.1 percent of loan applications granted in September 2006.[31] It makes sense that lenders would become more selective when case law subjecting grey zone interest to recovery claims caused the permissible interest rate to drop. According to questionnaires from 2008, lenders expect their screening to be even stricter when the prohibition of excessive lending is introduced.[32]

As a result, the amount of consumer debt outstanding has decreased. At the end of March 2009, outstanding debt reported to the FSA counted ¥22.4 million in number, a 12 percent decline from the previous year (¥25.4 million in debt in March 2008) and a 22 percent decline from the year before (¥28.8 million in debt in March 2007).[33] The trend seems to correspond to the decrease in the amount of outstanding consumer debt, which was ¥20.3 trillion in March 2007, ¥17.9 trillion in March 2008, and ¥15.7 trillion in March 2009.[34] Whether this reduction in consumer indebtedness spells an inconvenience or hardship for consumers is unclear. Looking at a longer period of time, the amount of consumer debt was ¥16.4 trillion a decade ago (March 1999); it gradually peaked in 2006.[35] Thus, the Supreme Court decision and the regulatory reform of 2006 shrank Japanese consumer credit markets back to the level of ten years ago from its boom.

Searching for a consumer credit system after the reform

As the government foresaw that tightened regulation would lead to a reduction in the market for consumer credit, it also looked to implement a policy package to address the problem of consumer over-indebtedness. Amending the moneylenders' regulation was considered insufficient if not accompanied by ad-

---

the year for the quoted data, the context implies that the data describes the situation before the reform.

31 Material no.1-3 submitted to the 11th meeting of the Experts Meeting to Combat Over-indebtedness, at13 (dated October 30, 2008).

32 Material no.1-3 submitted to the 11th meeting of the Experts Meeting to Combat Over-indebtedness, at 12 (dated October 30, 2008). It is noteworthy, in this respect, that major lenders recognize that quite a number of their outstanding loans will infringe upon the prohibition of excessive lending. Half of the eight major lenders respond more than 60 percent, and three others responded more than 40 percent, will be affected by the implementation of the prohibition of excessive lending (id., at14).

33 Material no.3 submitted to the 14th meeting of the Experts Meeting to Combat Over-indebtedness, at 35, (June 17, 2009).

34 Kin'yucho 2009, at 8.

35 Id., at 8.

ditional reform. A comprehensive policy package was viewed as necessary, including both enhanced provision of social services and police power enforcement. The government left about three and a half years between enactment of the reform package and prohibition of excessive lending comes into force.

Major amendments included in the 2006 reform

The 2006 reform included multiple amendments to be implemented step by step.[36] The first part increased the penalties on unregistered moneylenders as well as penalties on agreements on, requests for or receipt of hyper-expensive interest rates (109.5 percent per annum) by registered moneylenders. This amendment entered into force on January 20, 2007, roughly two months after the amendments passed the Diet.

The second part further strengthens the regulation of moneylenders. Moneylenders must, among other things, establish a system for handling customers' credit information, complying with enhanced disclosure and explanatory obligations now required before making loan agreements, refraining from becoming beneficiaries under life insurance contracts taken out by their borrowers, and respecting the new suitability standard when soliciting loan agreements. Further, the Federation of Moneylenders Association (*Zenkoku Kashikingyo Kyokai Rengokai*) was asked to reorganize itself into a nationwide Moneylenders' Association and to serve as the self-regulatory body authorized under the Moneylenders Law. These amendments entered into force on 19 December 2007 and the new Japan Moneylenders Association (*Nihon Kashikingyo Kyokai*) was incorporated on the same day.

As third part of the amendments, moneylenders were required to hold reserves (net assets) of ¥20 million or more, much larger than the equivalent qualification of ¥3 million for individuals and ¥5 million for corporations, respectively, under the previous regulation. Further, information sharing institutions, with which member moneylenders have to file each time they extend a loan, are to be certified by the government as a result of these amendments. The filed information must be shared with other certified institutions. These amendments entered into force on 18 June 2009 and the two information sharing institutions, Japan Credit Information Reference Center Corp. (JICC) and Credit Information Center (CIC), were certified.

The last, and most important, part of the law abolishes grey zone interest and penalizes interest above the rate allowed under the IRRL. It also imposes on lenders the duty to investigate the ability of a borrower to repay a loan, in par-

---

36 For details, see Pardieck 2008, at 576-580; see also Kozuka and Nottage 2008, at 224-225.

ticular by referring to the certified information sharing institution when the borrower is an individual. It also requires the lenders to decline extending such loans as are considered under the statute to constitute excessive lending – that is, making a loan when the total amount of the outstanding debt will exceed one third of the debtor's annual income. Finally, to become registered, moneylenders are now required to hold reserves of ¥50 million and are obligated to employ at each office one or more individuals that have passed the national examination for a "qualified moneylender." The last part came into force on June 18, 2010.

The headquarters to combat over-indebtedness

It was foreseen from the beginning that by the time the fourth part of the amendments entered into force, credit markets would shrink significantly and some borrowers would face difficulties in obtaining new loans or refinancing their pre-existing obligations. In order to resolve this anticipated problem, the government established in December 2006 the Headquarters to Combat Over-indebtedness. The Headquarters are led by the minister in charge of Financial Regulation and consists of all relevant ministers needed to promulgate a cross-sector policy package to address over-indebtedness.[37] The Headquarters convened an Experts Meeting (*Yûshikisha Kaigi*), similar to a traditional council (*shingikai*) in the Japanese political process.[38]

The Headquarters published its Policy Package in April 2007,[39] based largely on the report of the Experts Meeting.[40] The Policy Package is built on four pillars: (i) the provision of "carefully advising counseling," (ii) the extension of safety net lending "based on a human relationship," (iii) offering financial edu-

---

37 It is one of many "headquarters" that the Liberal Democratic Party (LDP) government established since the end of 1990s. Contrary to other types of Headquarters where the Prime Minister serves as the Director General and all the members of the cabinet become members, such as the Headquarters for Ocean Policy based on the Basic Act on Ocean Policy (law no.33 of 2007) and the Headquarter for Space Policy established by the Basic Act on Space (law no. 43 of 2008), the Headquarter to Combat Against Overindebtedness has no statutory basis and consists of only the relevant ministers, namely the Ministers for Consumer Affairs, Police, Internal Affairs and Communications, Justice, Finance, Education, Science and Technology, Health, Welfare and Labor, as well as Economy, Trade and Industry.

38 As regards the Council system of Japan, see Noble 2003, at 113.

39 'Tajû Saimu Kaizen Puroguramu' (The program to improve the overindebtedness), available on the website of the Headquarter <http://www.kantei.go.jp/jp/singi/saimu/kettei/070420/honbun.pdf>.

40 'Tajû Saimu Mondai no Kaiketsu no Muketa Housaku ni Tsuite' (On the measures toward resolving the overindebtedness problem), available on the website of the FSA < http://www.fsa.go.jp/singi/tajusaimu/01.pdf>.

cation as a means of preventing over-indebtedness, and (iv) a crackdown on illegal lenders.

Though not explicit in the Policy Package itself, theoretically the four pillars can be divided into two approaches. On one hand, there are some people in need of money who are incapable of repaying the needed amount, but cannot convince lenders of their credibility without committing to high interest rates. For this type of borrower, the Policy Package seeks a mechanism to replace high interest loans. "Safety net lending" may be intended to serve as such a mechanism, as indicated by the modifier "based on human relationship." The crackdown on illegal lending is related to this issue, because illegal lenders usually appear at first as the easy lender, tempting the borrower not to go through the rather complicated procedure of safety net lending. On the other hand, some borrowers cannot meet basic needs with their income and, therefore, are not appropriate borrowers to any reasonable lender. For these people, the Policy Package looks to improve household management. The Package seems to look to debt counseling in this respect, as it seeks to create not simple debt adjustment but "carefully advising" counseling. The aim of the financial education is also to educate future consumers to behave properly with regard to borrowing, saving, and spending.

Safety net lending coupled with counseling

In practice, safety net lending is offered together with counseling for over-indebtedness. This may be because the provider of safety net lending cannot identify appropriate borrowers without counseling applicants first. In other words, safety net lenders are themselves selective and can extend loans to only a fraction of applicants.

A well known scheme of safety net lending is the "help-the-consumer loan" offered for the past ten years by the local credit cooperative in Iwate Prefecture, the farming area of northeastern Japan. The local governments (33 cities, towns and villages) cooperate by contributing a certain amount of money deposited with local banks, which in turn creates a credit facility for the cooperative in an amount equal to four times the deposits made by the local governments. Thus, the risk is shared by the local governments and banks, besides the cooperative that serves as the lender. Before extending a loan, the credit cooperative counsels applicants. In 2005, more than 5,000 applicants were counseled, with loans extended to 842 of them. As a result of careful selection, the default rate in that year was 0.16 percent.[41]

---

41 Minutes of the 2nd meeting of the Experts Meeting to Combat Overindebtedness, at18 (dated February 7, 2007).

A similar scheme was started in 2006 by a cooperative in Fukuoka, a regional center in the western part of Japan. During the first two years, the cooperative received more than 3,000 telephone calls and counseled 1,500 borrowers in person.[42] Loans were extended to 160 people.[43] Although there has not yet been a default on these loans, the cooperative incurred a large loss because the counseling generates no profit and entails significant personnel expense. Finding the scheme useful, the local government has begun to aid the cooperative financially.[44]

More recently, Kurihara City, in another northwestern prefecture, commenced a scheme of safety net lending in 2008. The city government entered into an agreement with two local financial institutions (thrifts) and deposited ¥100 million with them. Over-indebted individuals contact the counseling section of the city government to meet the official counselor, followed by legal advice if necessary. Lawyers are cooperating according to the agreement between the local bar association and the city government. If new money is still found to be necessary after legal solutions are exhausted, including access to a bankruptcy proceeding with discharge, a loan may be extended by one of two participating thrifts. Ten loans were made in the first fifteen months of this program.[45]

These three schemes of safety net lending hold important policy implications. First, safety net lending is not itself a profitable business. Therefore, commercial institutions cannot engage in safety net lending without a commitment of assistance from a public body. Local governments seem to be suitable partners in this context, not the least because they have stakes in the welfare of the local residents. Second, the cases in which loans were extended under safety net schemes were small in number. Lenders tend to be selective in choosing those who are truly in need of finance and at the same time capable of making a plan for repayment. Third, in order to screen borrowers, counseling is necessary. However, lenders cannot afford to counsel without assistance from public entities because counseling does not itself generate profit.

The causes of over-indebtedness and the role of counseling

Over-indebtedness's causes can be seen from data collected through debt counseling in Iwate and Fukuoka. This data shows that 30 to 40 percent of the debtors in these programs started borrowing to support the household, including loans to pay for education and medical services. Less than 10 to 20 percent of

---

42 Minutes of the 9th meeting of the Experts Meeting to Combat Overindebtedness, p.10 (dated September 1, 2008).

43 Id. at 13.

44 Id. at 15.

45 Minutes of the 13th meeting of the Experts Meeting to Combat Overindebtedness, at 2-5 (dated May 19, 2009).

these debtors borrowed to pay for gambling debts and other entertainment expenses.[46] The counselor from Fukuoka also reported that the average household income of borrowers to whom the cooperative extended a safety net loan was ¥4.2 million,[47] 20 percent less than the national average of ¥5.47 million.[48] Thus, the cause of over-indebtedness appears to lie in the poverty of the households, rather than the expenditure pattern of the consumers.

The fact that over-indebtedness is the result of poverty does not mean that nothing can be done to improve the borrower's household finances. The same counselor of the cooperative in Fukuoka mentioned the case of a family that spent ¥30,000 on food each month and another ¥30,000 for the expenses of mobile phones. In order for safety net lending to be effective, counselors should provide borrowers with advice on personal financial management.

Advice of this nature creates a difficult issue that the policymakers have yet to face. If counseling is provided by a local government or another public body, questions arise as to whether public officials should intervene in individuals' private decision making. If the counselors of such a public body start advising borrowers on household management, the result will be quite a paternalistic intervention by the public authority into matters normally viewed as very private. Whether or not it is desirable for a government to "teach" its people not to spend as much money on mobile phones as on food is a difficult question to be answered.

Conclusion: Lessons from the Japanese experiment

Whether intentionally or not, the Japanese Supreme Court commenced a large-scale social experiment in January 2006 when it outlawed grey zone interest. The Court triggered legislative reforms that have impacted moneylenders significantly. These effects have already started to be felt. It also opened the door to a flood of recovery claims for excess payment by existing borrowers and caused an immense wealth transfer from lenders to borrowers. As a result, the market for consumer credit in Japan is in flux; where this transition will lead, no one knows.

---

46 Material no.2 submitted to the 2nd meeting of the Experts Meeting to Combat Over-indebtedness, at 7, (dated February 7, 2007); Material no.2-2 submitted to the 9th meeting of the Experts Meeting to Combat Overindebtedness, at 3, (dated September 1, 2008).

47 Material no.2-3 submitted to the 9th meeting of the Experts Meeting to Combat Over-indebtedness, at 6, (dated September 1, 2008).

48 The Statistical Bureau, Ministry of Internal Affairs and Communications, the Family Income and Expenditure Survey, statistics for total households, Table 1-1 (2012), < http://www.e-stat.go.jp/SG1/estat/ListE.do?lid=000001100812 >.

Such a social experiment might appear to be unique to Japan, where several statutes constituted a complex and somewhat ambiguous regulation of the interest rate cap. As opposed to this, many countries consider the problem of over-indebted borrowers as posing the agenda of bankruptcy law reform, under which the system of a discharge is the issue.[49] The two reforms, however, have much in common, since discharge of the debts of an insolvent borrower after bankruptcy means the partial abandonment of the loan by the lender and the release of the borrower from the obligation to repay. After all, both result in a kind of wealth transfer. In this respect, those considering seriously the problem of over-indebtedness may learn from Japan's recent experience with this regulation.

The first lesson is that, while wealth transfers of this sort can punish lenders and relieve borrowers from their obligations to repay existing debts, they do not prevent future borrowers from becoming over-indebted. Indirectly, future borrowers may benefit because, in this environment, moneylenders that cannot survive with only modest interest incomes will quit the market. However, once these "harsher" lenders are out of the market, there can be no assurance that borrowers' demands for credit availability will be met. Safety net schemes can replace some moneylenders, but only to a limited extent, as indicated by experiences in Japan.

The second lesson, related to the first, is that solutions to over-indebtedness should involve both regulation of financial markets and social policy. One overarching question inextricably related to the problem of over-indebtedness is, after all, how to address poverty and its effects on society. Counseling borrowers to improve their management of household expenses can be effective. But counseling also raises questions as to how paternalistic governments should be in this context. The issue is far more complicated than simply punishing greedy lenders.

In autumn 2009, just before the complete entry into force of the reform, the new coalition led by the Democratic Party of Japan (DPJ) came to power after an historical victory in the general election. They boldly claimed to be changing policy making processes and suspended all the existent Councils, alleging that bureaucrats dominated those Councils. Instead, the DPJ-coalition government established Project Teams that reflected the political will more strongly. According to this general policy, they suspended the Experts Meeting and established the Project Team on Moneylenders Regulation.

Interestingly, however, the Project Team did not radically change the reform designed by the previous government. After several meetings, it published "Ten

49 The bankruptcy law reform is not a major agenda with regard to consumer credit regulation in Japan, because the discharge for a bankrupt individual, which was introduced as early as in 1952, and the civil rehabilitation procedure for the individuals introduced in 2000 are available for an over-indebted consumer.

Measures to Meet the Demands of the Borrowers", which even compromised the strict application of the regulation over the excessive lending in order to remove some difficulties with implementing the regulation in practice. Further, the "Ten Measures" suggested supporting such seminal attempts of safety-net lending reported before the previous Experts Meeting. Thus, as far as over-indebtedness is concerned, the policy retained consistencies despite the alteration of the policy making body. The social experience that the judiciary commenced and the legislative branch took over has apparently survived the turnover of the governing coalition and is going to continue further.

References

Kin'yucho, (Financial Services Agency): Kashikingyo kankei tôkei shiryôshû (Statistics on moneylending industry). Tokyo: Financial Services Agency 2009.

Kozuka, Souichiro: 'Judicial Activism of the Japanese Supreme Court in Consumer Law: juridification of society through case law?' Zeitschrift für japanisches Recht, Nr.27, at 81.

Kozuka, Souichirou and Luke Nottage: 'Re-regulating Unsecured Consumer Credit in Japan: Over-indebted Borrowers, the Supreme Court and New Legislation'. in Parry, Deborah, Nordhausen, Annete, Howells, Geraint and Twigg-Flesner, Christian (eds): The Yearbook of Consumer Law 2009, Surrey: Ashgate publishing limited 2008, at 197.

Kozuka, Souichirou and Nottage, Luke: 'The Myth of the Cautious Consumer: Law, Culture, Economics and Politics in the Rise and Partial Fall of Unsecured Lending in Japan'. in Niemi, Johanna, Ramsay, Iain and Whitford, William C. (eds): Consumer credit, Debt & Bankruptcy. Oxford: Hart Publishing 2009, at 199.

Matsumoto, Emi: 'Adjusting an «imported» (or «received») law - an approach from the "precedent" in Japanese law'. in Hondius, Ewoud (ed), Precedent and the Law. Brussels: Bruylant 2007, at 323.

Nihon Kashikingyô Kyôkai (Japan Financial Services Association), JFSA Hakusho (Heisei 20 Nendo Ban) (The Annual of JFSA, 2008 edition), Tokyo: Japan Financial Services Association 2009.

Noble, Gregory: 'Reform and Continuity in Japan's Shingikai Deliberation Councils'. in Amyx, Jennifer & Drysdale, Peter and (eds): Japanese Governance: Beyond Japan Inc. Oxon: Routledgecurzon 2003, at 113.

Pardieck, Andrew M. (2008), 'Japan and the Moneylenders - Activist Courts and Substantive Justice', Pacific Rim Law & PolicyJjournal, 15(3), 5at 29.

Note:

1. The minutes of, and the materials submitted to, the Experts Meeting to Combat Over-indebtedness (*Tajû Saimusha Taisaku Yûshikisha Kaigi*) are available on the website of the Financial Services Agency (in Japanese) <http://www.fsa.go.jp/singi/tajusaimu/index.html>
2. Some of the cases cited in this chapter can be read in English translation on the website of the Supreme Court of Japan. <http://www.courts.go.jp/english/judgments/index.html>

Unemployment and Over-indebtedness in Germany

Michael Knobloch

Introduction

Over-indebtedness is a social phenomenon that affects millions of households each year. Its effects are wide ranging and often devastating, and can include inhibiting the ability of individuals to participate in society; social exclusion of families; and long term impacts for child development. Over-indebtedness also affects health and poverty levels. Taken together its effects result in a significant cost to the Germany economy of billions of Euros in lost output.

In Germany, unemployment is the most common trigger of over-indebtedness. To mitigate its impacts, government and providers both try to reduce unemployment levels and also provide assistance to unemployed people in order to help with debt problems.

This chapter investigates how successful these approaches have been. It is arranged in two parts. In the first part it examines the impact of unemployment on private households. The second part then examines to what extent there are indicators that can be used to measure the impact of unemployment on levels of over-indebtedness, especially with regard to the numbers of people seeking debt advice.[1]

---

1 The following representation results largely from the findings of the iff over-indebtedness reports (www.iff-ueberschuldungsreport.de). The annual iff over-indebtedness reports are produced by a team of sociologists and lawyers at the iff (institute for financial services) in Hamburg. First published in 2007, the 2009 edition is based on the examination of data from over 12,000 households collected from individuals having sought debt advice starting in 2004 until Q1 2009. The evaluation of the data, made anonymous, is based on collected information from nine debt advice centers located in five federal states. The data are process-generated, meaning that they have been assembled and produced from the debt advisory process, with debt advisors capturing data during the consultation with the client, and iff subsequently documenting, summarising, and presenting statistical analysis of the whole, through the use by debt advisors of its specialist debt advice software CAWIN. The analysis overwhelmingly covers private individuals that are not self-employed, however one in ten cases do involve a household where a former entrepreneur failed to be successful. In addition, and starting from 2009, a pilot project was designed to focus specifically on collecting data on the dynamics of the over-indebtedness process. The data, once again obtained through the use of the iff debt advice software, are able to shed light on the stages and phases of over-indebtedness, especially on the duration, timing and sequence of events over the process.

Effects of unemployment on the economy of private households

Analysis of the interaction between unemployment and over-indebtedness is not possible without first describing and defining the phenomenon of over-indebtedness. Attempts at reaching a generally valid and accepted interdisciplinary definition of over-indebtedness have so far remained elusive in both Germany and at the EU level.[2] This is not surprising, when one realizes that over-indebtedness is a social phenomenon, the effects of which are felt in many different areas of economic and social life. In this respect there is not one, but several appropriate definitions. These definitions reflect the point of view of the researcher or stakeholder and the respective disciplines of these observers. As a result, one finds judicial definitions; definitions from the suppliers' perspective (demand failures); medical (shopping addiction) or even psychological definitions. In addition, there also exist subjective descriptions and appraisals of the phenomenon (the feeling of not being able to manage one's debts or no longer coping with payment of one's bills on time).

In Germany, there are two main definitions in use. The judicial definition is fixed in §§ 17-19 of the Insolvency Statute (Insolvenzordnung, InsO): A person can make a demand to the procedure (an individual debtor is insolvent) if he is either unable to meet his due payment obligations having reached maturity (§17 InsO) or if the assets owned by the debtor no longer cover his existing obligations to pay (§19 InsO). A broader socio-economic definition also exists. In this case, over-indebtedness is defined as a situation in which a person's remaining income available to him/her after deduction of the normal costs of living is insufficient to cover the existing bills of debt over the foreseeable future. This definition has been used by the German government in its third report on wealth and poverty.[3] Furthermore (and linking to the above mentioned definitions), over-indebtedness can be understood as a dynamic process that follows its own logic. Thus over-indebtedness is not conceivable without indebtedness. Over-indebtedness triggers relative over-indebtedness, absolute over-indebtedness, consumer insolvency proceedings and finally debt-relief. Hence, a description and analysis of the over-indebtedness phenomenon should not content itself with one chosen definition, but should instead consider the varied aspects mentioned above.

As described, over-indebtedness can typically be understood as a process involving several phases.[4] A result from the latest *iff* study[5] showed that the duration of the entire over-indebtedness process, from the first recognised sign of

2 Davydoff et al 2008.
3 Bundesministerium für Arbeit und Soziales 2008, at 49.
4 Phases in support of Reis 1992, at 11 ff.
5 Knobloch and Reifner 2009, at 22.

over-indebtedness through to the granting of release from all outstanding debts and deleted entry from all credit registers, lasts an average of 13 years. Access to the labor market by the individuals concerned (or its antagonist, failed access: unemployment) plays a role of varying significance in each of the identified phases.

Employment and work are preconditions for loans and investment

Every over-indebtedness process begins with indebtedness, i.e., the taking on of credit, but indebtedness does not automatically cause or systematically lead to over-indebtedness. Indebtedness and over-indebtedness should therefore not be confused. Indebtedness, or credit use, is normal in today's modern society. It forms a key part of the market economy and using credit is an integral part of the economic processes taking place within private households. This is because the interaction and balance between the exchange of effort and reward between the contracting parties is seldom constant over time. Indebtedness may therefore be the result of ongoing obligations and financial commitments that are normal in our society. Even without formally or informally borrowing money, consumption patterns today mean that there is not always a perfect temporal match between the point in time at which actual use is made of a good or service (realizing its utility) and the point in time at which payment for this consumption is made (pre-payment or deferred payment). As such, a tenant's monthly rent is a debt when he has to pay his rent at the end of the month. There are numerous similar examples, especially in the area of consumption of utility services such as in electricity supply contracts or telecommunication contracts, where the supplier trusts the consumer and relies that the transaction will lead to him receiving his reward after performance, which in effect means he gives credit to the consumer.

While acknowledging that many of these creditor-debtor relationships arise from such "involuntary" credits, and appreciating that these are often unavoidable for the satisfaction of basic needs, credit relationships are also often entered into deliberately and intentionally.

This is particularly the case during the earlier phases of a person's life-cycle, where loans are increasingly becoming necessary for the majority of households. More than 50 percent of German households between the ages of 25 and 55 years make use of a bank loan (excluding credit facilities such as the extension of an overdraft on a current account). Credit from a financial provider allows for the realization of investment opportunities looking into the future, which would otherwise not be possible without it. The examples are many and varied. For example, a loan can be used for education, occupation, household needs including to support the raising of families, and to gain access to accommodation. Loans allow significant costs in these respects to be met in the present despite the fact that a person's current income is too low to meet all of these commitments during the early stages of adulthood. Consumer loans of such a form can therefore help people to invest in activities that result in increased or more stable incomes later in life. When used in these ways credit can therefore provide people with the essential opportunity to dispose of his expected future income today, thus allowing enabling that person to use it for investments in ones own advancement. This indebtedness is therefore not only something normal, but often something desirable.[6]

Figure 1: Credit use in the German population by age.

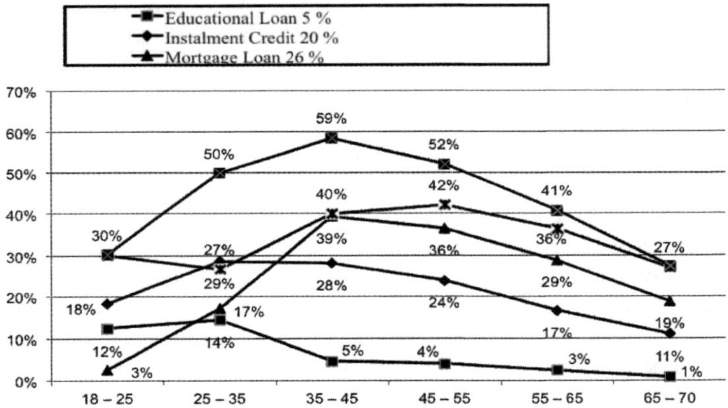

Source: German Federal Statistical Office – Sample survey of income and expenditure 2008

As a consequence, the decision to extend a loan should always be based on the forecasted future income (after investment) instead of only taking the present situation into account. Unfortunately, this principle is not yet realised in many areas. Over the "investing" phases of the life-cycle, a situation of employment and a steady income pattern make it attractive for banks to extend loans to prospective borrowers showing such characteristics, while on the contrary, a status of unemployment will often prevent that prospective borrower from successfully being granted a loan and therefore from realizing the planned investment. Many banks are not prepared to extend loans to unemployed persons or even to people who have obtained work but who are in a probationary period of the employment contract. A similar problem often arises for self employed people, for example those who have been self employed for less than three

6 Reifner 2004, at 1.

years. Exceptions to these lending rules are rare, even in cases where the purpose of the loan is to make an investment in activities that will make finding work easier such as training and education, measures to improve labor mobility, or for technical equipment. With perhaps the exception of student loans for education purposes, which has seen a rising trend, there are frequently no exceptions to this principle of "loan restraint" with regard to the loan applicant's employment situation.

After one year of unemployment, state benefits are often insufficient to balance expenditures

Out of the normal situation of indebtedness detailed above, a crisis can arise. In the majority of cases, this crisis begins with an unexpected event heavily affecting the financial liquidity of the household's finances. Such events may reduce income, cause additional financial burdens, or lead to both these effects arising.

Based on empirical evidence, the most significant variable causing a triggering of over-indebtedness is reported by debt advisors as being unemployment or a forced reduction in one's working hours. More then 40 percent of their clients state that unemployment was *a* trigger for over indebtedness and 30 percent state that unemployment was the *main* trigger. Other triggers of over-indebtedness include divorce or separation from a partner (13 percent), a failed business attempt at self-employment (12 percent) and consumption behavior (11 percent). Avoidable behavior plays only a minor role in explaining entry into over-indebtedness when compared to factors that are described as inevitable events outside the direct control of the borrower. Together, unemployment, forced short time work and failed self-employment, all shocks affecting the income side of a household's finances, constitute the triggers of over-indebtedness in 42 percent of all reported cases.

Figure 2: Main triggers of over indebtedness as seen by debt advisors, 2005-2009

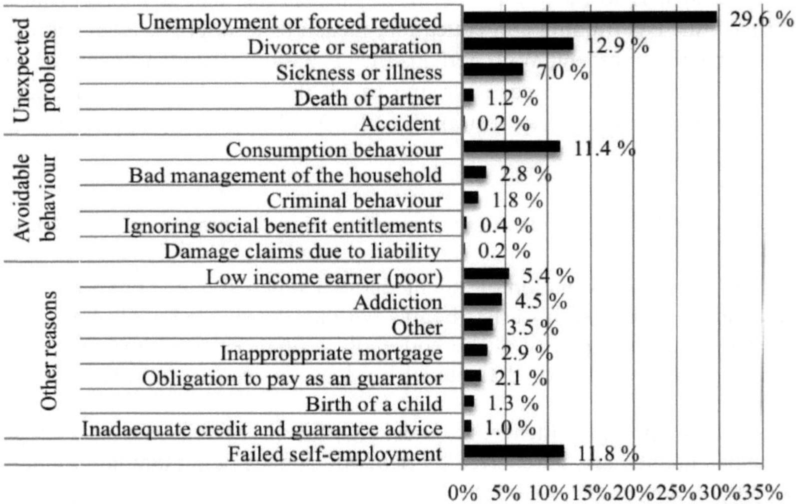

Source: Knobloch and Reifner (2008), at 23.

Because repayment of debt in installments according to contractual obligations depends on the cash flow situation of the household budget, the key indicator to monitor is household liquidity. The level of household liquidity in the event of unemployment – the main trigger for over-indebtedness – is determined on the income side by the discontinuation of the previously earned income and by the state transfer entitlements that are available to that person. When jobs are lost, the transfers that exist are the so-called "*unemployment benefit I*" (ALG I) regulated in the German social code III (SGB III), the "*unemployment benefit II*" (ALG II) regulated in the German social code II (SGB II) and the "*short time working allowance*" (Kurzarbeitergeld, Kug) regulated in the social code III. In terms of the amount of money received, whereas *unemployment benefit I* and the *short time working allowance* are calculated based on the level of the person's previously earned income ("wage principle") and the payments are limited in time, *unemployment benefit II* corresponds to the social aid level. As such and in contrast to *unemployment benefit I,* it is a transfer payment financed through taxation and not through the unemployment insurance scheme. The level at which it is set is directed by the household's basic needs and it can theoretically be granted indefinitely over time.

Since the beginning of the financial crisis in 2008, German firms have been allowed to respond to a temporary reduction in demand by reducing the number of contractual days their employees work each week or the number of hours in the working day. This *Kurzarbeit* called short time working hours (and not to be confused with either "short-term contract work" or "temporary work") is not seasonal and can last for periods of up to 18 to 24 months during which the employee works less or even in extreme cases not at all.[7] The loss of earnings originating from short time working hours is partly compensated for by the *short time working allowance*, legally based on §§ 169 – 182 social code III (SGB III). The funding for short-time work serves the purpose of bridging a phase of joblessness, preventing job redundancies and avoiding the costs of having to re-hire staff once jobs are available again. Short-time workers receive 60 percent of their net wage differential (normal working hours minus actual working hours) from the Federal Employment Agency (BA), or 67 percent if there is a child living in the household.

In cases where workers have been made redundant, the legal basis for the calculation of *unemployment benefit I* is found in the provisions in §§ 127 and 129 social code III. Two specific factors are decisive in the calculation: the prior duration of the employer-employee relationship subject to insurance before the entry into unemployment, and the age of the individual at the date of unemployment. The payment of the *unemployment benefit I* starts at the earliest of 6 months after entry and lasts up to a maximum of monthly payment until the 18th month (for a person of 55 years of age or more with at least having accumulated 36 months of compulsory insurance contributions). In general, the amount of the unemployment benefit entitlement is equal to 60 percent of the former net income (i.e., after subtracting insurance and other social security contributions from gross income) that was earned by that person in the fiscal year before he became unemployed. The amount of *unemployment benefit I* that can be claimed is capped. The highest monthly gross income to be taken into account when calculating the 60 percent is set at a threshold of €5,250. Therefore, a person who has been earning €7,000 of monthly gross income does not receive a greater benefit payment than a person who was earning only €5,250 last year. The pay-

7 At the beginning of 2009, the ruling grand coalition government of CDU/CSU and SPD initially extended the funding for short-time work from 6 to 18 months, and upped the period in spring 2009 to 24 months. In addition, social-security contributions are fully reimbursed by the BA if employees undergo training to upgrade their skills during this time. Also, the review and application procedure for companies was noticeably simplified. At the start of 2010, the government decided to set the funding period for companies applying to join the scheme in the current year at 18 months. Without this amendment, funds for short-time work would only have been available for six months again as of January 1, 2010. This means that companies can benefit from the Kurzarbeit scheme until mid-2012. As things stand now, the BA will from 2011 discontinue the practice of shouldering the related social-security contributions. However, there are hints that the government will once again extend parts of the regulation.

ment of the *unemployment benefit I* is always calculated for completed time periods and always executed at the end of the month.[8]

Persons with children receive a larger amount from the unemployment benefit insurance on the basis of two factors. On one hand, there are tax allowances for children that lead to tax deductions and thus to a higher net income. On the other hand, the proportion of previous income paid out is raised to a sum of 67 percent for unemployed persons with one or more dependent children.

The extent of the resulting decrease in the overall family net income situation will depend on the exact given household characteristics and type. If unemployment hits an individual in a household where several persons contribute to the family income, one would expect the reduction of the family net income to be relatively lower when compared to a household with only one breadwinner. In addition, a potentially acute liquidity gap arises in cases where the last salary from employment was paid and received at the beginning of the last month of employment and where *unemployment benefit I* is paid at the end of the first month of unemployment.

This time period taken to bridge the shortfall in income represents a significant liquidity risk for the debtor who has been made unemployed. This situation can also be exacerbated further because people do not always experience a smooth bureaucratic process when claiming entitlements and there are often delays in obtaining benefit payments. These delays are mainly due to a failure of the unemployed person in claiming their entitlements rather than a failure of state agencies. Nevertheless, a working assumption should be made that there will be on average one month of payment waiting time which should be taken into account for any impact assessment of unemployment on the household's finances.

In contrast to the *unemployment benefit I*, the *unemployment benefit II/social welfare* is an entitlement which is not means tested and is calculated independent of the prior income of the person applying. It is based on standard budgets for the protection of living standards. The budget is calculated using the costs faced by typical households by taking account of minimum acceptable expenditure patterns with regard to consumption of food, clothes, personal care, household belongings, energy-saving appliances and heating etc. Due consideration is taken of the basic material needs of everyday life, as well as those of a more social nature relating to relationships with one's social environment and participa-

---

8 Example 1: A gross income of €5,250 proves in tax class I with legal health insurance with a contribution sentence of 12 percent a net income of €2,857.48. As an unemployment benefit, 60 percent would be paid €1,714.49. The difference amounts to €1,142.99. Example 2: A gross income of €3,000 proves a net income of €1,815.45 with the same conditions. Sixty percent of it proves a sum of €1,089.27. The difference amounts to €726.18.

tion in cultural life. Regulated in § 20 SGB II, the monthly standard rate amounts to €345 for singles. Other family members fit for work are entitled to 80 percent of this rate (€276), and adjustments are made for households with children with an extra 60 percent of the basic rate paid with dependent children up to the age of 14, and 80 percent for older children. Additional social transfers are also available for housing and heating, provided that these costs remain moderate (§22 SGB II). Although provisions exist to make additional payments accessible if required in the case of increased demand (§21 SGB II),[9] the standard budgets themselves shall not be subject to an increase in cases were the benefit recipient applying for additional funds faces ongoing recurring instalment obligations.

Where people are making a transition from *unemployment benefit I* to *unemployment benefit II* a limited acceptance (§24 SGB II) is paid. It amounts to two thirds of the difference between the two transfer entitlements, taking any housing subsidy into account. The amount of this benefit payment, while valid in its entirety for the first year, is then halved during the months of the second year, before being cancelled completely in the third year.

Unemployed households face limited compensation possibilities

In response to the situation, several compensation strategies are possible. Household members may try to stabilise the financial situation by either liquidating assets, increasing the total size of current income, or reducing their expenditures. A possible option open to people who have experienced a sudden fall in income due to job loss at this stage is to borrow.

One measure with only a one-off effect on household liquidity is the decision to sell property. Measures with a more lasting effect are those that enable either a reduction in expenditures or a solution that allows re-generating a working income while controlling the level of spending. In the cases where either unemployment or short time working hours has triggered over-indebtedness, not all of the above mentioned coping mechanisms are available to that person. It is especially the more structural measures with the more lasting effects – re-generating a working income or reducing spending – that are very limited. Generating a new income often proves to be difficult because the reason that caused the unemployment will usually last for a period of time and, if part of a wider economic downturn, will continue to hinder the affected person's search for a new job. While unemployment is often caused by deterioration in the regional or

9 They shall be paid in cases of pregnancy (additional 17 percent of the standard rate after the 12th pregnancy week), care of children (additional 36 percent of the standard rate with a child less than 7 years or two or three children less than sixteen years), disability for work (additional 35 percent of the standard rate).

national macro-economic situation, this will also sometimes be the case because people have low levels of education or skills.

Both situations take time to overcome. Just as it is very unlikely to find a new job in the middle of a recession, it also takes time for an individual to improve her level of professional education, to retrain, and to improve her chances in the job market. The situation for these households is made more difficult when they try to reduce their expenditures. The amount of discretionary expenditure available to them to cut down is often small. Households being affected by unemployment often have less non-earmarked disposable income because they will often be using instalment credits or other bank loans that continue to require servicing.

As described above, investment often depends on employment and therefore the time for investing is the time of employment. The majority of the German over-indebted households falling prey to unemployment make use of bank loans.[10] Since these households are faced with the obligation to pay back their loans, they have already reduced their standard of living somewhat in order to be able to service the instalments falling due. Therefore, households affected by unemployment often have less renounceable income compared to those households where other factors have been the trigger of over-indebtedness.

Results from the iff pilot study[11] show that, in reality, only a very small proportion of households are successful in adopting measures to increase revenues, whereas running down pre-existing savings is resorted to more frequently. Findings also show that households are very restricted in their ability to borrow from professional providers and that they therefore struggle to smooth liquidity. The principal explanation is that the unemployed person loses his creditworthiness from the perspective of the provider. If the borrowing option is not completely closed, some unemployed debtors may have existing loans consolidated or converted, but otherwise individuals also resort to obtaining informal loans from family and friends. Other informal transfers may be used at this stage of the over-indebtedness process.

In the event of unemployment, the following mechanisms are therefore likely: Immediately after receiving notice of redundancy the affected household will try to reduce the ongoing recurrent outflows and postpone planned investments. Through these actions, a liquidity cushion can generally be formed for the duration of about two months. After a further waiting period that might last for 2 months, income is subsequently reduced to the level of *unemployment benefit I* (ALG I). At this stage, the reduced income is still sufficient to cover the reduced spending achieved by the household. If the person affected is not able to find a new job within the following 12 months, income will typically be reduced a sec-

---

10 Reifner and Knobloch 2007, at 39.

11 Knobloch and Reifner 2009, at 19.

ond time to the level of *unemployment benefit II* (ALG II). Again, the household will be compelled to try to reduce its spending yet further out of even greater necessity, but in some cases this reduction might not be sufficient. In such cases, spending will exceed the net income of the household. This leads to stage 4 of the over-indebtedness process.

Figure 3: Income and spending after notice.

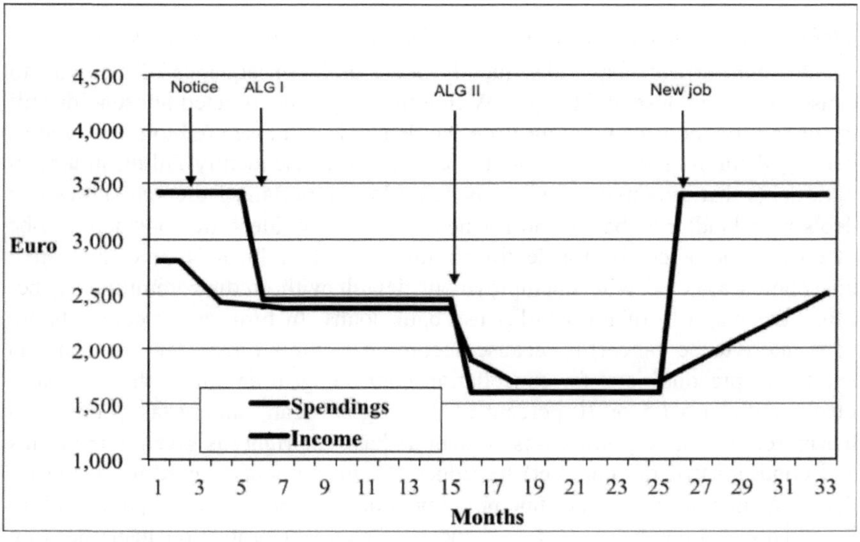

Source: Knobloch and Reifner (2008), at 43.

Balancing strategies of over-indebted households are often insufficient to erase due debts in time

Despite the coping mechanisms described above (life-style moderation, development of new opportunities to earn money, and use of liquid assets), the situation may arise where the remaining income simply becomes insufficient to allow the appropriate repayment of debts. At this stage, description of the situation using the definition of "relative over-indebtedness" is warranted. Relative over-indebtedness is used to describe situations where individuals are no longer in a position to pay back their debts within a foreseeable future, either by making payments from using existing assets or income, without compromising their own living standards beyond basic needs. Sometimes "property" or the "reduction of the life style" are excluded from this definition. Besides this "classical" definition, other breakdowns are also carried out. There are, for example, other definitions, where a high likelihood of repayment difficulty is seen as a sufficient condition for describing the observation that debts can't be paid back in time. These definitions, which do not take the actual impossibility of the repayment into account, are not followed up here. They nevertheless define a special form of poverty, which might lead into over-indebtedness.[12] By this they might provide indicators for a quantitative approach towards over-indebtedness as described below.

Default, loan notice and means of coercion (absolute over-indebtedness)

Payment arrears may subsequently occur as a consequence of a failure to consolidate the household budget. Within this stage, the affected households still try to service their debts by meeting the demands of those creditors they see as helping them satisfy their essential needs, while consequently falling in arrears with debts that they may consider as being less important. Research shows that debts with landlords, banks and financial service providers are considered to be of most importance from a debtor's point view. Finally, it is very likely that households affected with unemployment default with credit commitments, because the majority of households use bank loans. In turn, credit contracts are very likely to be canceled, because according to the German law there are no additional preconditions for cancellation then being in default with two instalments and at least 5 or 10 percent of the original loan amount taken out. Furthermore, only in very few cases do debtors have the right (as given in the terms and conditions of the contract) to reduce the installments according to the reduced income in the event of unemployment or in order to take a repayment holiday. Though debtors very often dispose of payment protection insurances on their loans, these financial services are unlikely to help in case of unemployment because unemployment is often not covered (efficiently) by insurance. Though there has been a rise in credit defaults from 2.3 percent in 2007 to 2.5 percent in 2008, insurance claims have decreased from 0.20 percent of the insured size to 0.18 percent.

12 Zimmermann 2007, at 19.

Table 1: Payment Protection Insurances in Germany 2001 – 2008 (size, claims, claims ratio).

year	Insurance claims (Euro)	Insurance size (Euro)	Insurance claims ratio according to insured size (Euro)
2001	49,000,000 €	24,761,000,000 €	0.20 %
2002	52,000,000 €	26,048,000,000 €	0.20 %
2003	53,000,000 €	27,658,000,000 €	0.19 %
2004	54,000,000 €	27,006,000,000 €	0.20 %
2005	56,000,000 €	24,320,000,000 €	0.23 %
2006	47,000,000 €	22,187,000,000 €	0.21 %
2007	43,000,000 €	21,900,000,000 €	0.20 %
2008	38,000,000 €	21,420,000,000 €	0.18 %

Source: German Insurance Association (GDV) – German Life Insurances by numbers.

Because the result of cancellation is the total amount of the credit falling due, payment default will often be accompanied by creditors turning to collateral pledged as surety for the loan, claims of securities, court enforcement actions, or sworn statements, and a loss of creditworthiness resulting from entry into credit registers of the SCHUFA or other credit bureaus. This situation, where so-called hard signs of over-indebtedness (payment arrears, loan cancellations, bank account closure, and examples of coercion such as collecting a sworn statement) are visible, is defined as "absolute over-indebtedness."

Menace of existence and suffering pressure lead to debtor's consultation

Over-indebtedness leads to an economically and psycho-social destabilization of debtors and their families. Resulting from execution attempts and other means of coercion, not only is the household economy affected, but also the health and human participation in social life are depressed. This is true for all household members, but it is especially children who are at the most risk of long-term harm. Only at this point do people generally seek help from debt advice centers.

It is estimated that it takes nearly four years from the first signs of over-indebtedness to the moment the average over-indebted person visits the debt advice center. This observed delay between the start of problems and the take up of external counseling services is caused not only by the fact that debtors make several attempts to deal with the problems themselves and do not arrive at a critical point until quite late in this process, but is also caused by the fact that debt advice centers often do not have sufficient or efficient capacities to serve people at an earlier point. Another reason for delayed entry into the advisory process in some federal states might be the financial incentives and revenue structures in place, whereby debt advice centers only receive reimbursements according to the number of insolvency registrations they perform.

Consumer insolvency

Following a three-month waiting period, the counseling service lasts on average nine months. In eight of ten cases reported at the debt advice centers, the households in question end up undergoing bankruptcy procedures. Studies show that more than 42 percent of individuals passing through the insolvency proceedings state that unemployment was a trigger of insolvency. This corresponds almost exactly with the proportion obtained from responses from the over-indebted persons applying for debt advice. The consumer insolvency proceedings introduced in Germany in 1999 allow for a complete waiver, through State cancellation of these debts within six years. Although the debt cancellation process takes approximately six years, about an additional two years need to be taken into account until the negative traces of the bankruptcy procedure disappear from the recorded entry in the register of the credit referencing agencies (particularly the SCHUFA). In total, the period from start to finish thus lasts approximately 13 years.

Indicators to demonstrate whether unemployment and over-indebtedness are linked

Resulting from the interdependency between unemployment and over-indebtedness as described above, it is very likely that the regional distribution of unemployment highly corresponds with the regional distribution of over-indebtedness. Regarding variations in time, it can also be expected, that the level of over-indebtedness follows the level of unemployment with delay. Provided this is true, quantitative data could be very useful for government and providers to measure the effectiveness of preventive and reactive measures.

There are a few indicators that may reflect the regional and inter temporal interdependency between unemployment and over indebtedness: The judicial definition corresponds with the number of insolvencies procedures being opened. Also the phases of over-indebtedness have their quantitative correspondences, e.g., "indebtedness" corresponds with the number and the volume of households with consumers loans, "relative over-indebtedness" corresponds with the number of households in default, "absolute over-indebtedness" corresponds with the number of households with "hard" signs of over-indebtedness or with the number of households seeking debt advice and the "disencumberment phase" corresponds with the number of households having already entered the insolvency procedure.

Indicators taken from credit bureaus

Published studies covering both unemployment and over-indebtedness and their interdependencies are as far as can be seen not available for Germany yet. Available investigations only cover either over-indebtedness or unemployment, but do not link the two phenomena. Regarding unemployment, regional data and maps are available from the Federal Employment Office or the Federal Statistical Office (based on the number of people who reported to be unemployed). The figures are updated regularly but do not show over-indebtedness indicators. Regarding over-indebtedness, regional investigations are available from the provider sight, namely the credit bureaus SCHUFA and Creditreform.

Since the German government has not supported quantitative research on over-indebtedness for some years now, there have been few independent investigations on this subject since 2002. This leaves us reliant upon the data available from suppliers, for example the number of enforcement attempts as registered at the credit bureaus like SCHUFA or Creditreform. As a result, there is a danger that the perception of over-indebtedness is narrowed to the supplier- relevant aspects.

In addition, the observance of scientific standards is not guaranteed because providers do not normally disclose the calculation methods used. Looking at the data it should be taken into account that "hard negative signs" are stored at the credit bureaux for only for a proportion of over-indebted households.[13] Therefore, it is uncertain whether the data are valid to represent over-indebtedness.

Furthermore, as discovered by recent investigations, the data stored at credit bureaus are partly faulty.[14] In spite of these deficits, quantitative data of credit bureaus might have explanatory power for relative temporal changes and regional differences.

In recent years, the largest German credit register, SCHUFA, has published its "private debt index" (PDI) calculated on the basis of SCHUFA´s total data portfolio. The private debt index provides figures of the individual debt risk in the Federal states and the 429 counties in Germany. The PDI figures are divided into four degree levels (slight, moderate, strong and very strong risk to become over-indebted). The risk levels are represented by colors with green representing a slight debt risk to red representing a very strong risk. According to the SCHUFA, the following debt indicators are taken into account: payment defaults at non-banks and banks ("soft" negative indicators), and "hard" negative indicators, such as information on the delivery of an oath of disclosure or personal insolvency proceedings. The maps therefore represent the regional distribution of the number of soft and hard debt indicators.

---

13 Reifner and Knobloch 2007, at 59, with reference to SCHUFA data.

14 Korczak and Wilken 2009, at 25.

Also, Creditreform publishes annual comparable maps based on their "defaulter rates" that show different levels of reported defaults plotted by federal states and counties. Creditreform also publishes the numbers of over-indebted individuals and households annually. The number is based on a set of different indicators. As for SCHUFA's indicator model, Creditreform uses data from their own register,[15] which have the same limits as SCHUFA's data.

Different approaches are necessary to prove the inter-temporal interdependency between unemployment and over-indebtedness. It is to be assumed that the trend of the number of over-indebted households follows the trend of the number of unemployed persons if the remaining influencing preconditions stay the same. It can be concluded from the analyses of Creditreform that there is a one and a half years displacement (mismatch/parallel offset) between the unemployment rate and the over-indebtedness rate: The unemployment rate in Germany decreased between beginning of 2006 to autumn 2008 from 12 percent to eight percent. This trend changed in September 2008. Since then, the unemployment rate has been increasing. The numbers of people on short time working arrangements has increased enormously (about approximately 1.1 millions between March 2008 and March 2009). The decline of the unemployment rate was followed by a decline of the debtor's rate. As stated by Creditreform the debtor's rate sank between 2007 and 2009 from 10.8 percent to 9.1 percent, after it had risen before.[16]

Similar conclusions can be made with regard to the number of consumer insolvency procedures in Germany. For the first time the number of consumer insolvency procedures decreased between 2007 and 2008 from 103,000 openings to 96,000 openings. Also an investigation of the Creditreform in 2006 showed a high regional correlation between the rate of unemployment and the debtor's rate.[17]

Indicators taken from debt advice agencies

To prove the inter-temporal interdependence, not only inter-temporal correlations between the number of unemployed individuals and the number of over indebted households can be considered. It is also possible to examine the people applying for debt advice and to indicate trends of unemployment indicators within that group. This has been done for the *iff* over-indebtedness report in 2009 for the first time. The period between the start of 2006 and the second

15 Creditreform uses a set of different indicators such as default rates, delivery of an oath of disclosure or applications of personal insolvency proceedings; See Creditreform (2009), at 1.

16 Creditreform (2009), at 4.

17 Creditreform (2006), at 19.

quarter in 2009 was investigated. The data from debt advice agencies analyzed for the over-indebtedness report contain five unemployment indicators:

- The person searching for advice is announced jobless.
- The debtor's adviser states that unemployment is *one among other* triggers of over-indebtedness.
- The debtor's adviser states that unemployment is the *main* trigger of over in-debtedness.
- The person seeking for debt advice obtains unemployment benefit I (ALG I).
- The person seeking for debt advice obtains unemployment benefit II (ALG II)

One or more of these indicators is found among households in debtors' consultation facing the problem of unemployment or diminished work. Regarding unemployment it is most likely that the composition of people being advised inside of the agencies is in accordance with the composition of people waiting for advice and with the composition of people being over-indebted. That is why it can be assumed that the portion of unemployed people in debt advice centres is following the trend of unemployment in the society. Furthermore, it can be assumed that the unemployment indicators react at different rates to changes in the job market.

For all five indicators, a delayed change of trend can be assumed in comparison to the rate of unemployment because of the balance strategies used by affected households as described above. The rate of unemployment benefit II (indicator 5) can be considered a rather "sluggish" indicator, because it is granted not earlier than one year after notice. On the contrary, indicators 2 and 3 (the statement that unemployment or diminished work is a trigger or main trigger) are supposed to be more reactive, because they cover households who seek advice very early, already when threatened by insolvency.

Regarding the course of all five unemployment indicators, there was a prominent reduction between 2006 through to the second quarter of 2009. A turn in the trend is only observed for the reactive indicators 2 and 3 (unemployment is a trigger or main trigger) in the first quarter 2009, however. The proportion of people for whom unemployment or diminished work is given as a trigger of over-indebtedness (indicator 2) has risen about relatively 5.9 percent in the first quarter in 2009 for the first time since 2006. In the same period of time the increase of indicator 3 (unemployment or diminished work is given as the main trigger of over-indebtedness) amounts to 1.9 percent. Although a reversal of trend is only visible for the most reactive over-indebtedness indicators, the immediate increase in the first quarter 2009 is surprising. There might be evidence that these two indicators respond with a mismatch of only half a year to changes in the labor market. A reason for this could be not only rising unemployment but also the huge increase in forced short time work in Germany. On the other hand, the portion of the ALG II subscribers (indicator 5) has still decreased among the over-indebted households as expected; also in the first quarter in 2009 in comparison to the last year's quarter (relatively about 6.9 percent). Here a turn in the trend is to be expected for 2010. Also with the remaining indicators (1 and 4) a turn in the trend and with it an increase stands out for those who were advice-searching; however, this is not noticeable in the first quarter of 2009.

In addition to the unemployment indicators for the population seeking debt advice, it is also possible to use the number of people applying for advice as an indicator to demonstrate the regional interdependency between unemployment and over-indebtedness. The 2007 edition of the *iff* over-indebtedness report examined data concerning the city of Wilhelmshaven closely, covering both unemployment and over-indebtedness. Calculations were carried out for a small sample (n = 420) of persons seeking debt advice in 2005 and 2006. The number had been related to the total population and this quota had been used as an indicator for over-indebtedness. This proportion had been calculated for five post codes where the respective persons there had permanent resistance. To represent unemployment, the number of people that reported as unemployed by the Statistical Bureau of the city of Wilhelmshaven had been calculated as a proportion of the whole population for the same post codes.[18] Resulting from the investigation, there is evidence of a very high correlation between the proportion of persons seeking debt advice and the rate of unemployment as calculated above.

Figure 4 shows the correlation between the rate of persons seeking debt advice and the rate of unemployed persons. It is obvious that a high unemployment rate is accompanied by a high rate of people applying for debt advice and vice versa (Pearson product-moment correlation coefficient: 0.94). A similar tendency has been discovered for two post codes in Hamburg.[19]

18 Origin of the unemployment figures: City of Wilhelmshaven, office for statistics and elections, 12/2005. The unemployment rate used above is based on the number of jobless people and the announced population and therefore does not comply with the rate used by the federal agency for work.

19 It was not possible to investigate in more regions because the unemployment rate was only available for very few post codes. Also, on this occasion, the unemployment rate was calculated as a proportion of the unemployed people in the whole population living in the post code district.

Figure 4: Regional correlation between unemployment and dept advice in Wilhelmshaven 2005 by post code.

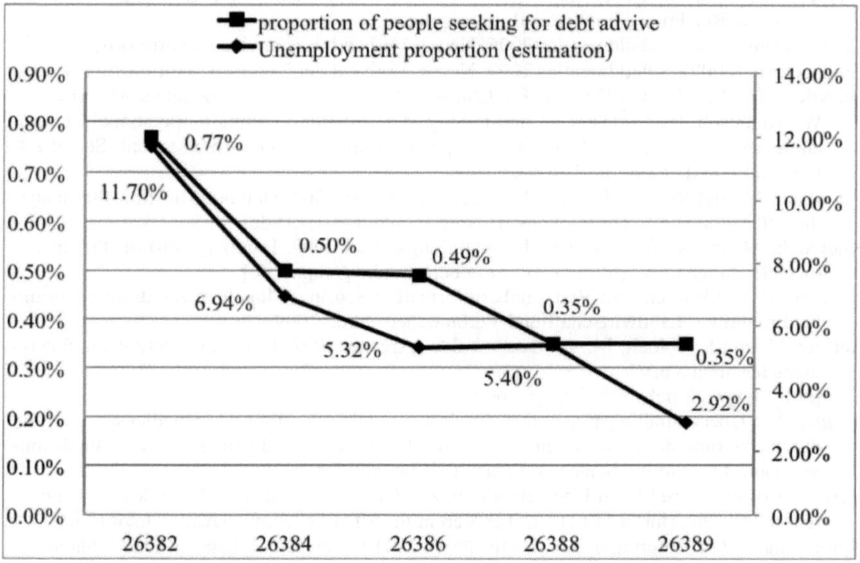

Source: Reifner/Knobloch (2007), at 31.

Conclusion

There is a strong correlation between unemployment and over-indebtedness in Germany. Preventive or reactive measures to protect unemployed people from becoming over-indebted are not sufficient to fully compensate the destabilisation of the single private households after notice. The interdependency between the two phenomena can be proved not only by using data from credit bureaus and the Federal Employment Office, but also by using data directly collected from debt advice agencies. There is evidence that the impact of Germany's rising unemployment rate since 2008 is already being reflected in some of the unemployment indicators of over-indebted people seeking for debt advice from the first quarter 2009, pointing to another increase in the number of over-indebted by the beginning 2010.

References

Bundesministerium für Arbeit und Soziales (2008), Lebenslagen in Deutschland. Der 3. Armuts- und Reichtumsbericht der Bundesregierung.

Creditreform (2006), Schuldneratlas 2006. Neuss: Verband der Vereine Creditreform e.V.

Creditreform (2009), Schuldneratlas 2009. Neuss: Verband der Vereine Creditreform e.V.

Davydoff, D., Naacke, G., Dessart, E., Jentzsch, N., Figueira, F., Rothemund, M., Mueller, W., Kempson, E., Atkinson, A. and Finney, A.: Towards a common operational European definition of over-indebtedness. European Commission: DG Employment, Social Affairs and Equal Opportunities. 2008.

Knobloch, M. and Reifner, U.: iff-Überschuldungsreport 2008. Hamburg: institut für finanzdienstleistungen e.V. [http://www.iff-ueberschuldungsreport.de]

Knobloch, M. and Reifner, U.: iff-Überschuldungsreport 2009. Hamburg: institut für finanzdienstleistungen e.V. [http://www.iff-ueberschuldungsreport.de]

Korczak, D. and Wilken, M.: Verbraucherinformation Scoring. München: Bundesministerium für Ernährung, Landwirtschaft und Verbraucherschutz. 2009.

Reifner, U. and Knobloch, M.: iff-Überschuldungsreport 2007. Hamburg: institut für finanzdienstleistungen e.V.
[http://www.iff-ueberschuldungsreport.de]

Reifner, U.: Überschuldungsprävention durch sozial verantwortliche Finanzdienstleister und durch Stärkung der finanziellen Bildung der Bürgerinnen und Bürger. Berlin: Bundesministerium für Familie, Senioren, Frauen und Jugend. 2004.

Reis, C.:Konsum, Kredit und Überschuldung. Zur Ökonomie und Soziologie des Konsumentenkredits. Frankfurt a.M.: Deutscher Verein für öffentliche und private Fürsorge. 1992.

Zimmermann, G.: Ermittlung der Anzahl überschuldeter Privathaushalte in Deutschland sowie weitere Kennzahlen zum Ausmaß privater Überschuldung auf Basis der SOEP 2006. Karlsruhe: Bundesministeriums für Familie, Senioren, Frauen und Jugend. 2007.

The Ultimate Victims of the Economic Crisis: A Portrait of Portuguese Overburdened Families

Cláudia Abreu Lopes *Catarina Frade* *Fernanda Jesus*

Introduction

Operating a material or symbolic function, consumption plays a central role in contemporary society. This role has been shaped by the availability of various complex financial products generally accessible to the consumer. Credit has become popular in most market economies and lost the negative connotation it had for so long. Nowadays it is a common tool in the family budget management and a structural component of market economies.

In Portugal, consumer credit started to expand in the 1990s, with Portuguese families taking advantage of the low interest rates to acquire, above all, their own house and also a car, computer, and domestic appliances. Using credit as a way of anticipating consumption enabled Portuguese consumers to obtain goods and services that would otherwise be inaccessible to them.

This positive side, however, also entails a negative one. Taking on medium and long-term financial commitments can become untenable not only when the amounts exceed the family's real capacities, but mainly when the financial conditions of the family decline.

There are several scenarios leading to over-indebtedness. Unemployment or the deterioration of working conditions are, undoubtedly, the primary causes. But there are also reasons inherent to the family itself, such as divorce or the death of a family member, as well as causes associated with consumption habits and the financial literacy of individuals.

In times of systemic financial crisis like nowadays, these scenarios tend to aggravate. It is difficult to predict how to overcome over-indebtedness, especially in a context of meager savings and growing unemployment. It is worth remembering that Portugal has a very significant poverty rate within the European context (18 percent, compared with the average of 16 percent in the European Union).[1] Several governments have tried various ways to combat extreme poverty. However, a fringe of new poor is now evident in Portuguese society, which escapes official measurements but mirrors the reality of a middle class that is

1 Alves 2009. With the current economic crisis and the austerity plan negotiated in 2011 by the Portuguese government with the IMF, the European Central Bank and the European Commission (the so called Troika), there are reasons to believe that the convergence path initiated two decades ago will be reversed or at least interrupted and the poverty rate will remain stable or even increase.

more and more impoverished because of the burden of debt, job loss and the government's austerity measures (tax raise, salary and social benefits cuts).

The main aim of this chapter is to contextualize the phenomenon of over-indebtedness in Portugal. It begins with a brief overview of the macro-economic and macro-social reality of Portugal in which over-indebtedness is clearly framed. Next, a profile of the over-indebted Portuguese is presented, based on an analysis of primary survey and interview data. Lastly, two over-indebtedness related policies proposed by the Portuguese government are discussed. These measures aim to help households in arrears to settle their mortgages. We also make an overview of bankruptcy system since this has been in high demand by households in current times.

The "new poor": heavily in debt, increasingly unemployed

Contrary to the experience of the US and other European countries, where the spread of credit was slow and occurred in different periods, over-indebtedness grew in Portugal rapidly over the past several years.

Portugal's growth in consumer credit was the result of a confluence of several factors: (1) initially, the context of the Portuguese economy was characterized by a rapid increase in net income, (2) the downward trend in unemployment and interest rates, (3) the liberalization of financial markets and a consequent increase in competition among the financial institutions.

By resorting to credit, many Portuguese families solved their housing problems, bought a car, furnished their home, and bought computers. They were able to take advantage of diverse commercial offers, which gave them access to goods and services that, until recently, had remained beyond the financial capacity of the majority of Portuguese households. In this way, family material well-being grew considerably during the last ten to twenty years. The rate of indebtedness (measured as a percentage of income affected to credit out of the disposable income) changed from a modest 18 percent in 1990 to 126 percent in 2011, with mortgages accounting for 80 percent of the total consumer indebtedness.

The increasing rate of indebtedness brought with it a growing risk of families becoming bankrupt. Over the last five years, more and more families have been burdened with credit and, for various reasons, they can no longer meet their debts. Even before the crisis was formally declared, families underwent a sudden deterioration in their living conditions. From 2007 to 2008, employment rates showed a very slow increase but families' financial well-being worsened because interest rates increased, which placed a burden mainly on mortgage contracts. With the financial crisis beginning in 2008, interest rates diminished, but this sudden relief didn't last long because at the same time there was a rapid growth of unemployment rate. In the first semester of 2012, unemployment rate peaked at 15percent.

In 2007, DECO – the Portuguese association providing consumers' assistance and legal defense – received more than twice as many requests for help from over-indebted families than in 2006 (from 905 to 1,976 cases, respectively). DECO was not the only organization that reported such an increase. At the same time, other organizations in the social assistance sector, including religious institutions, similarly reported an increase in requests for help since 2007.

The increase in the number of families seeking help from non-governmental associations was also observed in the following years and in a more exacerbated manner due to the impact of the financial crisis. In 2011, DECO received 3,238 requests and from January to September 2012 the association supported more than 4,000 cases (4,010). At the same time several organizations of civil society and of the church reported a huge unprecedented demand for support from households unable to provide food and clothes, to pay the rent or the utility bills.

The picture of Portuguese families' financial difficulties cannot be described only with numbers. The profile of consumers seeking help has changed. Requests for assistance come not only from low-income families, those in unstable jobs or with limited academic and professional qualifications, but also for the first time, institutions are dealing with families with social and professional standing, even with higher education, and with average incomes, who cannot keep their income to the end of the month even to buy food. Such requests arrive at these institutions mainly by email or mobile phone. Some consumers come in person at the end of the day, at times when there is less movement so as to hide their shame for having to beg for food or clothing. They live in big cities and have neither savings nor families willing to help. They feel uncomfortable showing their difficulties to their partners and find it difficult to prioritize their expenses. They seem willing to cut down consumption, but find it hard to do so. Many are unemployed and have already used up their unemployment benefits or do not have access to such benefits.

The social support organizations talk about a new class of poor, made of individuals and families who, in the past, had well-paid jobs, a stable financial life, diverse and complex consumer habits, and two or more loans. This is a class that has dangerously combined a intense consumption, meager savings, several loans, and deterioration in labor circumstances (unemployment or loss of wage benefits). This is a class for whom traditional methods of social assistance are neither adequate nor sufficient. Their financial future is a gamble, especially in light of the negative evolution of current labor markets and of the growing austerity measures implement by the Portuguese government in the shadow of the Troika's intervention of 2011. Economic forecasts are grim for the near future.

In the past several years the unemployment rate more than doubled in Portugal, being currently 15 percent.[2] Private and public investment is at a standstill and has not been sufficient to create new job posts to absorb the avalanche of new unemployed people. Family and company demands for credit have seen a drastic slump in the last two years. The protracted economic recession is delaying any positive signs of improvement in Portuguese families' financial health. It is the efforts of a still active welfare society that will ultimately ensure the financial recuperation of many families. The State is found wanting from many aspects.

In the next sections of this chapter, we present an outline of those who find themselves over-indebted and continue to rely, above all, on the efforts of their social networks (family and friends). Despite creditors' recent openness to the renegotiation of debt, these debtors remain at financial and poverty risk.

An empirical study of the over-indebted

In 2005, the Observatory of Consumer Indebtedness at the University of Coimbra (OCI) began a systematic empirical analysis of over-indebted Portuguese consumers. To this end, an online questionnaire was filled in to consumers seeking for help from the Advisory Offices for the Over-indebted (GAS-Gabinetes de Apoio ao Sobreendividado) of the Portuguese Association of for the Consumer Protection - DECO.[3]

The questionnaire covers standardized socio-demographic and financial data (income, number and type of credits), as well as socio-psychological data relating to motives for resorting to credit, the reasons for payment default and the characteristics of such default (number and type of credits in arrears).

In due course, as a way of triangulating data to obtain further insights, the OCI carried out semi-structured interviews with some of these over-indebted people (chosen convenience sample selected from the over-indebted database). Here, the trajectory of consumption habits and the behavior of individuals that lead to their situation of over-indebtedness, the financial, psychological and professional consequences of this situation, the individual and familial strategies, and the support consumers received towards the resolution of their financial difficulties were explored in depth.

---

2 See ine.pt

3 DECO is not the only institution providing advice and/or support to over-indebted consumers in Portugal. However, it is the most important debt counseling service available in Portugal. For these reasons, we monitored the cases of over-indebtedness that we encountered at DECO, outlining from them the personal and financial profiles that this phenomenon displays in our country.

The descriptive study presented here is based on a survey of 5,867 over-indebted individuals between January 2005 and April 2012, and on content analysis of the interviews to over-indebted consumers carried out in 2005 (28 interviews), 2009 (15 interviews) and 2011 (10 interviews). This survey does not include all the cases supported by DECO over these seven years. It only contains the questionnaires voluntarily completed by over-indebted individuals seeking assistance from DECO during that period.

Participants were mostly married or in a common-law partnership (59.5 percent) or divorced (21.5 percent), and aged between 30 and 49 (59.4 percent). The respondent's families comprised three (29.6 percent), two (26.4 percent) or four (19.9 percent) members, with one (41.4 percent) or two (31.3 percent) children to support. A couple with one child was the typical family. Regarding education levels, individuals with average schooling (12 or 9 years) predominated. In terms of occupational status, 62.3 percent of the respondents were working, 24.4 percent were unemployed and 10.8 were retired.

The socio-demographic profile of our sample remains relatively unaltered for these more then seven years under analysis, with an exception for the growing number of retired people, who are now in financial difficulties because their responsibilities as credit guarantors were activated, or because they borrowed credit themselves to help their offspring.

However, the financial and motivational variables oscillate during this period. From the total of respondents, 62.1 percent have incomes stemming from salary, 16.3 from retirement benefit and 16.1 percent from other temporary benefits. The monthly income of the households[4] are mainly between €501 - 1,000 (40.3 percent) or €1,001 - 1,500 (22.2 percent). It is worth noting the fact that in the last three years the group of €1,001-1,500 monthly income surpassed the €501-1,000 group. Situations of multi-indebtedness predominated (55.6 percent), although the number of cases where there was only one debt or none is also relevant (15.7 percent and 28.7 percent, respectively). As can be verified from the data, more than a quarter of the sample are individuals with no debt, but who find themselves in arrears when it comes to paying household bills such as condominium, communications, rent and other basic services.

The most frequent type of credit involved personal loans (48.3 percent have one personal loan, 31.9 two and 20.2 three). This is followed by mortgage loans (31.6 percent), credit card credit (30.3 percent with one credit card, 17.8 percent two and 9.6 percent with three credit cards) and car loans (25.6 percent with one). Other categories of credit have limited representation. The choice of the credit institution is governed above all by advertisement (46.8 percent). The conditions of the credit (23.6 percent) and the fact that the institution where the

4 The minimum wage in Portugal is €485 per month.

purchase were made proposed a credit sale (23.0 percent) were also represented in the motives for choosing a particular institution.

Their motives for resorting to credit are shown in Figure 1, where we can see that financial difficulties (57.7 percent) and access to essential goods (39.7 percent) were the main reasons that led the Portuguese in our sample to borrow.

Figure 1: Motives for resort to credit (%)

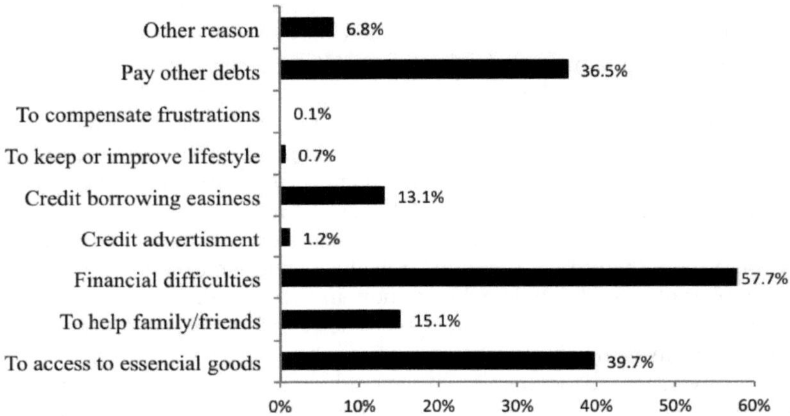

Regarding payment default, our sample shows that between one and 13 debts are in arrears. Specifically, 25 percent of the respondents have one debt in arrears and 13.6 percent are late with the payment of two of their debts. However, more than a third of these consumers (36.3 percent) have no debt in arrears.

Interviews allowed us to delve into the reasons why so many households seek debt assistance when they have no debt in arrears. We learned that some consumers approach DECO because they find themselves at the risk of failing debt commitments, but many more manage to comply with payments because they have the support of family and friends, or have opted for buying an additional credit. This fact mirrors what we have found in other studies:[5] the existence in Portugal of a welfare society that prevents many over-indebted consumers to fall into default. The financial and other material support of family and friends assumes a central role to refrain default.[6] In the same vein, over half of

5 Frade et al. 2006; Frade et al. 2008.

6 This support, often found among the over-indebted interviewed, translates not only as a gift of money or a loan to pay off the installments, but also as offers of food, meals and clothes, which reduce family expenses. This leaves more money to settle the monthly financial obligations, as is shown in the excerpts presented here.

the respondents surveyed (61.7 percent) state that they have receive support from social networks to pay debts or satisfy the family's daily needs.

> I didn't have any money to buy food to my kids. It was my sister who helped me. (Interview, 2011)
> I was living in my sister's. She was keeping me. (Interview, 2009)
> Lately it's my mother who gave my children's trainers. (Interview, 2009)
> I borrowed from my brother, but he got a loan for me...he's paying a loan he took out for me... (Interview, 2005)
> Very often our parents had to help to pay for the nursery. We ate at our families'. (Interview, 2005)
> We had some savings and it's true my wife's parents gave us financial help. Sometimes they bought clothes. If it wasn't for her parents, it would have been very difficult for us. (Interview, 2005)

Non-payment is greater in consumer credit than in mortgages, as is to be expected. Families make the greatest possible effort to meet installments on mortgage obligations in order to preserve the house, while perhaps sacrificing other debts.

Looking at Figure 2, it becomes evident that unemployment is the main reason for non-payment (44.3 percent). Respondents' next most common explanation for default is illness or accident of one of the family members (22.1 percent), increasing in the costs of credit (20.9 percent), deterioration of working conditions (20.5 percent) and bad management of the family budget (20.2 percent). In fact, resulting from wages decrease, the large number of people that were fired and the difficulty to get a new job, credit default is especially a work-related problem, that will only be mitigated with a structured macro level fight against unemployment.

Figure 2: Motives for payment default (%)

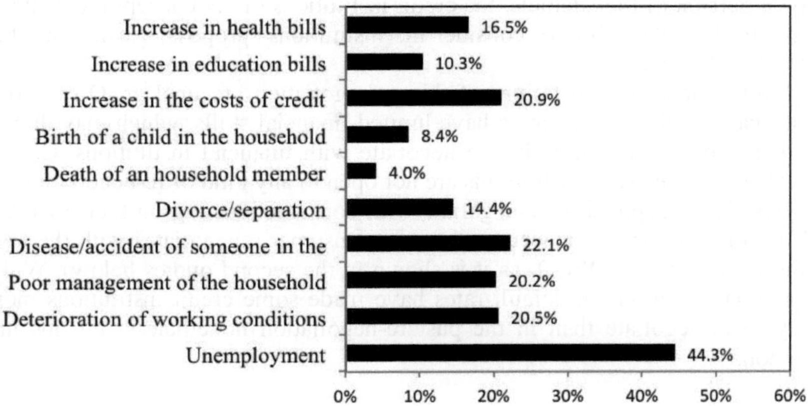

Considering unemployment as a cause, one may see that many respondents faced a drop in income. Figure 3 shows an increase in the lower income classes and a decrease in the highest ones after job loss. This reflects the dramatic reduction of available income to settle household regular expenses and explains much regarding the financial difficulties that these families suffer.

Figure3. Household income before and after unemployment (%)

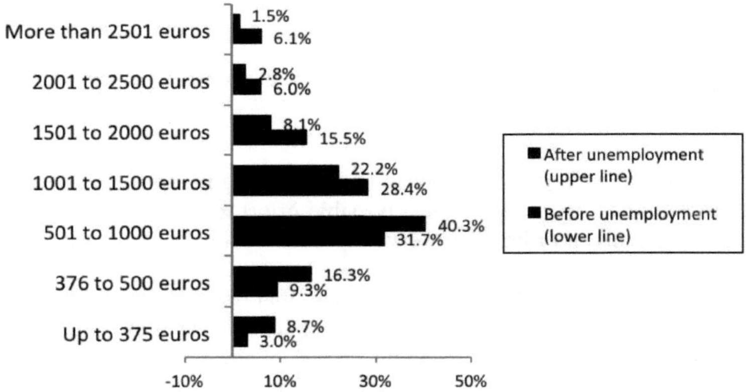

The information gathered, whether in the questionnaire or in the interviews, demonstrates the importance of the intervention of an association such as DECO in the renegotiation with creditors. Although 67.1 percent of over-indebted respondents had tried to renegotiate their debts with the creditors, only 21.7 percent had managed to reach an agreement and then only with a few entities. In 78.3 percent of the cases, over-indebted individuals' attempts were unsuccessful. In 67.8 percent of the attempts, the credit institutions did not accept the debtor's proposal; the debtor did not consider the institutions' proposal feasible in 10.5 percent of the cases.

Explanations for the failure of this re-negotiation are unclear. On the one hand, many of these consumers have limited financial skills, which may diminish their motivation and ability to negotiate with financial institutions. On the other hand, some credit institutions are not open to any kind of re-negotiation, or are especially skeptical to re-negotiate with consumers acting on their own behalf (a different behavior occurs when the consumer renegotiates with the help of an institution like DECO, as it is shown in the second quotes below). While recent changes in credit default rates have made some credit institutions more likely to re-negotiate than in the past re-negotiation nonetheless remains uncommon.

> I tried to renegotiate but it was not possible. I have all the e-mails with the negative answers from the banks. (Interview, 2011)
> Just the mention of DECO helped me. When I mentioned DECO, everything run quicker.(Interview, 2011)
> I did not [telephone], at the time. I was waiting to see what the letter was for the next month (…) so now I'm waiting for them to contact me. (Interview, 2009)
> Every time they phoned me it was a different person and I asked "Why can't I talk to someone responsible for my case?" (Interview, 2009)
> This was what I proposed to them [credit institution]. The reply was no… they wanted the four hundred odd Euros otherwise they would go to court. (Interview, 2005)

We also learned that the re-negotiation of debts is not the only, or even the first, step taken by consumers facing financial difficulties. The immediate reduction or suspension of some consumer goods was the first strategy of all those interviewed.

> I found a way of saving, for instance in feeding. I don´t need to eat meat every day (…) and I can use parts of foods that are usually discarded, like stalks of spinach. (Interview, 2011)
> If there are a few coppers for a coffee, we'll go out for one. If not, we simply stay at home. (Interview, 2009)
> My husband and I stopped smoking due to financial difficulties. And it's two years since I went to the hairdresser's. (Interview, 2005)

Overall, the data show that families' financial situation worsened over time, especially since 2007. The number of families going to DECO is increasing and those who go earn higher incomes and owe more unpaid debts, whether for credit or current expenses. This worsening is confirmed by the respondents' self-reported motives for incurring debt. The more recent questionnaires show that the predominant reason for borrowing is no longer to obtain essential goods (51.9 percent in 2005, compared to 39.7 percent in 2012); instead, it is now the need to confront the family's financial difficulties (38.1 percent in 2005, compared to 57.7 percent in 2012).

These results reveal a worsening of the economic and financial situation of the middle class, who see their income as insufficient to meet credit obligations and daily expenses. The social tension derived from this state of affairs has put pressure on public authorities for designing policies that help families in arrears. The most salient extrajudicial measures are described immediately below. Their dramatic failure and the exponential increase in bankruptcy filings are the most remarkable features of the current legal solutions provided to Portuguese over-indebted families.

Some anti-crisis governmental measures and the bankruptcy relief

Pressured by the worsening economic conditions and the drain of these conditions on family budgets, the Portuguese government adopted extrajudicial measures aimed at helping families with difficulties in paying their mortgages. One measure was the creation of an alternative renting system for those who cannot manage the monthly installment payments on their mortgage. The other was a partial and temporary moratorium to help with mortgage payments. These two measures were a complete flop.

The first measure – alternative renting – was instituted by the 2009 State Budget Law.[7] It involves the *Establishment of Residential Tenancy Real Estate Investment Fund* (FIIAH - Fundos de Investimento Imobiliário para Arrendamento Habitacional). These funds are destined primarily for people who have difficulty in paying their mortgage but wish to continue to live in the property. In line with this regime, the owner of the property sells it to FIIAH for an amount agreed with the respective management company and which will have as the limit the value of the evaluation undertaken by two independent experts. Following this, the former owner of the property can sign a rental agreement with FIIAH in which the tenant is given the option to buy the property by December 31, 2020. The tenant can exercise the option to purchase at any time the rental agreement is in force. Some estimates point to a rent 20 percent below the average value of the credit installment.

Only a public banking institution and a private bank, which control about 50 percent of the market for housing credit, can manage these funds. Although data on the results of this measure are scarce, it seems that the families have not adhered to it. The fact that those two banks favor their own customers to the detriment of those of other banks is one possible cause for these failures. Another reason could be the excessive delay associated with these processes, which demoralize potential beneficiaries and usually place people in a situation of great financial stress. Alternatively, the pronounced drop in interest rates in 2009 that still remain relieved the size of many families' mortgage payments, giving them some financial breathing space. We must emphasize that in Portugal housing credit is mainly contracted with variable interest rates, which makes it particularly sensitive to alterations in the Euribor rates. Additionally, the increase in household bankruptcies since the middle of 2010 and the voluntary settlement of the house to the bank registered in the last months deepened the insignificance of this measure.

---

7 Law no. 64-A/2008, dated December 31, 2009, together with regulations entered by Ministerial Order No. 1553-A/2008, dated December 31, 2009.

The second measure directed at people with mortgages, a transitory measure, was *the moratorium regime*, sanctioned in Decree-Law no. 103/2009 of May 12, 2009. In this case, the government provided aid to support up to 50 percent of individuals' installment or €500 per month for a period of 24 months (a period that has expired). To benefit from this procedure, it was necessary to have been unemployed for at least three months. During the period of the moratorium, the State substitutes as the debtor for the payment of half of the installment to the financial institution. At the end of the moratorium period, the debtor is obligated to repay the amount paid by the State plus interest equivalent to the Euribor rate over six months and a spread of 0.5 percent. This repayment can be attenuated throughout the time of the loan, and the deadline may be extended for up to two additional years. This moratorium measure is the equivalent to the State opening an exceptional line of credit for families so as to help them hold on to their house. Structural and contextual reasons explain the motivation this measure. On one hand, house-buying accounts for 80 percent of Portuguese families' indebtedness. At the European level, the Portuguese show one of the highest rates of home ownership (75 percent). On the other hand, unemployment has shown a high increase over the last two years. Taken together, these two factors emphasize the social and economic importance of avoiding evictions en masse and the concomitant depreciation of property values.

Contrary to the hopes of public authorities, recourse to this mechanism was also scarce. Although there are more than 1.6 million families with housing credit, by mid-October 2010 banking institutions had received only 1,431 requests. Of these, 887 were approved and 146 refused. Bureaucracy may explain this limited demand, together with ignorance of the moratorium law and the social shame that may be felt in taking advantage of it. Added to this is the fact that access to the regime was dependent on financial institutions' acceptance.

The medium-term impact of these anti-crisis measures was not at all significant. Their unusual and momentary character, the exclusion of other credit or rent debts and a certain resistance on the part of the financial actors to use them, provided for a very limited application for such instruments. In the case of the moratorium, for example, a period of 24 months was clearly insufficient to rebalance the family budget, above all because there was no improvement in the labor market. On the contrary, with the ongoing rise in unemployment, we suspect that some of the beneficiaries of the moratorium were unable to repay the unpaid installment principal plus interest. Because of this, relief was probably momentary, limited and ultimately ineffective. The lack of any official information on the success or failure of this measure does not allow for more than speculation, however assumptions are not needed when we take a look at the *bankruptcy* statistics.

In 2004, a new bankruptcy code for companies and private individuals – CIRE – came into force. Until mid-2010, personal bankruptcy filings remained scarce, presumably because households were unaware or ineligible to use this mechanism of last resort.

CIRE establishes some specific rules concerning personal bankruptcy, like the non-reporting obligation to the insolvency procedure for private individuals, the five years period of income assignment and the conditional debt relief.

When an individual or a household is declared bankrupt, a trustee is appointed by the court and proceeds with the liquidation of debtor's assets in order to repay to his creditors. After assets are sold, the debtor is forced to assign to the creditors the surplus of the income other than for living expenses to satisfy the remaining unpaid debts. It is only after expiration of a five years' probation period that the debtor is entitled to a discharge. This is not, however, a guarantee. In half of the cases, judges deny the relief even at the beginning of the procedure. They usually argue that the debtor should have filed for bankruptcy earlier and that because of that lack of initiative the creditors' position worsened. In cases in which discharge is denied, the debtor remains at the mercy of his creditors after expiration of those five years. Along the way he lost all the assets and any promise of regaining control of his financial life.

Not surprisingly, however, bankruptcy has become a kind of fashion in the last two years. The deterioration of the macroeconomic conditions of the country, the sharp rise in unemployment, and the income cuts approved by the government in the context of the austerity plan agreed with the Troika have thrown many households into default and insolvency. All this and the ineffectiveness of those extrajudicial solutions so far adopted have channeled households into bankruptcy as a last hope.

Bancruptcy has been sold as an ultimate solution, with promises of quick and assured relief. In many cases this is a hoax, because this expensive procedure frequently does not provide a fresh start for individuals. And yet the data show its success or most likely the despair of a growing number of families.

According to the Ministry of Justice statistical bulletin,[8] in the first quarter of 2007 personal bankruptcies accounted for 17 percent of the total number of bankruptcies declared by the courts. In the same period in 2010, they represented 25 percent, in 2011, 49.6 percent, and in 2012, 57.2 percent. For the first time in history, personal bankruptcy filings surpassed companies' filings during 2011.

Remarkably, only 5.9 percent of the claims recognized by courts in company and individual filings are recovered on the procedure. As a result, 94.1 percent of the amounts owed are not repaid to creditors. This shows that both companies and households resort to bankruptcy only after losing the bulk of their wealth, and that creditors do not recover any significant amount through the

8 See http://www.dgpj.mj.pt/sections/siej_pt/destaques4485/estatisticas-trimestrais8105/

procedure. Most of the time creditor simply obtain a fiscal statement of unpaid credit as a result of the bankruptcy proceeding.

This recent trend towards bankruptcy doesn't allow us as to know if individuals applying for bankruptcy are able to start all over again. We have to wait for the conclusion of the first cases to see if, after liquidation and those five years of income assignment, households are able to restart.

In our opinion, bankruptcy as it is designed in CIRE is a solution that falls short of resolving the financial difficulties of many households. It is expensive, legally demanding, too punitive and too long. The loss of all the assets, including the dwelling, the extensive period of assignment and the uncertainty of relief make us fear that this is a non-solution in the sense that it will not prevent people from falling into poverty and exclusion.

Conclusion

Although Portuguese consumer credit markets did not open until the mid-1990s, Portuguese consumers immediately felt the negative consequences of this increases access to credit. By 2000, families faced substantial difficulties in settling their obligations. This was when DECO created Support Centere for the Over-Indebted (Gabinetes de Apoio ao Sobreendividado).

Problems of over-indebtedness have grown since 2000, and most intensively since 2007. Long accustomed to restricting consumption and delaying projects, Portuguese families rapidly learned to take advantage of this new way of financing their expenses. Within Europe, Portugal has one of the highest indebtedness rates associated to consumer credit and residential mortgage debt. The largest portion of this debt is mortgage debt but, in the context of the current economic crisis, non-mortgage consumer credit is also increasing in amount, especially when used to pay other credits.

Problems of over-indebtedness are only partially a problem of debt. They are also a problem of reduced income. Portuguese families do not enjoy sufficient levels of income or savings to meet prolonged situations of unemployment or a pronounced increase in the cost of credit. And unemployment is increasing in Portugal at a rapid pace. The continuing rise in Portuguese unemployment rates is associated with a weak national economy, where economic growth is conditioned by the need to reduce budget deficits. The world economic and financial crisis only worsened the situation in Portugal, forcing the government to apply for international rescue from the EU and IMF.

Low economic trust indexes demonstrate the breadth of financial difficulties within Portugal (51 percent of the population, measured by the Genworth index).[9] Although the recent fall in the Euribor rate has alleviated many Portuguese families' interest obligations associated with mortgage installments, the cases in which incomes are insufficient to bear expenses and debt obligations continue to rise, especially after the salary and social benefit cuts and tax increases implemented by public authorities.

Our research demonstrates that the over-indebted in Portugal are mainly couples with one child and with an average socio-economic and educational level. They have several consumer credits and a mortgage. Their number continues to grow and the economic conditions in which they live have worsened. In fact, and mainly since 2007, families with higher incomes but with greater difficulties have begun to approach DECO. Their expenses are multiple and ever-growing and the non-fulfillment of their obligations shows not only in terms of credits taken out but also in terms of goods and essential services.

News reports confirm this tendency toward the impoverishment of the middle class, noting increases in requests for help from religious institutions and for social support by people who are or were until recently employed, are educated and of good appearance. More and more are asking for help via the Internet, through which their anonymity does not reveal the social shame that many feel. Most cite unemployment as the main reason for their difficulties and, although many receive State benefits, they know this has an end. They relate stories of short-lived employment and failed attempts to find a new job. They are sad, without motivation, and with little hope. Although we have not yet been able to measure fully the negative impact of the situations of failed obligations, we know that they play a great deal of havoc in psychological, social, and labor terms, and it is urgent to take steps.

The Portuguese government has not closed its eyes to this reality, especially at this time of crisis, having proposed measures to assist in alleviating the monthly burden of families' credit expenses. These measures only apply to families living in their own homes and not to renters, however. Moreover, they do not present a real solution to the problem, but offer only a temporary reprieve from mounting mortgage debt obligations. We underline their precise character and we question the future because we do not envision a long-term improvement.

That bankruptcy is becoming more and more a path followed by many families is positive in the sense that it provides, at least for (those with no assets and no job), a way out from the trap they have entered. But the punitive and prolonged procedure available makes us suspect that this will be an inadequate solution for a large majority of families.

9 Genworth Index 2010.

References

Alves, Nuno: Novos factos sobre a pobreza em Portugal. In Banco de Portugal, Boletim Económico, Primavera 2009, Lisboa: Banco de Portugal 2009, at 125-154. http://www.bportugal.pt/pt-PT/BdP%20Publicaes%20de%20Investigao/AB200902_p.pdf

Genworth Index: Measuring Consumer Financial Vulnerability in 18 Countries (vol. 4, 4th Quarter 2010). London: Genworth Financial 2010.

Instituto Nacional de Estatística, 2012. www.ine.pt

Frade, Catarina, Lopes, Cláudia, Nogueira, Cláudia, Magalhães, Sara and Brinca, Pedro: Desemprego e sobreendividamento dos consumidores: Contornos de uma "ligação perigosa". Coimbra: OEC/CES 2006. http://www.oec.fe.uc.pt/biblioteca/pdf/relatorio_desemprego_sobreendividamento.pdf

Frade, Catarina, Lopes, Cláudia, Jesus, Fernanda and Ferreira, Teresa: Um perfil dos sobreendividados em Portugal. Coimbra: OEC/CES 2008. http://www.oec.fe.uc.pt/pdf/Relatorio_Proj_Regulacao_Consumo.pdf

Over-indebtedness, Health and Social Network

Eva Münster Ulrike Zier Heiko Rüger Stephan Letzel

Introduction

As many as 6.59 million citizens in Germany may be restricted in their daily activities due to over-indebtedness and inability to pay.[1] For over-indebted people, there may be no long-term prospect of bill payment or debt settlement through earnings or other income, even if they reduce their standard of living. Such a condition jeopardizes the supply of basic goods. Economic and social participation is restricted, as well.

The share of over-indebted persons in Germany was 9.65 percent for 2012 and, thus, has increased slightly after reaching a low of 9.09 percent in 2009.[2] The increase in the rates of over-indebtedness despite the decreasing rate of unemployment in Germany between 2005 and 2012 and legislative regulations helping to handle unaffordable debts[3] might be a consequence of a high level of private consumption in 2011 and early 2012.[4] Already in 2011, inability to pay led 101,289 individuals to file applications to open personal insolvency cases in Germany, one of the highest levels since introduction of the new insolvency law in 1999.[5]

Scientific evidence of a relationship between poverty, generally defined by gross income, and health is well documented. This applies not only to less developed countries, but also for the western industrial nations, such as the Federal Republic of Germany.[6] Resolving the inequality that results from the relation-

---

1 Creditreform Wirtschaftsforschung 2012, at 4.

2 Cutoff day was October 1, 2012; Creditreform Wirtschaftsforschung 2012, at 4.

3 As a reaction to the increase in over-indebtedness in Germany, a new law for insolvency was introduced on January 1, 1999 ("Insolvenzordnung," or "InsO"). This law governs consumer insolvency, also referred to as personal insolvency. In the case of destitute but honest debtors, InsO permits the exemption from, that is the discharge of, the unpaid debt that remains after successful completion of the proceedings. This is being the case, if a debtor has shown good conduct over the course of six years and surrendered his sizable income and if there are no reasons for not allowing an exemption from the remainders of de discharged. This means that claims that are otherwise outstanding cannot be enforced compulsorily. However, they can still be performed voluntarily (InsO, § 301, paragraph 3).

4 Bundesagentur für Arbeit 2009; Bundesagentur für Arbeit 2012, Statistisches Bundesamt 2012a. Creditreform Wirtschaftsforschung 2012.

5 Statistisches Bundesamt 2012b, at 14.

6 Helmert et al. 1997b; 1997a; Mackenbach et al. 1997; Knopf et al. 1999; Marmot and Bobak 2000; Marmot 2001; Lampert and Thamm 2004; Marmot 2005.

ship between socio-economic factors and health has eluded German policy makers, despite various efforts.[7]

Commonly, poverty is defined to refer to the gross income of a person, with this definition sometimes further differentiated by educational level and training qualification. Conventional assessments of poverty fail to capture the multi-dimensionality and complexity of the problem, however, so that specific risk groups remain undetected. One of those specific risk groups may include the over-indebted, who show grave constraints in many areas due to their financial difficulties to the point of inability to pay, but who may earn income above the poverty level in Germany.

The relationship between over-indebtedness and health has not been studied. Few differentiated scientific analyses of over-indebtedness in association with health status have been carried out.

Existing research is restricted to psychological investigations abroad, which disclose a positive correlation between financial stress factors, especially debt, and psychological problems.[8] The chronological course of cause and effect is still unclear, however, longitudinal research hints at debts as the cause of psychological problems.[9] This relationship is stronger if the financial situation is perceived by the individual as a difficulty.[10] Two other longitudinal investigations[11] found that high financial pressure due to debt can result in a loss of self-confidence and self-esteem, and in the occurrence of depression. It is assumed that depression due to over-indebtedness is fostered by a deficient social network.[12]

Simultaneous with the rising prevalence of over-indebtedness in Germany, German models of co-payment for health care were introduced during the 1990s.[13] Because not all benefits could be paid for by the statutory health insurance, a financial equity contribution was implemented in addition to the general payment of contribution.

Recent legislation, introduced on January 1, 2004, sought to modernize the German health system, by requiring a co-payment of €10 for registration in general, specialist, dental and psychotherapy practices, as well as for urgent care. All patients insured by statutory health care are now required to pay this quarterly fee prior to medical treatment. Although the registration fee will be abolished in January 2013, other co-payments will remain. Co-payment for medication is

7 Bundeszentrale für gesundheitliche Aufklärung 2003.
8 Marmot et al. 1997; Weich and Lewis 1998b; 1998a.
9 Marmot et al. 1997; Stradling 2001; Webley and Nyhus 2001.
10 Wildman 2003.
11 Pearlin et al. 1981; Price et al. 2002.
12 Ziglio et al. 2003.
13 Busse and Riesberg 2005, 219 ff; Graf von der Schulenburg 2005.

calculated on the basis of the product's market price and accounts for up to €10 for drugs on prescription. Further co-payment is due for modalities, hospital stays, transportation costs, and cure.

The goal of this legislation was to stabilize the financial situation of the statutory health insurance and to strengthen the patient's individual sense of responsibility. Health-related, but also social and economic consequences for the individual, were not canvassed scientifically prior to the introduction of the law. Nor did legislators consider the possibility of discrimination against certain groups due to unequal access to German health care prior to the introduction of the law. Some of these issues were investigated after implementation,[14] but so far no one has questioned the extent to which over-indebted individuals who are unable to afford these co-payments are discriminated against in the German health system.

The present study draws on data in Rhineland-Palatinate, a federal state in south-western Germany with about 4 million inhabitants, and assesses health status, social networks, and utilization of the German health system by over-indebted persons.

After introducing the research methods in part 1, part 2 presents its results. There part A first presents the health status of over-indebted persons. Part B next analyzes the relationship between psychological disease and support of the social network for over-indebted persons. Finally, Part C examines the consequences of co-payment requirements in the German health care system, with a focus on the socially deprived group of over-indebted individuals.

Method

A cross-sectional study was conducted between July 2006 and March 2007 among over-indebted individuals in Rhineland-Palatinate in the form of an anonymous survey among clients of debt counseling centers. The survey was carried out with the cooperation of 53 centers for debt and insolvency counseling in Rhineland-Palatinate and with the Expert Debt Advice Center of the Johannes Gutenberg-University Mainz, a support agency for these local centers.

The questionnaire was developed exclusively for this study on poverty, debt and health (the "PDH-study"),[15] and contained 58 mainly closed questions on

---

14 For an overview of investigations see Mielck 2005. Further examples are Grabka et al. 2005; Grabka et al. 2006; and Winkelmann 2004.

15 The PDH-study was fully funded by the cluster of excellence "Corporate interdependence and social networks" of the Ministry for Science, Further Education, Research and Culture of Rhineland-Palatinate. The study was made possible by close cooperation with the specialized debt counseling center of the Johannes Gutenberg-University Mainz, by the support of the responsible bodies and members of staff of the debt counseling centers as well as by the participation of many clients of these centers. Special thanks therefore

the participant's health status and utilization of the health care system, his or her debt situation, and the structure and quality of the available social network.

All clients of the debt counseling centers were selected according to certain inclusion criteria, namely that they had to be at least 16 years of age and had made use of a counseling center at least twice. No exclusion was made with regard to nationality. Only one person per household was interviewed. If possible, this was the person seeking advice. Participants were informed about the study by one of the debt counselors and received documents about the study.

All in all, 2,235 questionnaires were distributed among 53 centers for debt and insolvency counseling by the coordinating center of the study at the Institute for Occupational, Social and Environmental Medicine at the Johannes Gutenberg-University Mainz. Of these, 1,876 questionnaires were passed on to clients. All questionnaires, which had been completed in written form and had arrived at the coordinating center by the end of March 2007, were collected and checked for plausibility using the Scan-System "Readsoft."[16]

Questions were asked regarding health status, social network and fees for medical visits and co-payment for medication. For example, to determine existent diseases respondents were asked:

> Do you or did you ever have one of the following diseases: hypertension, heart diseases, respiratory disorders, diseases of the stomach, inflammable intestinal diseases, liver diseases or hepatitis, thyroid diseases, diabetes, kidney diseases, cancers, diseases of joints or spine, nervous diseases, psychological diseases, addiction?

A case was defined, if a respondent answered *"I have now"* or if they stated *"I don't have any more"* and were still under medical treatment due to this disease. All other answers were defined as control. To measure support of the social network, the standard measure *"F-SozU"*[17] and a few supplemental questions were used.

The following questions were posed in order to investigate the utilization of the health care system:

> Did you ever refrain from visiting a doctor due to the 10 Euro fee for medical registration? If so, how often did this happen within the last 12 months?Did you ever refrain from buying prescribed medication because of financial reasons? If so, how often did this happen within the last 12 months?

---

goes to the specialized center at the University, to everyone involved with debt counseling and to all study participants.

16 Further details on how the study was implemented can be found in Münster et al. 2007.

17 Fydrich et al 2002; Sommer and Fydrich 1989.

If a participant answered affirmatively in either of the two cases, the case was defined as *"problem fee medical registration"* or *"problem co-payment for medication."*

The participant's socio-economic situation, debt situation and health status were considered as variables possibly influencing utilization of the heath care system. Participants were asked whether they suffered from a chronic disease; they were also asked to self-report their subjective well-being by filling in the *"Gießener Beschwerdebogen"* (complaint form developed in a town called Gießen).[18] This questionnaire covers 24 complaints, which can be merged to four areas of complaint (disposition for fatigue, rheumatic pains, stomach-related problems and complaints concerning the heart) and to one general complaint score. The results are based on the subjective appraisal of the participant. For the present analysis, a predefined classification into categories was used. Values ranging from 0 to 1 indicated hardly any complaints, values from 1 to 2 moderate complaints, and values between 2 and 4 considerable and strong complaints.

Uni-variate group differences were tested, using a χ^2 test. Continuous variables were categorized in order to prove non-linear effects. All tests were conducted using the statistical software SPSS, version 14.0.

Results

All in all, 666 individuals (51.1 percent female) aged 18 to 79 (mean 40.99 years; standard deviation 11.18 years; median 41 years) participated in the study. This corresponds to a response rate of 35.5 percent. About one third were married; 5 percent were of non-German nationality. Approximately two thirds of the participants had completed only basic education or had no formal education at all, with 30 percent not having completed any vocational training.

Health status of over-indebted persons

Out of the 666 participants, 79.1 percent (n = 467) reported at least one illness. Table 1 shows the prevalence of the most relevant diseases and significant gender differences. Multiple answers were permitted. On average, one participant reported two diseases. Psychological illnesses appeared most frequently with a share of 40 percent, followed by diseases of joints or spine with a share of 39 percent. Both diseases were significantly more often stated by women (46 percent and 42 percent, respectively) than by men (both 35 percent). Only addic-

18 Brähler and Scheer 1995.

tion was stated more often by men (18.5 percent) as compared to women (8.5 percent).

Table 1: Prevalence of diseases by gender in the over-indebted study population

	Total N=666	%	Male N=324	%	Female N=340	%	p-value
Psychological disorders	269	40.4	112	34.6	157	46.2	<.001
Diseases of joints or spine	259	38.9	114	35.2	144	42.4	.06
Hypertension	168	25.2	91	28.1	76	22.4	.09
Respiratory disorders	153	23.0	63	19.4	90	26.5	.03
Diseases of the stomach	139	20.9	56	17.3	83	24.4	.02
Thyroid diseases	90	13.5	23	7.1	66	19.4	<.001
Addiction	89	13.4	60	18.5	29	8.5	<.001
Cancers	23	3.5	5	1.5	18	5.3	.01

Source: Münster et al. 2007, at 631.

Concerning the relationship between over-indebtedness and health, both directions of cause and effect were indicated by the participants. On one hand, health related reasons were indicated as one of the main reasons for the situation of over-indebtedness by 32.6 percent (n = 217) of the participants. Health related reasons were inquired as accident (2.3 percent), disease (23.3 percent) and addiction (12.6 percent). On the other hand, 37.8 percent stated that they had fallen ill due to their over-indebtedness.[19]

Social network, over-indebtedness and psychological health

Of the 666 participants in the PDH-Study, 18.9 percent stated that their family and friends had withdrawn themselves since financial problems arose, and 29.5 percent stated that either their family (7.7 percent) or their friends (21.8 percent) had withdrawn. This finding may indicate a strong social exclusion and stigmatization of over-indebted persons and those who are unable to pay. Furthermore, 62.9 percent of the participants specified that they had withdrawn themselves.

Social exclusion varies strongly with stated psychological diseases. Of those whose family as well as friends withdrew, 58.7 percent stated psychological diseases, whereas only 30.3 percent of those whose family and friends did not withdraw stated psychological diseases.

19 For further detail on this finding, see Münster et al. 2007.

Examining a scale measuring social support from the social network *("F-SozU"*[20]), results show that 61.8 percent of those who report a lack of social support also self-reported psychological diseases. If social support from the network increases, prevalence of psychological diseases decreases. This finding is statistical significant in multivariate analysis.[21]

In addition, prevalence of addictive disorders (alcohol, illegal drugs, and medical drugs) varies with the quality of social support received from the relevant networks. Among those whose received social support can be described as problematic, 21.3 percent reported an addictive disorder, whereas among those who can rely on intact social support, only 11.3 percent reported an addictive disorder (cp. Figure 1).

Figure 1: Prevalence of addictive disorders in over-indebted participants of the PDH study, stratified for quality of social support (F-SozU)

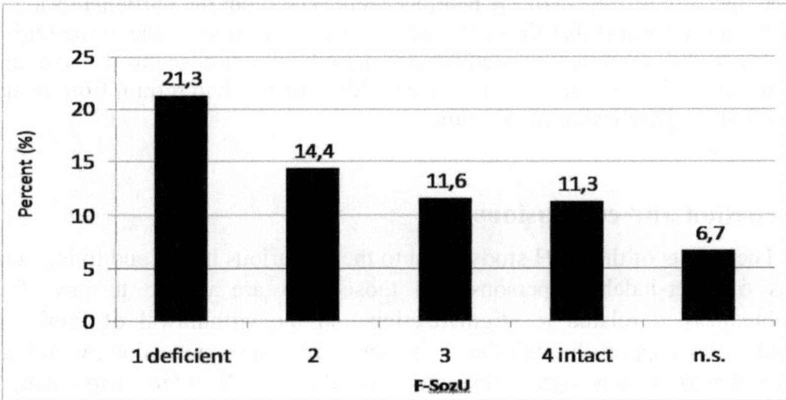

Source: PHD-study, own calculations

Utilization of the health system

The majority of all participants stated that they had refrained from a doctor's visit (60.8 percent) or from buying prescribed medication (65.2 percent) due to their financial situation, their debts, and their obligations for co-payment.

Regarding the utilization of health system services in relation to the debt situation, neither the variables *"amount of indebtedness"* and *"duration of indebt-*

20 Fydrich et al. 2002; Sommer and Fydrich 1989
21 For further information, see Rüger et al. 2009

edness" nor the existence of an affidavit[22] have significant influence on omission of medical visits or the purchase of drugs. It is striking that participants who filed for personal insolvency were more likely to refrain from purchasing prescribed medication (70 percent) than other respondents.

Health status measured via the *"Gießener Beschwerdebogen"*[23] and by direct questions about certain diseases does correlate with the omission of medical visits and purchase of drugs. The worse the health status of the respondent, the higher the likelihood that he or she will not consult a doctor or will not purchase prescribed medication. Utilization of the health system is further associated with self-reports about the importance of the respondent's own health. Individuals who are very strongly or strongly concerned about their health are less likely to refrain from a medical visit or from purchasing prescribed medication.

There is also evidence for a background influence of socio-economic factors on the utilization of health care services. A significant correlation is found between age and utilization of the health system. The older the participants are, the less often they report that they refrained from a medical visit due to the registration fee or did not purchase medications. Family situation seems to have an influence as well. Respondents who have children more often refrain from medical visits and not purchasing medications.[24]

Discussion and conclusions

The results of the PDH-study point to the precarious health and living conditions of over-indebted persons and those who are unable to pay. Over-indebtedness is related to stigmatization and the withdrawal of family and friends. Low support through the social network, in turn, goes along with higher prevalence of psychological diseases and addictive disorders. Moreover, the study discloses low utilization health care system services due to obligations for co-payment.

---

22 An affidavit, in this context, can be understood as the disclosure of the financial situation of the debtor. Upon a creditor's request, the debtor has to disclose his financial situation if during compulsory enforcement the attempt for garnishment of personal property remains unsuccessful. The purpose of an affidavit is to give creditors insight into the financial situation of the debtor in order to enable them to appraise the potential success of further enforcement measures. The bailiff of the county court at the debtor's dwelling place is responsible for the acceptance procedure of an affidavit.

23 Brähler and Scheer 1995.

24 For further detail, see Münster et al. 2009.

Health status

Out of 10 participants, 8 reported at least one disease, with psychological diseases and diseases of joints and spine stated most frequently. Reference data of the telephonic health survey 2003 of the Robert-Koch Institute, finding a lifetime prevalence of persistent diseases of 20.6-53.2 percent depending on age group for the lowest social stratum in Germany,[25] indicate that the high prevalence found in the PDH-study is not to be explained by a social stratum model. The high prevalence of 79 percent appears to be a particularity of over-indebted persons. Here, both ways of cause-effect are stated: one third of all participants refer to health related problems as a main reason for their financial situation; at the same time, one third declared they had fallen ill due to over-indebtedness.

Psychological diseases

The results show a close relationship between over-indebtedness and the withdrawal of relatives and friends. Within the population of over-indebted persons a close connection between the status or functioning of the social networks on one hand and the prevalence of psychological diseases or addictive disorders, on the other hand, is to be found. It can be assumed that over-indebtedness and psychological disorders come along with changes in social networks and social contacts.

Utilization of the health care system

The PDH-study demonstrates that the majority of the participating over-indebted individuals refrained from buying prescribed medication and from medical visits due to financial distress and the medical registration fee of €10. More than 60 percent reported a limited utilization of the health system and of medical services. With respect to health care research, it is particularly interesting that younger people, those with children, those with stronger medical problems and those who are less concerned about their health are less likely to make use of the doctor or to buy prescribed medication. People who have filed for private insolvency are further at higher risk to be excluded from those medical services that require co-payment.

Using the example of Rhineland-Palatinate, these results show for the first time for Germany that populations with high financial burdens, e.g., an inability to pay due to over-indebtedness, are disadvantaged with regard to access to health care requiring co-payment.

25 Lampert 2005.

Our results are contrary to prior studies in Germany, which did not find any sign of exclusion based on medical registration fees.[26] Although there is little empirical analysis of the effect of policies of cost-sharing, the new scheme has already been presented as a successful strategy to limit the number of redundant medical visits and examinations.[27] From this perspective, medical registration fees sensibly reduce *"moral hazard,"* an economic phenomenon describing incentives for reliance on unnecessary insurance benefits.[28] However, when examining scientific studies in detail, findings from the US as early as the 1970s and 1980s pointed to the discrimination of lower socio-economic groups.[29] The *"Health Insurance Experiment"* randomly allocated 2,750 families, that is, more than 7,700 individuals below 65 years of age, to five different models for health insurance. The findings showed that:

- Co-payment reduces the utilization of necessary and unnecessary medical services to a similar degree.
- Particularly among the lowest socio-economic groups, co-payment was linked to the following negative health effects: higher mortality of patients with high blood pressure, worse eye sight, limited dental care, and higher prevalence of certain symptoms like back pain, bleeding, loss of consciousness, shortness of breath and weight loss of more than five kilograms.

This US study found that the 6 percent of the population who had been poorest and most ill at the start of the study showed the best state of health when allocated to a health system that paid for everything. The experiment also showed that co-payment did not encourage more responsibility on the part of the individual. Risk behavior did not change in the long term for individuals required to pay extra for health care.

In two recent articles comparing the health systems of France, Spain and Germany, Lostao and colleagues similarly conclude that co-payment for medical visits leads to a reduction of health visits.[30] For their study, this reduction is increasingly visible among lower socio-economic groups. Given that disease prevalence is higher among lower socio-economic groups,[31] the limited utilization of medical services is counterproductive to health improvement and the treatment

26 Grabka et al. 2005; Grabka et al. 2006; Zentralinstitut für die kassenärztliche Versorgung in der BRD 2005; Streich 2004.

27 Grabka et al. 2005; Grabka et al. 2006.

28 Winkelmann 2004.

29 Brook et al. 1990; Brook, Lohr 1987; Brook et al. 1983; Keeler et al. 1985; Keeler et al. 1987; Lohr et al. 1986; Lohr et al. 1986; Newhouse 2004.

30 Lostao et al. 2007a; Lostao et al. 2007b.

31 Mielck 2005.

of diseases. Berth and colleagues[32] also point to socio-economic inequalities as affecting health care. They find a significantly higher risk of not having been to the doctor in the year 2004 among unemployed persons without training qualification.

The results of the PDH-study suggest that the higher complaints are, the more often medical visits are avoided, and the less often prescribed medication is purchased. They also point to the fact that over-indebted individuals ignored necessary treatment. The PDH-study did not measure the extent to which over-indebted individuals make use of hardship regulations of the compulsory health insurance,[33] but several factors nonetheless suggest that they underutilized these regulations. First, problematically, these regulations refer to the gross income of a person. As a result, over-indebted individuals may be disadvantaged as their financial exigencies would be underestimated. While according to these regulations individuals may earn too much income to qualify for an exemption from required co-payments, their payments towards creditors would not be taken into account. Furthermore, high bureaucratic efforts are necessary to apply for a hardship regulation since receipts have to be collected during the year and applications have to be filled every year anew. Both factors taken together suggest that, in practical effect, the regulations require over-indebted individuals to choose between paying their creditors and paying for access to health care by means of co-payments. The abolishment of the registration fee may lead fewer to refrain from medical visits, but will not entirely resolve the problem of co-payments and therefore the need for hardship regulations applicable for over-indebted persons.

It is also questionable whether persons with a small gross income know about their rights under German law. Nor is it clear that that the professionals who counsel the over-indebted, for example consultants for the unemployed, for debtors and for insolvent estates, are informed about the law. So far, few scientific studies have investigated the awareness level of this law in Germany. According to a written survey and a subsequent interview among the members of a German compulsory health insurance (AOK) conducted in the year 2000[34] – prior to the health reform and prior to the law which modernized the German compulsory health insurance – more than 60 percent of those who would be entitled

32 Berth et al. 2003; Berth et al. 2005.

33 These regulations release insured persons with low income or who are highly burdened by co-payment from the obligation to pay extra for one calendar year. In paragraph 62 of the German social code book (Sozialgesetzbuch V), the limit is defined according to gross income. Persons insured via compulsory health insurance are generally exempt from co-payment if co-payment would exceed 2 percent of the yearly gross income. For those with chronic diseases, this limit rests at 1 percent, if they took part in certain early detection examinations.

34 Eller et al. 2002.

to exoneration from co-payment had not applied for exemption due to a lack of knowledge.

Health system research is urgently needed particularly as to lower socio-economic groups in order to countervail socio-economic health inequalities. Given the results of this study, over-indebted individuals should be informed about their rights to seek exoneration from co-payment.

Reasons for limited utilization of the health care system

Despite methodological limitations of the PDH-study, it identified limited utilization of the health care system due to a lack of financial resources and due to the debt situation in Rhineland-Palatinate. The over-indebted individuals surveyed in the PDH-study seem to seek exoneration from co-payment rarely. There might be several reasons for this:

- The law allowing exoneration is unknown to them.
- The law does not apply as it refers to the gross income of the over-indebted person, which does not reflect the real financial burden.
- The bureaucracy related to an application for exoneration is too challenging for over-indebted individuals who are already strongly burdened. They therefore refrain from applying.

The data of the PDH-study demonstrates the problem of reduced and limited utilization. However, final evaluation requires further research to explain the causal chain in greater detail.

Although over-indebted individuals are a group difficult to reach in epidemiological studies, overburdened marginal groups of society should not be excluded from scientific research. It is internationally known that individuals with low socio-economic status are less likely to participate in scientific research.[35] Public health measures and health system changes deriving from "representative" samples of the general population can therefore lead to incomplete assessment, particularly with respect to lower socio-economic and fringe groups of society. Research aimed specifically at these groups should additionally be initiated in Germany.

While over-indebted individuals often are exposed to a diversity of stresses and burdens likely to reduce their participation in scientific studies, such as low education, high divorce rates and the fact that over-indebtedness is a taboo in Germany, the PDH-study shows that quantitative research is possible when trusted contacts and gatekeepers are used. The present sample was collected by

35 Burg et al. 1997; Cunradi et al. 2005; Galea, Tracy 2007; Hille et al. 2005; Partin et al. 2003; Richardi et al. 2002; Shaher et al. 1996.

using a setting approach and contacting debt counseling centers. This strategy portrays a group at high risk for poverty, which has so far not been captured in scientific research.

Limitations

Because cross-sectional, the PDH-study was not designed to provide scientific evidence of the chronological relationship between influencing parameter and dependent variable. However, it can investigate certain links. According to the specific structure of the questions of the PDH-study, it can be assumed that a debt situation in combination with a lack of financial resources is a cause of discrimination with respect to medical services requiring co-payment.

A response rate of 35.5 percent may have created possibilities for bias. The study participants were tested in terms of their representativeness as relates to all debtors in Rhineland-Palatinate by comparing them to the provincial statistics of all debt counseling centres.[36] Comparing provincial statistics on 11,520 debtors for the year 2006 with the 666 debtors participating in this study, the participants differed from provincial debtors in statistically significant ways with respect to family status, nationality and debt categories. In the PDH-study, participants of non-German nationality are under-represented, as are married participants and those living apart from their partners. There are significantly more singles and more divorcees in the PDH-study. The lower debt categories up to €5,000 are also under-represented in the PDH-study. Although differences are only marginal and selective, biases are possible.

The possibility that individuals who were excluded from the German health system were more likely to voice their complaints cannot be eliminated. This would have caused a rise in the prevalence of this response. It is also possible that those who are, due to their debt situation, heavily burdened with respect to health issues were less likely to participate in the study. This would imply that the real occurrence of non-utilization of the health care system is higher than the one presented. It has to be considered that, according to statements of debt counselors, some clients are not capable to read or write or to concentrate on a single action for more than a few minutes. As such basic abilities are necessary when taking part in a written survey, it may be that there are disadvantaged sub-groups within the group of over-indebted individuals who did not participate in the study. These individuals may be even more likely to be excluded from medical services for financial reasons, as these abilities are also necessary to apply for exoneration from co-payment.

In order to ensure equal opportunities for this marginal group of over-indebted individuals to participate in socio-medical studies and also to apply for

36 Münster et al. 2007.

exoneration from co-payment, an individual face-to-face survey and individual counseling would be necessary.

Conclusion

The health of over-indebted persons is at risk. Evidence suggests that two mechanisms interact here: over-indebtedness leads to disease and disease leads to over-indebtedness. An interdisciplinary approach is needed to reduce the burden of debt and health deprivation by combining debt counseling with medical counseling, both to do justice to the circumstances of the persons concerned and to allow for resolution of the over-indebtedness.

Health-related preventive programs for over-indebted persons should be developed to improve the health of persons concerned and to give them an opportunity to counter the indebtedness by their own means.

Counseling of over-indebted persons should include psycho-social aspects. Social support of over-indebted persons should also be promoted. When treating psychological diseases, patients' financial situation should be taken into account and, if necessary, the assistance of debt and insolvency counselors should be engaged at an early stage.

The German system of co-payment for a doctor's visit or the purchase of medication may discriminatorily limit over-indebted individuals' access to health care. Because co-payments are required, health services may be inaccessible to individuals with limited financial resources. Thus, equal access to healthcare services may be threatened by a patient's inability to pay. Empirical data collected by US scientists in the 1980s[37] found such an effect. From a socio medical point of view, co-payment obligations should be eliminated in Germany for poor populations and particularly for those with chronic diseases and burdens. The PDH-study corroborates these earlier studies. The over-indebted participants in the PDH-study did not make comprehensive use of claims for exoneration from co-payment, which are supposed to avoid discrimination against such groups.

First steps towards an improvement of the German health care system with respect to the deficiencies stated above would be to supply tailored support for over-indebted individuals. Claims for exoneration of co-payment should be investigated in greater detail. Specific consultants like debt counselors or unemployment counselors should assist over-indebted individuals in applying for exoneration from co-payment. Approval of private insolvency proceedings could immediately be linked to exemption from co-payment. In addition, professionals

---

37 Brook et al. 1990; Brook, Lohr 1987; Brook et al. 1983; Keeler et al. 1985; Keeler et al. 1987; Lohr et al. 1986; Lohr et al. 1986; Newhouse 2004.

involved with counseling over-indebted individuals (in whatever role) should be informed about the lack of utilization of health services requiring co-payment. It is further essential to introduce a simple system of applying for exoneration from co-payment in order to make health services as accessible for over-indebted persons as for the general population. Regulations specifying grounds for such exonerations should consider applicants' disposable income, rather than their gross income levels.

References

Berth, Hendrik, Förster, Peter and Brähler, Elmar. Unemployment, job insecurity and life satisfaction: results of a study with young adults in the new German states. Soc Prev Med: 2005; 50(6), at 361-369.

Berth, Hendrik, Förster, Peter and Brähler, Emlar: Unemployment, job insecurity and their consequences for health in a sample of young adults. Gesundheitswesen 2003; 65(10), at 555-60.

Brähler, Elmar and Scheer, Jörn W.: Der Gießener Beschwerdebogen. Handbuch, 2. completed and revised ed.. Bern: Hans Huber 1995.

Bundesagentur für Arbeit: Aktuelle Daten. Arbeitsmarkt in Zahlen. November 2009. Nürnberg: 2009.

Bundesagentur für Arbeit: Der Arbeits- und Ausbildungsmarkt in Deutschland. Monatsbericht Oktober 2012. Nürnberg: 2012.

Bundeszentrale für gesundheitliche Aufklärung: Strategies to reduce Health Inequalities. Cologne: 2003.

Busse, Reinhard and Riesberg, Anette: Gesundheitssysteme im Wandel. Deutschland. Kopenhagen: WHO Regionalbüro für Europa im Auftrag des Europäischen Observatoriums für Gesundheitssysteme und Gesundheitspolitik 2005.

Brook, Robert H., Kamberg, Caren J., Lohr, Kathleen N., Goldberg, George A., Keeler Emmett, B. and Newhouse, Joseph P.: Quality of ambulatory care. Epidemiology and comparison by insurance status and income. Med Care 1990; 28(5), at 392-433.

Brook, Robert H. and Lohr, Kathleen N.: Monitoring quality of care in the Medicare program. Two proposed systems. Jama 1987; 258(21), at 3138-3141.

Brook, Robert H., Ware, John E., Jr., Rogers, William H., Keeler, Emmet B., Davies, Allyson R., Donald, Cathy A., Goldberg, George A., Lohr, Kathleen N., Masthay, Particia C. and Newhouse, Joseph P.: Does free care improve adults' health? Results from a randomized controlled trial. N Engl J Med 1983; 309(23), at 1426-1434.

Burg, Je Anne, Allred, Sarah L. and Sapp, James H., 2nd: The potential for bias due to attrition in the National Exposure Registry: an examination of reasons for nonresponse, nonrespondent characteristics, and the response rate. Toxicol Ind Health 1997; 13(1), at 1-13.

Creditreform Wirtschaftsforschung: SchuldnerAtlas Deutschland 2012. Neuss: Verband der Vereine Creditreform 2012.

Cunradi, Carol B., Moore, Roland, Killoran, Moira and Ames, Genevieve: Survey nonresponse bias among young adults: the role of alcohol, tobacco, and drugs. Subst Use Misuse 2005; 40(2), at 171-185.

Eller, Martina, Baumann, Hans and Mielck, Andreas: Bekanntheitsgrad der Härtefallregelung in der gesetzlichen Krankenversicherung. Gesundheitswesen 2002; 64(11), at 565-571.

Fydrich, Thomas/ Sommer, Gerd and Brähler, Elmar: F-SozU - Fragebogen zur sozialen Unterstützung. In: Brähler, Elmar, Schumacher, Jörg & Strauß, Bernhard: Diagnostische Verfahren in der Psychotherapie. Göttingen: Hogrefe 2002, at 150-153.

Galea, Sandro and Tracy, Melissa: Participation Rates in Epidemiologic Studies. Ann Epidemiol 2007; 17(9), at 643-653.

Grabka, Markus M., Schreyögg, Jonas and Busse, Reinhard: Die Einführung der Praxisgebühr und ihre Wirkung auf die Zahl der Arztkontakte und die Kontaktfrequenz - eine empirische Analyse. DIW Discussion Paper 506, 2005.

Grabka, Markus M., Schreyögg, Jonas and Busse, Reinhard: The impact of co-payments on patient behavior: evidence from a natural experiment. Med Klin (Munich) 2006; 101(6), at 476-483.

Graf von der Schulenburg, J.-Matthias: German health care system in transition. The difficult way to balance cost containment and solidarity. Europ J Health Econ 2005: 6, at 183-187.

Helmert, Uwe, Mielck, Andreas and Shea, Steven: Poverty and health in West Germany. Soz Präventivmed 1997a; 42(5), at 276-285.

Helmert, Uwe, Mielck, Andreas and Shea, Steven: Poverty, health and nutrition in Germany. Rev Environ Health 1997b; 12(3), at 159-170.

Hille ET, Elbertse L, Gravenhorst JB, Brand R and Verloove-Vanhorick, S. Pauline: Nonresponse bias in a follow-up study of 19-year-old adolescents born as preterm infants. Pediatrics 2005; 116 (5), at e662-666.

Keeler, Emmet B., Brook, Robert H., Goldberg, George A., Kamberg, Caren J. and Newhouse, Joseph P.: How free care reduced hypertension in the health insurance experiment. Jama 1985; 254(14), at 1926-1931.

Keeler, Emmet B., Sloss, Elizabeth M., Brook, Robert H., Operskalski, Belinda H., Goldberg, George A. and Newhouse, Joseph P: Effects of cost sharing on physiological health, health practices, and worry. Health Serv Res 1987; 22(3), at 279-306.

Knopf, Hiltraud Ellert, Ute and Melchert, Hans-Ulrich: Social class and health: Gesundheitswesen 1999; 61 Spec No, at S169-177.

Lampert, Thomas: Schichtspezifische Unterschiede im Gesundheitszustand und Gesundheitsverhalten. Berliner Zentrum Public Health, Berlin: 2005.

Lampert, Thomas and Thamm, Michael: Social inequality and smoking behavior in Germany. Bundesgesundheitsblatt Gesundheitsforschung Gesundheitsschutz 2004; 47(11), at 1033-1042.

Lohr, Kathleen N., Brook, Robert H., Kamberg, Caren J., Goldberg, George A., Leibowitz, Arleen, Keesey, David R. and Newhouse, Joseph P.: Use of medical care in the Rand Health Insurance Experiment. Diagnosis- and service-specific analyses in a randomized controlled trial. Med Care 1986; 24(9 Suppl), at S1-87.

Lohr, Kathleen N., Kamberg, Caren J., Keeler, Emmet B., Goldberg, George A., Calabro, Thomas A. and Brook, Robert H.: Chronic disease in a general adult population. Findings from the Rand Health Insurance Experiment. West J Med 1986; 145(4), at 537-545.

Lostao, Lourdes, Regidor, Enrique, Geyer, Siegfried and Aiach, Pierre: Patient cost sharing and social inequalities in access to health care in three western European countries. Soc Sci Med 2007; 65(2), at 367-376.

Lostao, Lourdes, Regidor, Enrique, Geyer, Siegfried and Aiach, Pierre: Patient cost sharing and physician visits by socioeconomic position: findings in three Western European countries. J Epidemiol Community Health 2007; 61(5), at 416-420.

Mackenbach, Johann P., Kunst, Anton E., Cavelaars, Adrienne E., Groenhof, Freikje and Greuts, José J.: Socioeconomic inequalities in morbidity and mortality in western Europe. The EU Working Group on Socioeconomic inequalities and Health. Lances 1997; 349(9066), at 1655-1659.

Marmot, Michael: Economic and social determinants of disease. Bull World Health Organ 2001; 69(10), at 988-989.

Marmot, Michael: Social determinants of health inequalities. Lancet 2005; 365(9464), at 1655-1659.

Marmot, Michael and Bobak, Martin: International comparators and poverty and health in Europe. BMJ 2000; 321(7269), at 1124-1128.

Marmot, Michael, Ryff, Carol D., Bumpass, Larry L., Shipley, Martin and Marks, Nadine F.: Social inequalities in health: next questions and converging evidence. Soc Sci Med 1997; 44(6), at 901-910.

Mielck, Andreas: Soziale Ungleichheit und Gesundheit. Einführung in die aktuelle Diskussion. Bern: Hans Huber Verlag 2005.

Münster, Eva, Rüger, Heiko, Ochsmann, Elke, Alsmann, Christine and Letzel, Stephan: Überschuldung und Gesundheit. Sozialmedizinische Erkenntnisse für die Versorgungsforschung. Arbeitsmedizin Sozialmedizin Umweltmedizin 2007; 42(12), at 628-634.

Münster, Eva, Rüger, Heiko, Ochsmann, Elke, Letzel, Stephan and Toschke, André M.: Over-indebtedness as a marker of socioeconomic status and its association with obesity: a cross-sectional study. BMC Public Health 2009; 9:286 (August 7, 2009).

Newhouse, Joseph P.: Consumer-directed health plans and the RAND Health Insurance Experiment. Health Aff (Millwood) 2004; 23(6), at 107-13.

Partin, Melissa R., Malone, Michael, Winnett, Mary, Slater, Jonathan, Bar-Cohen, Annette and Caplan, Lee: The impact of survey nonresponse bias on conclusions drawn from a mammography intervention trial. J Clin Epidemiol 2003; 56(9), at 867-73.

Pearlin, Leonard I., Lieberman, Morton, Menaghan, Elizabeth and Mullan, Joseph: The stress process. J Health Soc Behav 1981; 22, at 337-356.

Price, Richard H., Choi, Jin and Vinokur, Amiram: Links in the chain of adversity following job loss: low financial strain and loss of personal control lead to depression, impaired functioning, and poor health. J Occup Health Psychol 2002; 7, at 302-212.

Richiardi, Lorenzo, Boffetta, Paolo and Merletti, Franco: Analysis of nonresponse bias in a population-based case-control study on lung cancer. J Clin Epidemiol 2002; 55(10), at 1033-40.

Rüger, Heiko, Löffler, Isabell, Ochsmann, Elke, Alsmann, Christine, Letzel, Stephan and Münster, Eva: Psychische Erkrankung und Überschuldung. Psychische Erkrankung, soziale Netzwerke und finanzielle Notsituation bei Überschuldung. Psychother Psych Med 2009; DOI: 10.1055/s-0029-1202364.

Shahar, Eyal, Folsom, Aaron R. and Jackson, Rodney: The effect of nonresponse on prevalence estimates for a referent population: insights from a population-based cohort study. Atherosclerosis Risk in Communities (ARIC) Study Investigators. Ann Epidemiol 1996; 6(6), at 498-506.

Sommer, Gerd and Fydrich, Thomas: Soziale Unterstützung, Diagnostik, Konzepte, Fragebogen F-SozU. Tübingen: Deutsche Gesellschaft für Verhaltenstherapie 1989.

Statistisches Bundesamt: Volkswirtschaftliche Gesamtrechnungen. Private Konsumausgaben und Verfügbares Einkommen. 3. Vierteljahr 2012. Beiheft zur Fachserie 18. Wiesbaden: 2012a.

Statistisches Bundesamt: Unternehmen und Arbeitsstätten. Insolvenzverfahren. Dezember und Jahr 2011. Fachserie 2 Reihe 4.1.Wiesbaden: 2012b.

Stradling, Steve: The psychological cost of student debt. Student dept: The consequences of undergraduate borrowing in the UK. Bristol: Policy Press 2001.

Streich, Waldemar: Reaktionen auf die Praxisgebühr - was antworten die Betroffenen. Gesundheitsmonitor. 2004.

Webley, Paul and Nyhus, Ellen: Life-cycle and dispositional routes into problem debt. Br J Psychol 2001; 92(Pt 3), at 423-446.

Weich, Scott and Lewis, Glyn: Material standard of living, social class, and the prevalence of the common mental disorders in Great Britain. J Epidemiol Community Health 1998a; 52 (1), at 8-14.

Weich, Scott and Lewis, Glyn: Poverty, unemployment, and common mental disorders: population based cohort study.BMI 1998b; 317 (7151), at 115-119.

Wildman, John: Income related inequalities in mental health in Great Britain: analysing the causes of health inequality over time. J Health Econ 2003; 22(2), at 295-312.

Winkelmann, Rainer: Co-payments for prescription drugs and the demand for doctor visits-evidence from a natural experiment. Health Econ 2004; 13(11), at 1081-1089.

Zentralinstitut für die kassenärztliche Versorgung in der BRD: Dauerhafter Rückgang der Inanspruchnahme durch Praxisgebühr bestätigt. Pressemitteilung vom 24. Januar 2005, Bonn.

Ziglio, Erio, Barbosa, Rogerio, Charpak, Yves and Turner, Steve: Gesundheitssysteme stellen sich der Armut. Kopenhagen: WHO; 2003.

The Role of Government as a Creditor of the Disadvantaged

Stephanie Ben-Ishai Saul Schwartz Jeremy Barretto

Introduction

Jorge,[1] a Portuguese immigrant, wanted his daughter, who has Downs Syndrome, to join him in Canada from Portugal. Jorge was earning high wages as a construction worker and felt able to sponsor her immigration to Canada. Upon her arrival, Jorge was advised by a social worker that she would qualify for benefits under the Ontario Disability Support Program (ODSP). Unfortunately, the social worker failed to tell Jorge that he was only two years into a ten-year responsibility period for any social assistance received by his daughter and might be asked to pay back any aid given to her.

Subsequently, Jorge suffered a series of setbacks. First, he was injured and was forced onto ODSP himself. Then his wife passed away and he had to use all of his available resources to pay for the funeral. Finally, the Ontario Ministry of Community and Social Services (MCSS) sent Jorge a letter claiming a $57,112 sponsorship debt, based on the ODSP benefits received by his daughter after her arrival in Canada. Jorge laments that had he been properly advised of the consequences, he would not have applied for ODSP for his daughter. Bankruptcy is not a viable option for him because he cannot come up with the $1600 in fees quoted by a bankruptcy trustee.

Jane[2] is unable to work due to a disability, but her ODSP application is pending. She is currently receiving $572 per month from Ontario Works (OW), which is less than her monthly rent. She used credit cards to meet her living expenses, and now owes $24,600 to four creditors. She is very nervous about her debts and is bothered by frequent calls from collection agencies. However, Jane had previously declared bankruptcy in 1996 because of her student loan debts. Jane recently consulted two Toronto-area credit-counseling organizations, Credit Canada and In-Charge Debt Solutions, but was told that her income was too low to qualify for their debt management plans. Bankruptcy, however, could be an

---

1 Pseudonym. The authors ran a pilot debt advice clinic at Parkdale Community Legal Services in January 2009. The purpose of the clinic was to provide neutral, informed advice and referrals to individual debtors. Clients who visited this clinic had debts ranging from $35 to $57,112. Most of the clients were on either Ontario Works (OW) or the Ontario Disability Support Program (ODSP), and had few if any assets. The following two stories from the Debt Advice Clinic are illustrative of the issues analyzed in this article.

2 Pseudonym.

attractive option for Jane. She visited five bankruptcy trustees, including four from a list provided by the Bankruptcy Assistance Program administered by the Office of the Superintendent in Bankruptcy. Partly because of her previous bankruptcy, she was quoted fees between $1,600 and $1,800, approximately three times her current monthly income.

For middle-class people, unforeseen events such as marital disruption, job loss and illness can set in motion a process that leads to insolvency. If they can no longer pay their debts, they can resort to one of the two main remedies available to Canadian consumer debtors to address insolvency-credit counseling and bankruptcy. As these two stories suggest, however, such events typically have very different outcomes for low-income people who depend on government transfers. Adverse economic events can set in motion processes that lead to changes in their benefit levels. Sometimes these changes cause benefit overpayments, which then become debts to the province. Faced with such debts, low-income people are left with few escape options, if any, because they do not have access to credit counseling, consumer bankruptcy or any form of neutral debt advice.[3]

In this chapter, we show that debts owed to the government are especially important in the lives of low-income people.[4] One well-known type of government debt arises from government-subsidized student loans designed to help post-secondary students who come from families with relatively low incomes. Post-secondary education might give such students access to good jobs at high salaries. But post-secondary education is a risky undertaking, and does not pay off for everyone. Those who borrow and do not find well-paying jobs after leaving school may find themselves with low incomes and significant debts to the government. Another sort of government debt, and the one on which we focus in this article, arises when government transfer programs overpay benefit recipients. Such overpayments can arise from errors on the part of recipients, including the deliberate provision of incorrect information, or errors by program ad-

---

3 Such overpayments are not a small issue, as demonstrated by work on the European consumer bankruptcy system. For a discussion of social problems caused by consumer overindebtedness, see Kilborn 2009, at 155. See also Kilborn 2009, at 307. It is also important to acknowledge that imprudent use of credit is also a cause of overindebtedness in some cases.

4 For the purposes of this paper, the term "low-income" is used to describe those individuals who are poor even before they incur debts leading to insolvency. However, it is important to clarify that insolvency is an issue that affects Canadians of varying income levels. Yet, despite the wide range of consumer debtors in Canada, our insolvency system remains tailored to meet the needs of middle-income debtors. This paper will explore the unique situation faced by low-income debtors and the way in which Canada's current insolvency system further disadvantages them.

ministrators. In either case, the overpayment becomes an involuntary debt to the transfer program.

To illustrate the debt problems that low-income people may face, we focus on overpayments that occur within Ontario Works (OW) and the Ontario Disability Support Program (ODSP), but similar stories could be recounted in the context of other transfer programs. The debt problems faced by government transfer recipients are nearly invisible. Some believe that transfer recipients cannot incur large amounts of debt because lenders will be reluctant to extend credit to them. Moreover, many transfer recipients are "judgment-proof"--any court judgment will have limited practical impact because they have no means of repayment. This leads some to believe that low-income people have few debts and little pressure to repay what they do owe, and therefore have little need for bankruptcy or credit counseling.

This chapter uses the statutory framework, interviews with government program officials and data on OW and ODSP overpayments to challenge the idea that low income people do not need bankruptcy or credit counseling. That belief rests in part on the presumption that those with low income have always had low income and always will. In fact, there is substantial movement in and out of poverty, as well as in and out of government transfer programs.[5] As a result, those who are receiving transfers at any given moment in time might well have accumulated large debts in their more prosperous past. And those who are now on government benefits and are judgment-proof may be looking forward to a time when they need no longer rely on government transfers and will no longer be judgment-proof. Without a mechanism through which recipients can deal with their debts, the current system can operate as a disincentive to leaving social assistance, since becoming independent may revive one's debts.

Using OW and ODSP as examples, our goal here is to demonstrate that transfer recipients are doubly disadvantaged in their efforts to resolve their debt problems. First, the two most common remedies for debt problems--credit counseling and personal bankruptcy--are out of their reach. Second, the government, which is often their most important creditor, controls their income and has more collection options than private creditors.

The most common methods of debt resolution in Canada are credit counseling and personal bankruptcy. Credit counseling often provides little more than debt management plans (DMPs) that require the full repayment of the debts.[6]

---

5 See, e.g., Finnie 2003, at 291.

6 Typically, a debt management plan requires that 100 percent of the existing debt, including interest, be repaid. However, the future accumulation of interest on most debts may be halted once the debt management plan is in effect.

Because transfer recipients often do not have any discretionary income on which to institute a DMP, credit counseling is not a viable option. Consumer bankruptcy does offer the discharge of most debts but it is costly--a private bankruptcy trustee typically charges about $1,500 over nine months.[7] The first disadvantage for transfer recipients is therefore that credit counseling is unavailable and personal bankruptcy is too expensive to be feasible.[8]

The second disadvantage is that the government, the main creditor of many low-income debtors, has more debt collection options than private sector creditors do. For example, most transfer programs have agreements with the Canada Revenue Agency (CRA)[9] that authorize the CRA to intercept some tax refunds and tax credits and turn them over to the transfer programs as debt payments.[10] Moreover, the government is in the enviable position (for a creditor) of being able to exert substantial control over the economic lives of its debtors by controlling their use of income transfer programs.

The rest of the paper will proceed as follows. Part 2 describes how the government of Ontario, through its OW and ODSP programs, comes to be a major creditor of some social assistance recipients. Other government programs, such as Employment Insurance, the Canada Pension Plan and federal and provincial student loan programs, also become creditors of the poor, but the OW/ODSP case best illustrates the salience of the two disadvantages referred to above. Part 3 explains and assesses the range of collection options open to the Ontario government as it tries to collect debts owed to OW or ODSP, options that include the reduction of benefit levels, referral to private collection agencies, court action and the set-off of tax refunds by the CRA. Part 4 outlines the options for low-income debtors attempting to address their debt problems. This section makes clear that in recent years the government has made various efforts to improve and centralize its debt collection efforts, but there has been no corresponding change in the availability of remedies that would allow economically disadvantaged people to deal with their debts.

---

7 Ben-Ishai 2007, at 510. For specific examples, see supra notes 1-2.

8 The Office of the Superintendent of Bankruptcy operates a Bankruptcy Assistance Program (BAP); see Office of the Superindendent of Bankruptcy Canada 18 September 2009 [BAP Directive No. 20]. Despite its name, the program does not offer lower cost bankruptcies, nor does it guarantee that a trustee will agree to administer the debtor's bankruptcy. The program is poorly advertized, little used and offers few if any benefits to debtors. The advertising that does exist is misleading. It gives the strong impression that a lower fee will be charged, but that is not true.

9 Canada Revenue Agency Act, S.C. 1999, c. 17.

10 See Ministry of Community and Social Services 2008 [MCSS, OW Policy Directives], Interview of Staff from the CRA's Refund Set-Off Program (6 March 2009).

Ontario Works (OW) and Ontario Disability Support Program (ODSP)

How Social Assistance Recipients Incur Debts to Ontario Works and the Ontario Disability Support Program

Social assistance in Ontario is divided into two separate programs. ODSP provides financial assistance and employment support to people with disabilities.[11] OW provides benefits, as well as help in finding work, to employable people in financial need.[12] ODSP is administered and delivered by the province, while OW is delivered by Ontario municipalities.[13]

OW and ODSP recipients come to owe money to the Ontario government when, for one reason or another, an overpayment is made to them by the government. Under section 19 of the Ontario Works Act[14], if a benefits recipient is paid more than he or she is entitled to, the overpayment may be deemed a debt to the Crown. Section 19(3) allows for recovery of overpayments from other government benefit programs, including those made under the Ontario Disability Support Program Act[15] and those made under the legislation which preceded the Ontario Works Act.

An important class of overpayments involves benefits paid to sponsored immigrants. A significant number of immigrants to Canada are sponsored by family members who are already living in Canada.[16] The Immigration and Refugee Protection Act[17] requires that the sponsor provide financial support to partners and to children 22 years of age or older for three years after the sponsored person becomes a permanent resident. Sponsored dependent children must be financially supported for ten years, or until the child turns 25.[18] If the sponsored person receives financial assistance from OW or ODSP despite the sponsorship

---

11 For a brief MCSS description of ODSP, see Ministry of Community and Social Services, About social assistance in Ontario. For a lengthier version, see Ministry of Community and Social Services 2006.

12 "1.1 Overview of Ontario Works" in MCSS, OW Policy Directives, supra note 10.

13 The local administration of Ontario Works is directed by "delivery agents." A delivery agent is either a municipality or a First Nation. The 47 municipalities and 100 First Nations that comprise the set of delivery agents are listed in O. Reg. 136/98, Sch. 1 & 2 [Delivery Agents][Municipalities].

14 S.O. 1997, c. 25, Sch. A, section 19.

15 Ibid., Sch. B.

16 Citizenship and Immigration Canada, 25 August 2009. Overview for 2008 listing: 65 000 Family Class (sponsored), 149 000 Economic Class and 22 000 Refugees (numbers have been rounded to the nearest thousand). See also, Carment 2008.

17 S.C. 2001, c. 27 [IRPA].

18 Prior to June 28, 2002, the Immigration Act, 1976, S. C. 1976-77, c. 52 required that sponsors provide financial support to partners and dependent children for 10 years from the date when the sponsored person became a permanent resident.

agreement, that assistance is treated as an overpayment and becomes a debt owed to the government by the sponsor.[19]

How Ontario Works and the Ontario Disability Support Program manage the collection of overpayments

The collection of OW and ODSP overpayments is complicated by the administrative structures of the two programs. The province administers and delivers ODSP through the regional and local offices of the Ministry of Community and Social Services (MCSS), which takes responsibility for collecting overpayments.[20] For "active cases"-- individuals who are currently receiving ODSP benefits--the Ministry reduces ODSP benefit payments by up to ten percent until the overpayment has been repaid. For "inactive cases"--people who have an overpayment but who are no longer receiving ODSP benefits--a central body known as the Overpayment Recovery Unit (ORU) takes charge of collection efforts.[21] The ORU will be discussed below.

The OW program is delivered on behalf of the MCSS by Ontario municipalities.[22] Eighty percent of OW benefits and employment assistance costs are paid by the province, with the other twenty percent paid by the municipalities; the administrative costs of the program are split evenly between the province and the municipalities.[23] When overpayments occur, the responsibility for collection falls on the municipality. As is the case for ODSP, overpayments among active cases are handled by reducing benefit levels by up to ten percent. For inactive cases, however, the program's financing scheme discourages collection efforts by municipalities, because they must bear fifty percent of the collection costs but must return to the provinces eighty percent of any money collected.[24]

---

19 IRPA, supra note 17 at s. 13(3). Because Section 13(3) of the IRPA states that "[a]n undertaking relating to sponsorship is binding on the person who gives it", ODSP or OW payments made to a sponsoree while the sponsor is still obligated to provide financial support become a debt to ODSP or OW.

20 Ministry of Community and Social Services 2008 [MCSS, ODSP Income Support Directives].

21 Interview of Darlene MacDonald Forsyth, Wendy Kaltiainen, Maxine Daley and Elizabeth Roy, Ontario Works Staff (6 February 2009) [Interview of Forsyth et al.]. Ibid.

22 See Delivery Agents, supra note 13, for a discussion of OW "delivery agents".

23 Interview of Forsyth et al., supra note 21. The same funding structure is in place for ODSP, with the province and the municipalities splitting the costs of benefits 80/20 and splitting administrative costs 50/50. That said, plans for changing the funding structure of OW were announced in the fall of 2008. See Ontario, Ministry of Municipal Affairs and Housing 2008. These changes would see the funding of OW return entirely to the province by 2018.

24 MCSS, OW Policy Directives, supra note 10.

Over time, the amount of uncollected social assistance overpayments grew to be quite large and drew the attention of the Ontario Auditor General (OAG) in studies done on OW in 2002 and on the ODSP in 2004. In a review of ODSP operations, the OAG wrote:

As of December 2003, information contained in the SDM system [the OW/ODSP computer system] indicated that outstanding overpayments for more than 61,500 active accounts (that is, amounts owed by people who were still receiving benefits) totaled $179.9 million. Outstanding overpayments on approximately 71,000 inactive accounts (that is, amounts owed by people who were no longer receiving social assistance benefits) totaled $303 million as of that date.[25]

By December 2008, a total of $202 million in outstanding ODSP overpayments was owed by 54,866 active cases, while $473 million was owed by 95,217 inactive cases.[26] In comparison, expenditures by ODSP in 2007/2008 were about $2.8 billion for financial assistance and $53 million for employment assistance.[27] New overpayments of $20 million were identified in 2008, while $17 million of the stock of outstanding overpayments was recovered.[28]

In its 2002 report dealing with OW, the OAG noted that: As of February 2002, Ministry records indicated that overpayments outstanding on over 49,000 active accounts totaled $77.4 million. Overpayments outstanding for approximately 274,000 inactive accounts totaled $336.9 million as of that date.[29]

By December 2008, a total of $107.2 million in outstanding overpayments was owed by 54,055 active OW accounts, while $487 million was owed on 319,133 inactive accounts. Expenditures for financial assistance by OW in 2007/2008 were approximately $1.6 billion. New overpayments of $24 million were identified in 2007/2008, while $21.2 million of the outstanding OW overpayments were collected.[30]

In the 2004 report, the OAG criticized the ODSP program for being lax in its efforts to collect the overpayments, in both active and inactive cases. In par-

---

25 Ontario, Legislative Assembly, Office of the Auditor General of Ontario 2004 [2004 OAG Report] at 97.

26 In the wake of a meeting of ODSP and OW staff (Interview of Forsyth et al., supra note 21), we requested further information about the nature and extent of overpayments and about the collection process. Much of the current information in this section arises from that request. We would like to thank the Ministry staff for their complete and timely response. We will refer to this information as the information from Darlene MacDonald Forsyth, Wendy Kaltiainen, Maxine Daley and Elizabeth Roy, MCSS Staff (May 2009) compiled at the request of the authors [MCSS Information].

27 MCSS Information, ibid.

28 Ibid.

29 Ontario, Legislative Assembly, Office of the Auditor General of Ontario 2002 [2002 OAG Report] at 53.

30 MCSS Information, supra note 26.

ticular, the program was criticized for not applying the directive, which provides that benefits on active accounts can be reduced by up to ten percent.[31] The OAG noted that at the offices visited, an average of about one-quarter of the active ODSP recipients with overpayments were not making repayments through automatic deductions. According to the OAG, this was because recipients claimed that reductions would cause them hardship. Turning to OW, the 2002 OAG report noted that the efforts of municipalities to collect overpayments on inactive OW accounts were "minimal," amounting to about two percent of the outstanding balances in 2001.[32]

The 2002 report led the Ontario MCSS to set up an overpayment task group in December 2003 to review how overpayments were created and managed in both the OW and ODSP programs.[33] In October 2004, the Ministry increased its capacity to recover overpayments from inactive social assistance cases and defaulting sponsors by consolidating collection activities into an Overpayment Recovery Unit (ORU). The ORU currently collects outstanding inactive delinquent overpayments from former ODSP recipients, outstanding inactive delinquent overpayments from OW participants who had been clients of Toronto Employment and Social Services (TESS), and Ontario Works and ODSP debts owed by defaulting sponsors.[34]

Operating as a 22-person unit within the MCSS, the ORU attempts to contact inactive cases that owe the program money resulting from an overpayment and set up repayment plans where possible. If these efforts fail, cases are referred to the Refund Set-Off (RSO) program operated by the CRA.[35] The CRA can then set off tax refunds and tax credits being issued to those with overpayments, and return the money to the province; the CRA Refund Set-Off Program is discussed in greater detail below.

In 2008, 4638 new inactive ODSP cases and 1815 inactive TESS OW cases were referred to the ORU.[36] The ORU was able to set up voluntary repayment plans for 1134 of these cases, and 3458 cases were referred to the CRA's RSO program.[37]

The special treatment of OW overpayments in Toronto deserves particular mention. The funding structure of OW discourages municipal collection efforts

31 MCSS, OW Policy Directives, supra note 10.

32 2004 OAG Report, supra note 25.

33 Ibid., at 361. This is a follow-up to the recommendations from VFM Section 3.01, ibid. at 23-61.

34 The inclusion of TESS overpayments in the activities of the ORU is discussed below.

35 MCSS, ODSP Income Support Directives, supra note 20.

36 MCSS Information, supra note 26.

37 Ibid. According the ORU, the remaining cases--ones for which the ORU has neither referred to the RSO program nor established voluntary repayment plans--required further administrative work because of the particular circumstances of the cases.

because, as noted above, municipalities must pay 50 percent of the collection costs but receive only 20 percent of what is collected.[38] In the summer of 2005, Toronto Employment and Social Services (TESS), which handles one-third of all OW cases, indicated its interest in participating in a pilot project for an enhanced provincial debt collection initiative. In December 2005, the City of Toronto outlined its plans for TESS to utilize the provincial ORU for the collection of overpayments.[39] In May of 2006, TESS confirmed its participation in the pilot project and agreed to turn over the collection of inactive, delinquent overpayment accounts to the ORU. The ORU pays all of the collection costs and returns 20 percent of the amount collected to the City.

The City of Toronto is the only municipality that has such an agreement with the ORU.[40] The Ministry is planning to expand debt recovery in OW by identifying other municipalities who are willing to work with the Ministry to refer inactive delinquent OW overpayments to the ORU.[41] Based on the results of the pilot project, the Ministry hopes to phase in the ORU's recovery of inactive delinquent OW overpayments across the province over 2009 and 2010.[42]

Collection options available to the government

When efforts are made to recover ODSP and OW overpayments, three general collection methods are available:

a. Internal efforts by the Ministry of Community and Social Services (MCSS) or by the municipalities who deliver OW;
b. The hiring of private collection agencies to recover the overpayments; and
c. Referral of the cases to the CRA's Refund Set Off (RSO) program.[43]

Internal efforts

When it is discovered that a person who is currently receiving OW or ODSP benefits has received an overpayment, the debt is most commonly collected through internal actions by the Ministry (in the case of ODSP), or by the municipalities (in the case of OW). As noted above, benefits can be reduced by up to ten percent when an overpayment debt exists. As of February 2009, there were

38 MCSS, OW Policy Directives, supra note 10. The funding structure of OW/ODSP collection efforts was discussed earlier in this paper.
39 Toronto, Social Services Division 2005, at 5 [Proposals].
40 MCSS Information, supra note 26.
41 Ibid.
42 Ibid.
43 MCSS, ODSP Income Support Directives, supra note 20.

about 44,900 ODSP cases and about 51,500 OW cases with overpayment reductions.[44]

Reducing benefits to recover an overpayment creates a conflict between the goal of providing financial assistance to needy people and government accountability. On the one hand, benefit levels are not generous at the best of times, and any reduction can lead to real hardship for the recipient.[45] On the other hand, it is incumbent on the provincial government to make sure that people receive only the amount of financial assistance for which they are eligible, and that overpayments are recovered.

The tension between providing adequate support to benefit recipients and properly handling public funds is reflected in the determination of the percentage reduction that is imposed in active cases. Our interviews with program administrators suggested that the default benefit reduction rate was five percent, but that it can be reduced if it seemed likely to cause hardship, or increased to ten percent if there was evidence of an ability or willingness to pay more.[46] However, the experience of staff at the non-governmental social service agencies has led them to believe that the "default" reduction rate is ten percent and can be lowered to five percent only by negotiating with program staff.[47] The data compiled in Figures 1 and 2 suggest that the reductions in benefits are less than 10 percent in most cases.[48]

---

44 MCSS Information, supra note 26.

45 We are assuming here that the amount overpaid has been spent long before any benefit reduction takes place and is therefore not available to support current consumption.

46 Interview of Forsyth et al., supra note 21.

47 E-mails from Jacqueline Esler, Social Assistance Violence and Mental Health Staff Lawyer Parkdale Community Legal Services, 16 January 2009 and MCSS Information, supra note 26.

48 MCSS Information, ibid.

Figure 1: Ontario Works – Percentage Reduction of Benefits Cheques due to Overpayments

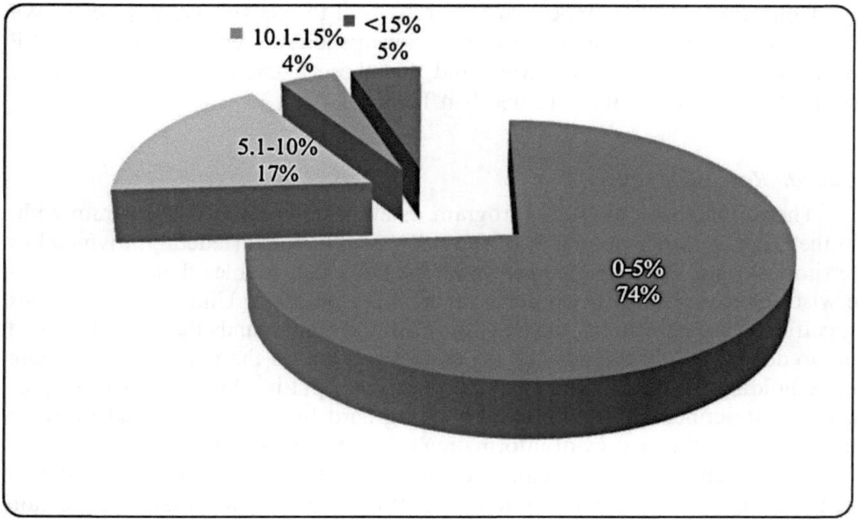

Figure 2: ODSP: Percentage Reduction of Benefits Cheques due Overpayment

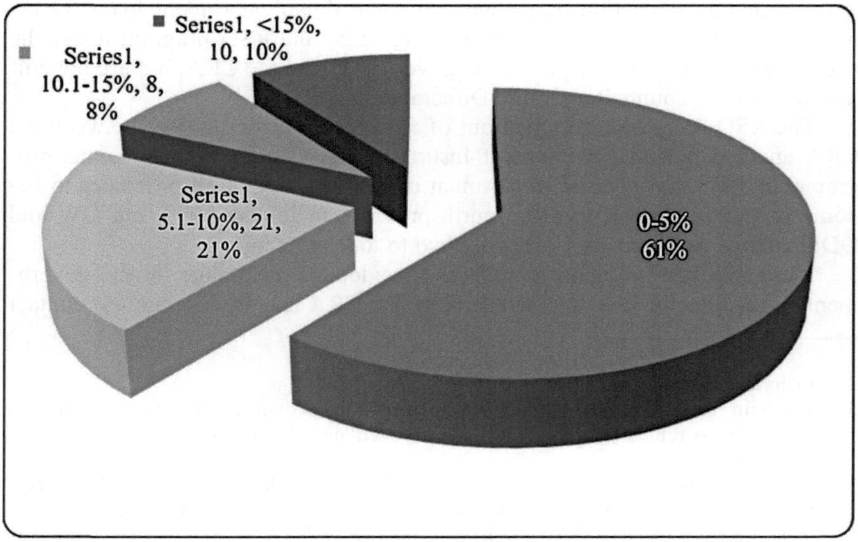

Collection agencies

Collection agencies appear to be rarely used to recover overpayments. We were told that the ORU did not use collection agencies to recover inactive ODSP overpayments. However, we were told that these agencies might be used by some Ontario municipalities (other than Toronto).[49]

Canada Revenue Agency

The Refund Set-Off (RSO) program, established in 1992, is a program within the CRA. In order to be part of the RSO, governments (federal, provincial or territorial) must sign an agreement with the CRA that enables them to refer otherwise unrecoverable Crown debts to the RSO program. Under the conditions specified in the agreement, the RSO program intercepts funds that would be paid out to debtors as tax refunds and tax credits and directs them to the government body holding the debt.[50] The CRA has, however, put in place a number of procedures, described below, to avoid creating hardship for debtors and to avoid compromising the privacy of information provided for tax purposes.

At the outset, it is important to distinguish between two types of collection activities that go on within the CRA. The RSO program is a "passive" collection method, as it simply sets off refunds and credits rather than actively seeking out the debtor and attempting to collect the money owed. Another part of the CRA--the Accounts Receivable Directorate--takes charge of more active collection efforts, including collection of unpaid taxes and defaulted student loans. Overpayments to ODSP and TESS can be handled by the RSO program under the MOU between the Ontario provincial government and the CRA, but are not collected by the Accounts Receivable Directorate.

The RSO program developed out of agreements made in 1992 between the CRA and the federal Employment Insurance and Canada Student Loans programs. In 1998, the Federal Department of Finance invited all provinces to become partners. Ontario was the fourth province to join in 1999, but OW and ODSP started requesting set-offs only two to four years ago.[51]

Using the RSO program confers a considerable advantage on the government-as-creditor for several reasons. First, the CRA usually has the best contact

49 Interview Forsyth et al., supra note 21.

50 The term "set-off" is used by the CRA to refer to the activities related to using the proceeds of a tax refund toward a crown debt. We will use the term "set-off" here to refer to that process.

51 Interview of Staff from the Canada Revenue Agency, 6 March 2009 [CRA Interview]. Each province signs an agreement with the CRA; that agreement allows many government programs (such as ODSP) to become partners in the RSO program. There are now more than 180 active partners. See Canada Revenue Agency 2008, at 4 [CRA Program Guide].

information for debtors because most Canadians file income tax returns and thereby provide a reasonably accurate address. Second, the CRA only allows the RSO program to be used only for unrecoverable Crown debts; no private creditor can use the program.

Before requesting a refund set off, partners must establish both that the debt is legally collectable and that they have established provisions to determine whether the set-off of refunds and credits would cause hardship for the debtor. Then the partner must make its own unsuccessful efforts to collect on the debt, thus establishing the debt as "unrecoverable".[52]

The relevant tax credits and refunds are generated by the review of individual tax returns. Before any of those refunds and tax credits can be set-off, any monies owing to the CRA itself or to the Department of Justice for alimony and child support are deducted. Any remaining amounts can be set-off to the RSO program partner.[53] When a refund has been set off, the CRA notifies the taxpayer and provides him or her with information about how to contact the partner, about why this has happened, and about how to appeal the set-off or claim hardship.

The CRA will set off some tax refunds and credits for its partners but cannot or will not set off others. For example, the CRA will not set off credits arising from the National Child Tax Benefit or from the Universal Child Care Benefit because the Income Tax Act--the legislation underlying these programs--prohibits their set-off.[54] The major refunds and credits that can be set off include: 1) income tax refunds, 2) the Goods and Services Tax (GST) credit and 3) the Working Income Tax Benefit.[55]

The various partners agree to ensure that the set-off will not cause hardship to the debtor. Nonetheless, the CRA has also established a number of policies under the RSO program that are aimed at preventing hardship for taxpayers. If the family income of the taxpayer is below various income thresholds (which vary according to the tax credit or refund involved), the CRA will not set off the refund. Income tax refunds, however, are set off regardless of the taxpayer's family income.

The CRA also concerns itself with maintaining the integrity of the tax system by protecting confidential information about taxpayers. For example, if the RSO program has not set off a tax refund or credit because the debtor has a fam-

52 CRA Program Guide, ibid., at 18.

53 The set-off request remains in force until the debt is paid off. As long as the debt remains unpaid, eligible refunds and tax credits can be intercepted.

54 Income Tax Act, R.S.C. 1985 (5th Supp.), c. 1, section 122.61(4).

55 Others include the British Columbia Low Income Climate Action Tax Credit, the Saskatchewan Sales Tax Credit, other provincial refundable tax credits and the refundable Medical Expense Supplement.

ily income below the relevant threshold, the CRA will not tell the partner why no refund is forthcoming since to do so would implicitly reveal the debtor's income. Perhaps more importantly, the RSO program does not reveal the address of the debtor to the partners, even though having that address might make it easier for the partner to pursue its own collection efforts.

The creation and growth of the RSO program would seem to have ratcheted up the pressure on current and former OW and ODSP recipients. Essentially, the RSO program is a new and effective collector of Crown debts. That said, CRA staff have not noticed any particular intent to increase the pressure on those who owe debts to the Crown. They acknowledge, however, that enhanced computerization and an increase in the number of partners has made it easier to identify debtors and collect money from them.[56]

Debt resolution options for government overpayments

There is no specific debt resolution option designed for economically disadvantaged people dealing with government overpayments or any other debts that they might have incurred. Bankruptcy is financially inaccessible and is not the solution for all debtors; Canadian "credit counseling" is really a mechanism for rearranging the debts of the middle-class. Further, with a few notable exceptions, there is no agency or service to which a low-income debtor can turn for neutral debt advice.

Credit counseling

A diverse array of organizations provide "credit counseling" in Canada and the United States. At one end of the spectrum are low-budget, local organizations that serve low-income individuals who need help dealing with the social assistance system, the tax system or ordinary financial matters. Such organizations charge no fees and are funded by charitable donations or local governments.[57] At the other end of the spectrum are non-profit organizations that seem to act much as profit-maximizing entities might (regardless of their status as registered charities) and seem to function essentially as debt collectors. They provide little in the way of education or counseling, and simply create and administer debt management plans (DMPs), receiving "fair share" payments from creditors in return. Somewhere in the middle of the spectrum are a set of non-profit credit counseling agencies that have a relatively long history of operation in

56 CRA Interview, supra note 51.

57 We describe two such organizations (Entraide Budgétaire and the Financial Advocacy and Problem Solving program) later in this section of the paper.

Canada, untainted by any hint of improper behaviour, which provide educational activities along with DMPs.[58] Another point on the spectrum is occupied by for-profit creditcounseling agencies that perform the same sort of debt consolidation function as the non-profits but do not provide education or counseling.

DMPs, regardless of the organization creating and administering them, typically require that debtors repay 100 percent of their debts including any interest accumulated up to the point when the plan goes into effect. The credit-counseling agency consolidates the debts of the client and negotiates a freeze on further interest accumulation with most creditors. The debtor sends the credit-counseling agency a single monthly payment and the agency divides the payment among the creditors. The debtor pays a set-up fee (on the order of $50) and a monthly service fee ($30-$50 per month). The credit-counseling agency receives a "fair share" payment from the creditors (on the order of 20-25 percent of the funds collected) in addition to whatever fees are paid by the debtor.[59] Credit counseling in this form is best viewed as a way of negotiating and rearranging debts.

There has been little systematic investigation of the credit counseling industry in Canada. In the United States, a Senate investigation in 2004 uncovered a wide array of illegal and unethical practices, generally involving high fees, poor service and violations of the laws concerning the operation of non-profit organizations.[60]

---

58 The extent to which Canadian non-profit credit counseling organizations provide services beyond the creation and administration of debt management plans is unclear. Henrietta Ross, the executive director of the Ontario Association of Credit Counseling Services (OACCS), told us that 80 percent of the work of agencies accredited by the OACCS involves educational activities; only the remaining 20 percent is related to debt management plans. When we asked In-Charge Debt Solutions, a relatively new non-profit credit counseling agency that is not accredited by the OACCS for a summary of their educational activities, we were given a list of workshops that it had provided, free of cost, to various organizations.

59 Until recently, Canadian banks provided funds to non-profit credit counseling agencies under the aegis of the "national donation policy" of the Canadian Bankers Association. Under that policy, banks "donated" 22 percent of the monies recovered by the credit counseling agencies to the credit counseling agencies. According to the CBA, the donations "recognized" the counseling and education provided by the credit counselors. As of November 1, 2009, each bank will develop its own policy with regard to paying credit counseling agencies for the money that they collect. Email from Andrew Addison, Canadian Bankers Association, 22 September 2009.

60 Such firms were the focus of an investigation by a US Senate Committee in 2005. See U.S., Permanent Subcommittee on Investigations of the Senate Committee on Homeland Security and Governmental Affairs 2005. In the wake of this investigation, as the US Government Accounting Office reported in 2007, the IRS ... [undertook] a broad examination effort of credit counseling organizations for compliance with the Internal Revenue Code, including the propriety of the organizations' tax-exempt status. Between January

It seems clear that Canadian credit counseling organizations provide services primarily to debtors who can afford to make regular payments to their creditors within the parameters of a debt management plan (DMP). The monthly payments required by a DMP are beyond the financial reach of most low-income people and certainly beyond the reach of benefits recipients. When benefits recipients contact a credit counselor, they are told that the agency cannot help them.[61] Since legal aid clinics do not generally offer debt resolution services, there are few, if any, places where a low-income person can obtain legal advice and counseling to address the debts caused by government overpayments.[62]

Bankruptcy

Unlike credit counseling, bankruptcy in its current form could be quite useful to low-income debtors. For example, the involuntary debts owed to the Ministry of Community and Social Services (MCSS) by active and inactive OW and ODSP recipients as a result of benefit overpayments are dischargeable in bankruptcy.[63] Directives from both programs contain information for program staff on how overpayments should be handled in cases where debtors file for bankruptcy. Therefore, one might expect that a non-trivial percentage of overpayment cases would end in bankruptcy.

According to the MCSS, the number of Overpayment Recovery Unit (ORU) bankruptcy cases for the 2008/2009 fiscal year can be broken down as follows. In the "sponsorship" category, there were sixteen OW-related bankruptcies and nineteen ODSP-related bankruptcies. In the "social assistance" category, there were sixty OW-related bankruptcies and 254 OSDP-related bankruptcies.[64] Note

---

2005 and March 2007, [the] IRS had revoked or terminated the federal tax-exempt status of 19 credit counseling agencies, and as of March 2007, [the] IRS had proposed revocations for an additional 28 agencies. See United States Government Accountability Office 2007, at 12-13.

61 During a pilot Debt Advice Clinic at Parkdale Community Legal Services in January 2009, an unemployed low-income client disclosed that he was instructed to "come back when he had a job" by a credit counseling agency. The credit counseling agencies we talked to agreed that successful debt management plans require a higher level of income than typically available to benefits recipients.

62 Staff were consulted at Parkdale Community Legal Services, Rexdale Community Legal Clinic and St. Christopher House in Toronto, as well as Entraide Budgetaire in Ottawa.

63 Bankruptcy and Insolvency Act, R.S.C. 1985, c. B-3, section 178(2) [BIA]. It is worth noting that the Government of Canada has expressly made efforts to make debts stemming from Employment Insurance overpayments non-dischargeable in bankruptcy. Indeed, under the BIA, the government's right to collect unremitted Employment Insurance ranks above both wage claims and the rights of unpaid suppliers to repossess goods (s. 81.1 of the BIA). See Office of the Superintendant of Bankruptcy Canada 2009.

64 E-mail correspondence with Ministry of Community and Social Services (August 6, 2008).

that the bankrupts in such cases are not usually current recipients of benefits: sponsors cannot be assumed to be receiving OW or ODSP, and other ORU cases are inactive cases, meaning that the individuals involved are no longer receiving benefits.

As far as we can tell, it seems that very few current benefits recipients utilize the Canadian bankruptcy system, likely because they do not have the financial means to access it.[65] Two options seem to exist for those who cannot afford to pay the usual fees charged by trustees for administering their bankruptcy: 1) the Bankruptcy Assistance Program (BAP) of the Office of the Superintendent of Bankruptcy (OSB) and 2) *pro bono* efforts by bankruptcy trustees.

(i) The Bankruptcy Assistance Program

The Office of the Superintendent of Bankruptcy (OSB) does not administer bankruptcies, leaving this task to private bankruptcy trustees. Under Directive 20, however, the OSB supervises a program called the "Bankruptcy Assistance Program" (BAP).[66] The target group for the BAP is debtors who are having difficulty finding a bankruptcy trustee willing to take on their case; this group includes low-income Canadians in general and benefits recipients in particular.[67] Since trustees are not required to take on any particular case, some debtors may not be able to use the bankruptcy system. In such situations, Directive 20 states that the OSB will facilitate the assignment of a participating trustee to the case of the debtor.[68] However, the directive does not specify that the trustee must charge a lower-than-normal fee; it says only that "[t]he application for a bankrupt's discharge is not to be delayed due to the lack of full payment of a trustee's fee."[69] The meaning of this section is obscure at best and falls well short of assuring debtors that the net cost of their bankruptcies will be low.

James Callon, the current Superintendent of Bankruptcy, interprets the BAP as a program that "is not necessarily a zero cost program to a debtor, but at the same time a debtor is not to be turned away by a designated trustee due to the inability to pay the fees."[70]

In our view, the BAP program is structured in a manner that seems to discourage, rather than encourage, its use. A debtor must be "unable to obtain the services of a trustee" after seeking out and consulting with two trustees.[71] He or

65 For example, one Debt Advice Clinic client received three quotes between $1,600 and $1,800 from bankruptcy trustees. His income is $572 per month and his debts total $24,600.

66 See BAP Directive No. 20, supra note 8.

67 Ibid.

68 Ibid.

69 Ibid. at para. 11.

70 E-mail from James Callon (July 7, 2009).

71 BAP Directive No. 2, supra note 8, at para. 5.

she must then apply to the OSB, which eventually assigns the case to a participating trustee.[72] Even then, as we pointed out in a previous paper, the fee paid by a BAP participant is likely to be quite close to the average fee charged to any other bankrupt.[73] Neither bankruptcy trustees nor the OSB see the BAP as guaranteeing a low-cost bankruptcy; part of the trustee's responsibility is to realize money for the estate from tax refunds, from the sale of assets or from any other source allowed by the *BIA*. The BAP simply ensures that debtors who manage to navigate the program requirements will have a trustee assigned to their case; there is no guarantee that the amount eventually paid will be lower than what trustees normally charge.

Few bankruptcies are filed under BAP and the distribution of cases across Canada is quite uneven. For example, almost no cases are filed in the Toronto area.[74] The program is poorly advertised and the advertising that does exist is misleading. Service Canada's summary of the program reads as follows: "The Bankruptcy Assistance Program helps individuals seeking to file for bankruptcy hire a bankruptcy trustee if they do not have the means to do so on their own." We do not see BAP, as it currently operates, as a mechanism that brings bankruptcy within the financial reach of the low-income debtors who might benefit from it.

(ii) Pro bono work by trustees

The professional organization of trustees, the Canadian Association of Insolvency and Restructuring Professionals (CAIRP), does not have a formal program that offers low-cost bankruptcies administered by its members. In our previous paper, we documented the efforts by trustees in Edmonton and in Halifax to undertake bankruptcies for less than the normal fee in cases where the trustee felt that the debtor could not afford the normal fee.[75] We have not heard of any

---

72 Ibid. at para. 6.

73 Ben-Ishai & Schwartz, supra note 7, at 481. The fee paid "out of pocket" by the bankrupt may be lower than that asked of a non-BAP client but, after the trustee has filed the BAP debtor's tax return and incorporated the tax refund into his or her estate, the overall fee can increase significantly.

74 In the first fiscal quarter of 2009-2010, a total of 107 bankruptcies were administered through the BAP program. None occurred in the Western region (Vancouver, Calgary, Winnipeg and Edmonton) and only three occurred in the East (Quebec, Montreal and Halifax). The remaining 104 all occurred in the Ontario Region (Toronto, Ottawa, London and Hamilton) and almost all of these were in London and Hamilton. Ottawa had none and Toronto only 15. We thank the OSB for providing these numbers; E-mail from Patricia Alferez (23 September 2009). Because BAP has disproportionately few cases in Toronto, the experience of the clients who came to our pilot debt advice clinic may not be representative of the experience of low-income debtors in other regions.

75 Ben-Ishai & Schwartz, supra note 7, at 511.

similar efforts elsewhere in Canada, but it is clear that while *pro bono* work by trustees undoubtedly exists, it is not systematically available.

Debt advice and access to bankruptcy

Debtors with government overpayment debts currently operate on an uneven playing field with the government. The government has shifted its collection efforts and policies to be more in line with those of private creditors.[76] However, because the existing remedies available to most Canadian debtors are not available to low-income debtors, the intensification and centralization of collection efforts has a harsh and unequal effect on low-income debtors.

In addition to access to bankruptcy, a missing element in the debt relief situation for low-income debtors in Canada is low-cost debt advice.[77] Bankruptcy is not the solution for all debtors and, as we have noted, Canadian "credit counseling" is really about rearrangement of debts and is available only to the middle class. Two examples of agencies that provide free debt advice to the poor are the Financial Advocacy & Problem Solving (FAPS) program, coordinated by Miryam Zeballos at St. Christopher House in Toronto, and Entraide Budgétaire (EB) in Ottawa.[78]

St. Christopher House provides a wide range of services to low-income people in the west end of Toronto. The FAPS program, which started operations in 2003, provides general financial information to St. Christopher's clients, in addition to help with income taxes, advice on how to apply for social assistance benefits and help obtaining bank accounts.[79] Depending on clients' situations, FAPS can refer them to a bankruptcy trustee who is often able to administer their bankruptcies at a lower-than-normal cost, or to a local credit counseling agency.

EB, funded by the City of Ottawa and the United Way, is a nonprofit agency that has served Ottawa's Vanier neighbourhood for the past 25 years. Unlike credit counseling agencies, EB has no financial interest in directing debtors to any particular debt remedy.[80] The advice and counsel provided by EB is holistic

76 See, e.g., the discussion in Proposals, supra note 39.

77 In Quebec, ACEF (Association Coopérative Economie Familial) provides financial services in a number of locations as does Option Consommateurs.

78 See St. Christopher House, "Financial Advocacy and Problem Solving."

79 FAPS prefers to be described as providing financial information rather than financial advice. In their words, FAPS helps its clients "make informed decisions by providing support, information, resources and training." FAPS, ibid.

80 EB notes that the minimal amount of bankruptcy counseling that they undertake is an exception to this rule. Debtors filing for bankruptcy in Canada are required to attend two mandatory counseling sessions. Those leading the sessions receive $85 per session from the estate of the bankrupt. EB derives a small amount of its budget (about 1 percent)

in nature in that the personal situations of clients--situations that can involve very low incomes, mental challenges and drug addictions--are considered before any financial recommendations are made. Importantly, EB continues to advise its clients as they go through whatever remedy they have chosen. Beyond advice on how to deal with indebtedness, EB also provides basic budget counseling, help with personal income tax for the poor and the elderly, and financial literacy sessions. EB is quite small, with an annual budget of about $350,000, and focuses its activities in one neighbourhood.

For low-income debtors lucky enough to live in the areas served by FAPS or EB, the services they provide are extremely valuable. For example, staff at both St. Christopher House and EB have developed personal relationships with one or two bankruptcy trustees to whom they can refer debtors, but those arrangements can break down at any point in time. For the vast majority of low-income Canadian debtors though, at least in English Canada, no such services exist.

Low-income debtors and the Bankruptcy and Insolvency Act

The situation described in the last three sections suggests that the Canadian bankruptcy system is not meeting the objectives set out in the *BIA*, the case law and subordinate legislation. The bankruptcy system in Canada essentially has three main objectives: 1) liquidation and distribution of debtor's assets; 2) rehabilitation of the individual debtor; and 3) enhancing commercial morality and protecting the credit system.[81]

The first objective is not significant for the current discussion since low-income debtors rarely, if ever, have significant assets. The second objective is supposed to be met by providing access to the bankruptcy system and by the "fresh start" offered by the resulting discharge of pre-bankruptcy debts.

The third objective provides the justification for limiting the access to bankruptcy by certain categories of debtors. For example, debtors who have committed fraud or other offences should accordingly be limited in their access to the bankruptcy system so as to maintain commercial morality and preserve access to credit.[82] Debtors who have involuntarily accrued a debt to the government through an overpayment, however, do not fall into the category of debtors who should be denied access to the bankruptcy system in order to preserve commercial morality. Accordingly, the tenets of the Canadian bankruptcy system do not justify limiting their ability to be rehabilitated through access to the fresh start that a bankruptcy offers. Bankruptcy should be brought within the financial

---

from such counseling. E-mail from Helene Menard, Executive Director of Entraide Budgetaire (March 3, 2009).

81 See, e.g., Wood 2009, at 36.

82 See BIA, supra note 63, section 198.

reach of low-income debtors, as this will level the playing field in negotiations with the government, and will better allocate risk between debtors and creditors by providing both parties with equal opportunity to address an insolvency situation.

Conclusion

Low-income individuals are no different than higher-income people in their need for remedies to insolvency-related issues. Without the same access to a fresh start, lower-income people will be further marginalized, and their ability to contribute to Canadian society will be further hindered.

The main objective of this article is to challenge the view that low-income people do not need debt remedies because they have few debts and are judgment-proof. Such commonly held assumptions are both factually incorrect and short sighted. Many low-income people do have significant debts, and even if a debtor is currently judgment-proof, the lingering debt provides a disincentive to improve his or her situation (and thereby lose judgment-proof status). Relief for these debts might allow the debtor to escape poverty. In fact, this is one of the goals of most government transfer programs.

The debts of low-income people include many of the same kinds of debt incurred by higher income individuals. Because people are continually moving in and out of poverty, they can run up significant debts--including credit card balances and bank lines of credit--when they have a source of steady income. However, the debts of low-income people, and especially those of transfer recipients, are disproportionately likely to be debts to the various levels of government.

The central focus of this article has been on creating symmetry between the debt resolution options available to low-income people in Ontario with government debts and the increasing centralization and intensification of the government's collection practices. The process by which some low-income people acquire debts through the overpayment of benefits in the first place also needs further investigation. For example, OW program officials are confident that sponsors are adequately warned of their responsibility should the sponsored person receive social assistance.[83] However, there are some indications that such policies are not always followed. For example, a third party sponsored the son of a former Parkdale Community Legal Aid Services client. When the son received social assistance, the provincial government attempted to collect from the mother rather than the third party. Another challenge is that legal clinics or social agencies occasionally advise sponsored persons to apply for social assistance

83 Interview of Forsyth et al., supra note 21.

without realizing the potential implications for their sponsors.[84] OW claims that, in response, notification letters are sent to sponsors and outreach activities have targeted settlement workers.[85]

This study does not represent a comprehensive examination of the situation facing low-income families who find themselves deep in debt. We were able to study only OW and ODSP, which are the largest transfer programs in the most populous Canadian province, but other transfer programs in other provinces may handle matters differently. The specific cases referred to in the text are drawn from a small number of debtors who came to our pilot debt advice clinic in Toronto; the situation in other Canadian cities, and perhaps even in other parts of Toronto might well be different.

The next phase in our research requires further investigation of the issues surrounding bankruptcy and low-income individuals. This involves developing a better understanding of the lived experiences of low-income individuals in Ontario, and their interactions with government programs that can result in overpayments. This research will involve extensive interviews and consultations, in order to better comprehend how debts affect economically disadvantaged Ontarians. Increasing our understanding of this issue will not only bring more awareness of the unique position of low-income people in dealing with government debt and with insolvency in general, it will also allow us to explore the ways in which Canada can develop a more inclusive insolvency framework.

At this point in our research, however, our tentative conclusion is that, as a counterbalance to the government's move toward acting more like a private creditor, the same remedies that are available to middle-class debtors should be made more accessible to low-income debtors.

References

Ben-Ishai, Stephanie and Schwartz, Saul (2007): Bankruptcy for the Poor? 45 Osgoode Hall L.J. 471 at 510.

Canada Revenue Agency: Refund Set-Off Program for Individuals: Program Guide. Canada: August 2008.

Carment, David & Bercuson, David, eds.: The World in Canada: Diaspora, Demography, and Domestic Politics. Montreal: McGill-Queen's University Press 2008.

Citizenship and Immigration Canada (25 August 2009): Canada--Permanent residents by gender and category, 1984-2008, online: Citizenship and Immigration Canada <http://www.cic.gc.ca/english/resources/statistics/facts2008/permanent/01.asp>.

Finnie, Ross & Sweetman, Arthur (2003): Poverty dynamics: empirical evidence for Canada. 36 Can. J. Econ. 291.

---

84 E-mail from Geri Sadoway, Immigration Staff Lawyer at Parkdale Community Legal Services (January 15, 2009).

85 Interview of Forsyth et al., supra note 21.

Kilborn, Jason (2009): Twenty-five Years of Consumer Bankruptcy in Continental Europe: Internalizing Negative Externalities and Humanizing Justice in Denmark. 18 Int'l Insovency Rev. 155.

Kilborn, Jason (2009): Two Decades, Three Key Questions, and Evolving Answers in European Consumer Insolvency Law: Responsibility, Discretion, and Sacrifice, in Niemi, Johanna/Ramsay, Iain and Whitford, William C.: Consumer Credit, Debt and Bankruptcy: Comparative and International Perspectives. Portland, Oregon: Hart 2009.

Ministry of Community and Social Services, About social assistance in Ontario, online: MCSS <http:// www.accesson.ca/mcss/english/pillars/social/odsp>.

Ministry of Community and Social Services, "Ontario Disability Support Program: Preamble" 2006.

Ministry of Community and Social Services, Ontario Disability Support Program: Preamble (September 2006), online: MCSS http://www.cfcs.gov.on.ca/NR/MCFCS/ODSP/ESDIR/en/0_0.pdf.

Ministry of Community and Social Services, Ontario Disability Support Program-Income Support Directives, 11.1 Recovery of Overpayments (Toronto: Queen's Printer for Ontario, 2008), online: MCSS <http:// www.mcss.gov.on.ca/en/mcss/programs/social/directives/ODSP_incomesupport.aspx>

Ministry of Community and Social Services, Ontario Works Policy Directives, "9.3 Recovery of Overpayments" (Toronto: Queen's Printer for Ontario, 2008), online: MCSS <http:// www.mcss.gov.on.ca/en/mcss/programs/social/direCTives/ow_policy_directives.asp>

O. Reg. 136/98, Sch. 1 and 2, online: Service Ontario e-Laws < http://www.e-laws.gov.on.ca/html/regs/english/elaws_regs_980136_e.htm>

Office of the Superindendent of Bankruptcy Canada, Directive No. 20: Bankruptcy Assistance Program (18 September 2009), online: Office of the Superindendent of Bankruptcy Canada <http:// strategis.ic.gc.ca/eic/site/bsf-osb.nsf/eng/br02138.html>

Office of the Superintendant of Bankruptcy Canada, Summary of Key Legislative Changes in Chapter 47 of the Statutes of Canada, 2005, and Chapter 36 of the Statutes of Canada, 2007 (17 September 2009), online: Office of the Superintendant of Bankruptcy Canada <http://www.ic.gc.ca/eic/site/bsf-osb.nsf/eng/br01782.html>

Ontario, Legislative Assembly, Office of the Auditor General of Ontario, 2002 Annual Report of the Provincial Auditor of Ontario (3 December 2002), online: Office of the Auditor General of Ontario <http:// www.auditor.on.ca/en/reports_2002_en.htm>

Ontario, Legislative Assembly, Office of the Auditor General of Ontario, 2004 Annual Report of the Provincial Auditor of Ontario (30 November 2004), online: Office of the Auditor General of Ontario <http:// www.auditor.on.ca/en/reports_2004_en.htm>

Ontario, Ministry of Municipal Affairs and Housing, Provincial Municipal Fiscal and Service Delivery Review (Toronto: Queen's Printer for Ontario, 2008), online: MAH <http:// www.mah.gov.on.ca/Pagel81.aspx>

St. Christopher House, Financial Advocacy and Problem Solving, online: St. Christopher House <http://www.stchrishouse.org/adults/financial-advocacy/> [FAPS]; and Entraide Budgetaire, online: Entraide Budgetaire < http://www.ebottawa.org/>.

Toronto, Social Services Division, Proposals for Implementing Toronto Social Services response to the Auditor General's Report on Recovery of Social Assistance Overpayments (June 2005). Toronto: Social Services Division 2005.

United States Government Accountability Office, Bankruptcy Reform: Value of Credit Counseling Requirement is Not Clear (Washington, D.C.: U.S. Government Accountability Office, 2007), online: United States Government Accountability Office <http://www.gao.gov/new.items/d07203.pdf>

U.S., Permanent Subcommittee on Investigations of the Senate Committee on Homeland Security and Governmental Affairs, Profiteering in a Non-Profit Industry: Abusive Practices in Credit Counseling (S. Rep. No. 109-55). Washington, D.C.: United States Government Printing Office 2005.

Wood, Roderick J.: Bankruptcy and Insolvency Law. Toronto: Irwin Law 2009.